GUITAR WORLD PRESENTS

Metal Guitar
LESSONS

ISBN 978-1-4950-0967-9

HAL•LEONARD®
CORPORATION
7777 W. BLUEMOUND RD. P.O. BOX 13819 MILWAUKEE, WI 53213

In Australia Contact:
Hal Leonard Australia Pty. Ltd.
4 Lentara Court
Cheltenham, Victoria, 3192 Australia
Email: ausadmin@halleonard.com.au

Visit Hal Leonard Online at
www.halleonard.com

Contents

INTRODUCTION

So you want to play like your favorite guitarist. Would you rather learn Metallica licks from someone who knows a lot about Metallica, or from Kirk Hammett himself?

The answer is obvious. Which is why, over the years, *Guitar World* has made it a point to go straight to the source to bring you the absolute finest in guitar instruction. Whether you want to become a deity of distortion, a chord-crushing master of metal, a Satan of the strings or a cool jazz, blues or acoustic dude, we don't have to tell you that the shortest way to greatness is to learn from the masters themselves.

Since the early Nineties, *Guitar World*'s monthly columns have featured advice and instruction from players like Angus Young, Brian May, Tony Iommi, Buddy Guy, Tom Morello, B.B. King, Steve Vai, Joe Perry, Marty Friedman, Kerry King, Joe Satriani and Dickey Betts. Electrifying licks and timeless insights? We've printed them by the truckload, and we've compiled some of the best columns by our most revered heavy metal guitar teachers right here in this book.

So the next time your buddy asks you if you're taking guitar lessons, just grab your dog-eared copy of *Guitar World* or this very book, smile and say "Yup." If he asks you who from, just say "Oh, Zakk Wylde, the dudes in Shadows Fall and Dave Mustaine."

And, you know what? It'll be the god's honest truth.

—Jeff Kitts
Managing Editor
Guitar World

CHAOS THEORY

by Chris Broderick of Megadeth

Right-Hand Way
Getting a handle on essential pick-hand techniques.

Hello and welcome to my new *Guitar World* instructional column, *Chaos Theory*. Over the next several months I'm going to show you a variety of the techniques that I consider essential to my approach to the electric guitar.

This first column features an exercise that emphasizes a variety of pick-hand techniques that are intrinsic to my style: sweep picking, alternate picking and multiple-finger fretboard tapping (see **FIGURE 1**). In putting this exercise together, I was looking to create a convergence of these different playing techniques within a musical-sounding piece.

All the examples demonstrated in this column are played on seven-string guitar in standard tuning (low to high, B E A D G B E). Let's start with bar 1 of **FIGURE 1**: I begin with an ascending run based on a Gmaj7 arpeggio (G B D F♯). All the pick-hand-tapped notes in this bar are sounded with the middle finger (indicated by *m*). There is no picking in the first two bars of this figure, and some of the notes are sounded by firmly hammering the fretting finger down onto the string.

7-string guitar (tuning, low to high: B E A D G B E)
FIGURE 1

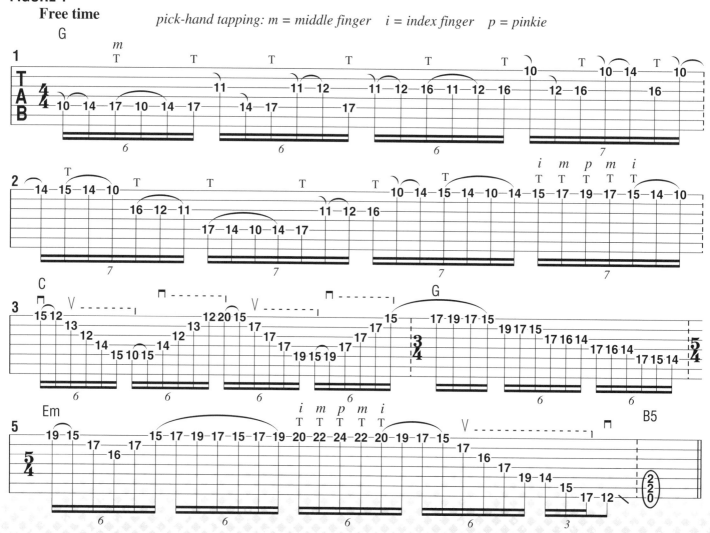

Although the run is phrased mostly as sextuplets and septuplets, it ascends in four-note patterns, with each successive four-note group starting one note higher within the arpeggio: the first four notes, G B D G, are all sounded on the fifth string, with the D at the 17th fret as the tapped note. The next four-note group is B D F♯ B, followed by D F♯ G D and then F♯ G B F♯; the pattern then starts with the first four notes again, G B D G, but one octave higher.

In bar 2 I descend and ascend straight through the Gmaj7 arpeggio in two octaves. Then, on beat four, I employ *multiple-finger* pick-hand tapping to play a scale fragment on the high E string, moving from the index finger (*i*) to the middle-finger (*m*) to the pinkie (*p*) and back down, followed by fret-hand pull-offs.

I switch to sweep picking in bar 3, descending and ascending through a C major arpeggio (C E G) in two octaves, followed in bar 4 with a primarily alternate-picked descent through the G major scale (G A B D C E F♯).

The run wraps up in bars 5 and 6, starting with a tonal shift from G major to its relative minor triad, E minor. On beat one I play a quick descending and ascending Em arpeggio, followed on beat two by some *legato* scalar movement, with all the notes sounded on the high E string with hammer-ons and pull-offs. Beat three brings multiple-finger tapping back into play, as I roll on the high E string from index to middle to pinkie and then back down, followed by fret-hand pull-offs. The phrase ends with a three-octave descending Em arpeggio, played across beats four and five of bar 5, followed by a big, low B5 power chord.

A question I hear all the time is, "How do I develop my pick-hand tapping ability so I can execute multiple-finger tapping techniques?" The first thing I tell people is to observe your fret-hand technique and imitate it. My multiple-finger tapping technique is still developing, so if there is a pick-hand tapping figure that I'm having trouble with, I'll play it with the fret hand first and watch the motion of the fingers. Then I'll try to imitate those mechanics with my pick hand.

It's good to start with something simple, like the ascending three-notes-per-string scale shown in **FIGURE 2**. Once you become comfortable playing scales this way, try moving on to arpeggios, as shown in **FIGURE 3**, which are more challenging. This technique also lends itself well to pentatonic scales, as demonstrated in **FIGURE 4**.

In order to move seamlessly between normal playing and multiple-finger tapping, I invented a "pick clip," which affixes my flatpick (I use a Dunlop Sharpie) to my thumb; this device conveniently allows my index finger to let go of the pick without dropping it so I can use all four pick-hand fingers to tap. I initially tried using thumb picks, but the design and shape never worked for me; with the pick-clip, I can use any type of pick. It would be much more difficult, if not impossible, for me to play the multiple taps in **FIGURE 1** without this useful accessory. I'm looking to patent it so I can make it available to others.

—reprinted from *Guitar World*, June 2010

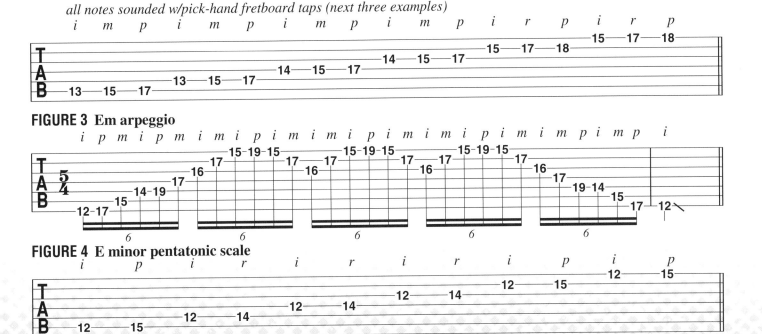

FIGURE 2 F major scale

FIGURE 3 Em arpeggio

FIGURE 4 E minor pentatonic scale

Across the Board

Adapting keyboard-style arpeggios to fretboard tapping, part 1.

This month's column focuses on an original composition of mine that acknowledges the influence of classical pianists on my playing style, specifically the way in which pianists will play arpeggios across several octaves very quickly (see **FIGURE 1**). In order to emulate that sound on the guitar, I've devised a few fretboard tapping techniques. In fact, much of my two-hand tapping technique is based on that goal and approach.

The idea is to break down the arpeggios into different sequences, such as four-note groups, and play them in a way that would be quite difficult, if not impossible, to play conventionally. This example is also cool because it has some unusual "advanced classical" chords in it, such as a Neapolitan chord, an augmented III (three) chord, and some diminished seventh chords.

Let's examine the first half of **FIGURE 1**. I start with a *second-inversion* G minor arpeggio (G B♭ D). "Second inversion" means the arpeggio begins (and ends) on the fifth, which in this case is D (see bar 1, beats one through five). On beat six, I switch to a *root-position* G minor arpeggio, which means that it starts (and ends) on the G root note.

All of the phrases in bar 1 are executed with sweep picking. On beat one, I begin with a pull-off from the pinkie to the index finger, and then I *reverse rake* (or *reverse sweep*) by dragging the pick in a continuous upstroke across the top five strings through beat two. Beat three begins with a hammer-on and is followed by a *forward rake* (or *downsweep*) as the pick is dragged in a continuous downstroke across the strings. The same sweeping techniques are utilized throughout the remainder of the bar.

In bar 2, I begin with a G natural minor (G A B♭ C D E♭ F) legato scalar run across beats one and two but then switch immediately to down-up alternate picking, using notes from the G harmonic minor scale (G A B♭ C D E♭ F♯). Bar 3 features a reference to the VI (six) chord, E♭, and then the II (two major) chord, A, followed in bar 4 with a *first inversion* (third "in the bass," or positioned as the lowest note in the chord voicing) Gm/B♭ voicing and a *second inversion* (fifth in the bass) D7/A chord.

Bar 5 initiates the section of the piece wherein all of the phrases are executed with tapping, hammer-ons and pull-offs. One can analyze the rhythmic subdivisions of these phrases in a variety of ways, but the prevailing sound is that of an eighth-note triplet feel, with a 16th-note triplet played on each (or the majority of) the eighth notes. In other words, the overall feel is "ONE-trip-let, TWO-trip-let, THREE-trip-let," etc. This triplet rhythm disguises the fact that the notes are actually phrased in four-note groups, in terms of the line's melodic contour.

The highest note in each four-note melodic group is tapped. This results in two tapped notes per octave, which is a little different than the tapped arpeggios played later in the piece, which include only one tapped note per octave.

Beats one and two of bar 5 cover the first octave, and starting on beat three the pattern is repeated an octave higher. Once we reach the highest note in the phrase—D, first string, 22nd fret—at the beginning of bar 6, we descend through G harmonic minor on beat one and then shift to the Neapolitan chord, E♭maj7, and descend through a series of four-note arpeggios based on the chord tones E♭ G B♭ D. We then ascend back though the same arpeggiated shapes. This phrase can also be analyzed as G natural minor because these notes all live within the G natural minor scale.

This is definitely a complex piece that will require a great amount of practice to get a handle on. The hardest thing of all when playing a piece like this is to keep the idle open strings from ringing. The best advice I can give it is use the palm of your pick-hand to mute the strings as much as possible, keeping it over the strings that aren't being played as consistently as you can.

I'll be back next month with part two of this challenging piece. Stay tuned.

—reprinted from *Guitar World*, July 2010

FIGURE 1

7-string guitar

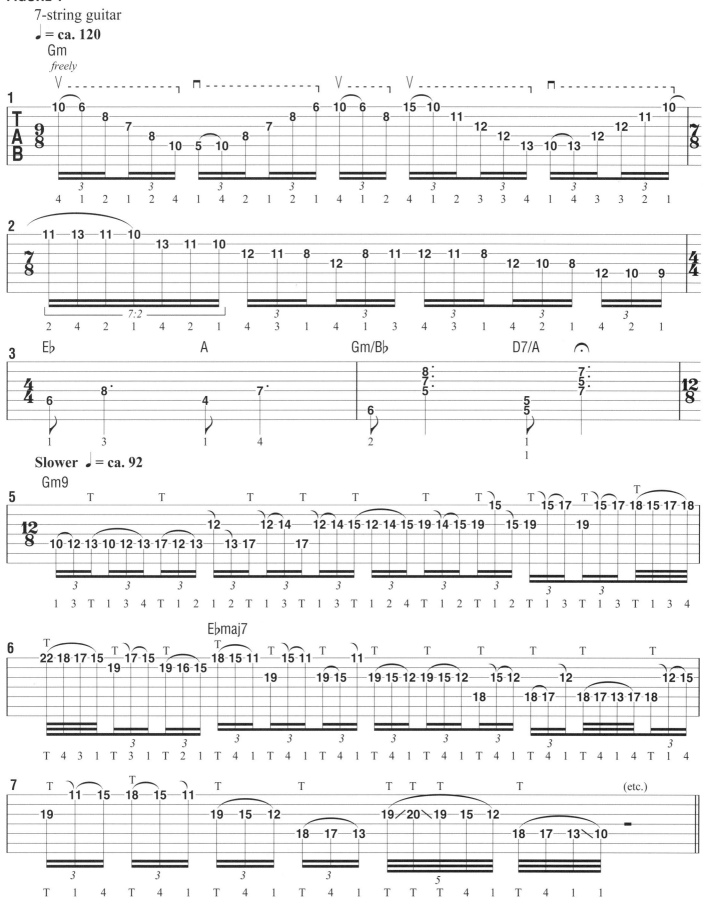

Across the Board

Adapting keyboard-style arpeggios to fretboard tapping, part 2.

Last month I introduced an original composition that involved the use of quickly played arpeggios, as well as utilized two-hand tapping techniques to emulate the way in which classical pianists play fluid-sounding arpeggios across multiple octaves. As you may have discovered, this is a very challenging piece that requires great patience and practice time to master. The key is to break each phrase down to its basic elements and practice it slowly and carefully.

This month's example, which is part two of the same piece, continues in a manner similar to last month's excerpt, with sequences consisting of steadily ascending four-note groups, i.e., each successive group begins one note higher in the arpeggio.

Let's begin by looking at what is essentially the second half of the piece as a whole, illustrated in **FIGURE 1**. In bar 1, all the notes are based on a Gdim7 (G diminished seventh) arpeggio (G B♭ D♭ E). After playing the first three notes, G B♭ D♭, I turn this into a four-note Gdim7 arpeggio and then repeatedly invert it by starting one note higher in the sequence each time. Notice that as the sequences progress, I use fret-hand "hammer-ons from nowhere"—sounding notes by firmly tapping a fret-hand finger onto a given string.

FIGURE 1

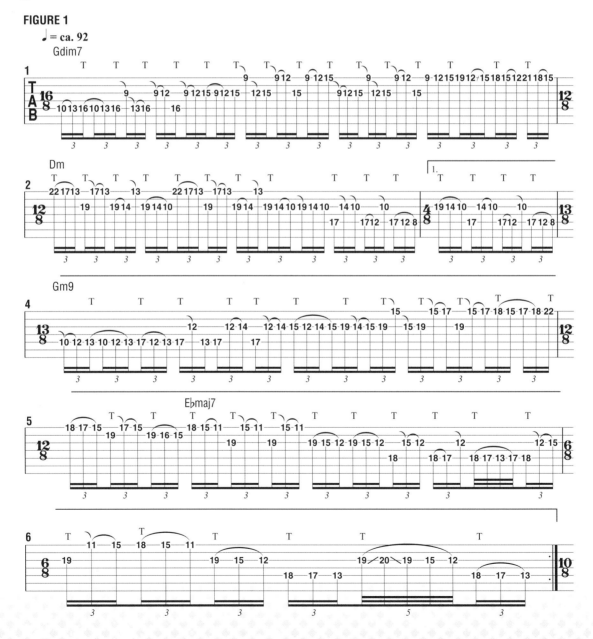

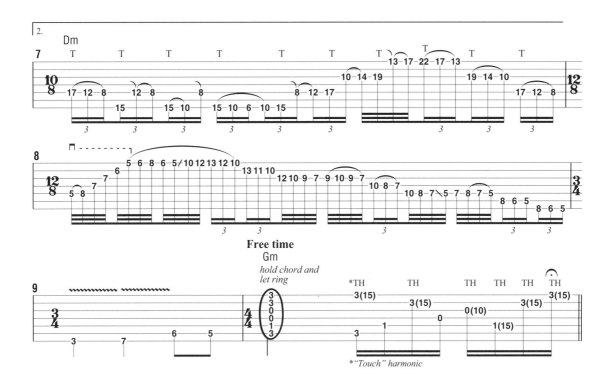

While the melody ascends in four-note patterns, it is phrased with the "feeling" of eighth-note triplets, with a 16th-note triplet played on each eighth note of the eighth-note triplet. Across the last beat and a half of bar 1, for the sake of varying the contour of the phrasing, I switch from four-note patterns to four groups of three-note patterns.

I return to four-note groupings in bar 2, based here on a Dm arpeggio (D F A) with the highest note doubled an octave lower, and descend the fretboard. During these descending arpeggios, the pick-hand tap always initiates the shift to notes sounded on a lower string. Notice also that I always jump two strings when switching to the next pick-hand tap. These four-note groups continue to descend through bar 3, bringing us into bar 4, which initiates a recap of the tapped Gm9 arpeggios (G B♭ D F A) played in part one of the piece.

On beat one of bar 5, I switch to a straight scalar descent down G harmonic minor (G A B♭ C D E♭ F♯), and then move to E♭maj7 (the Neapolitan chord in D minor) and descend through a series of four-note arpeggios based on E♭maj7 (E♭ G B♭ D).

At this point, I return to the Gdim7 arpeggios at the start of this excerpt and repeat bars 1 and 2 of **FIGURE 1**, and then move to the second ending, which continues the four-note arpeggiations of Dm, descending and then ascending, through four octaves.

In bar 8 I return to conventional picking with a good old-fashioned Dm sweep arpeggio, followed by fast alternate-picked phrases based on the D Aeolian mode (D E F G A B♭ C). I change things up harmonically in bar 9 by playing a D major arpeggio (D F♯ A), which serves as a V (five) chord to set up a resolution back to Gm, which ends the piece in bar 10.

While sustaining the Gm chord, I sound "touch" harmonics by lightly placing the fingers of my picking hand on certain strings exactly 12 frets above the fretted notes, and plucking the string simultaneously.

This is a challenging piece filled with difficult twists and turns, but if you apply yourself, you will learn a great deal about how different arpeggios are formed on the fretboard, and how to use tapping to execute them quickly and efficiently.

—reprinted from *Guitar World*, August 2010

Altered Awareness

Examining altered chords through arpeggiated sequences, part 1.

This month, I'd like to dissect another composition of mine, one that I wrote specifically to examine arpeggiated altered chords in various fretboard positions as applied to an assortment of chord voicings. In putting the piece together, I tried to use some interesting chord qualities, such as an augmented III (three) chord, a *tritone* substitution and a few other neat altered chords. There are also some twisty positional jumps on the fretboard when moving from one arpeggiated sequence to the next. This is a fairly complex piece, so I've broken it up into two parts, the first of which is presented here. I hope you have fun with it because it has tortured me for years!

FIGURE 1 illustrates the first half of the piece, which begins with an arpeggiated G minor triad (G B♭ D) played on the top three strings. At the end of bar 1, on beat three, I substitute C for D for melodic interest, then repeat the G minor triad shapes in bar 2, followed in bar 3 with a descent into the next lower octave of the G minor arpeggio.

Proper execution of this challenging piece requires careful attention to both pick- and fret-hand technique, so I have included fret-hand fingerings and picking directives throughout. A♯ a rule, when playing a descending pattern, I use an *upsweep* (drag, or *rake*, the pick in a steady motion across the strings, moving from higher to lower strings); when ascending, I employ a *downsweep* (drag the pick across the strings, from low to high). Be sure to practice each bar—or each beat—slowly and carefully, striving for clean execution.

At bar 4, I jump up to 10th position and play a similar sweep arpeggio, this time outlining a Daug (♯5) chord; at the end of beat one into beat two, I "roll" the tip of the middle finger from the B to the G string at the 11th fret, which allows me to get up and down the arpeggio quickly and comfortably. At the end of bar 4 and into bar 5, however, I switch to using the index finger for the same F♯ note at the 11th fret on the G string, as this alternate fingering choice facilitates the continual descent through the arpeggiated triad shapes, all the way across to the seventh string.

In bars 7–9, I play arpeggiated Dm triad shapes, beginning in 10th position with a *first inversion* voicing, starting on F, the minor third of D, and utilizing F two octaves lower as the first note in bar 9. In bar 7, there is a big positional jump on beat three, as I quickly shift down to fifth position, where I remain through the end of bar 8, shifting up to seventh position in bar 9.

This sets up the change to A7, starting with what I think of as a second-inversion A7 arpeggio because it begins with E, the fifth of A, as the lowest note. So remember, a first-inversion chord voicing or arpeggio places the third as the lowest note, and second-inversion means the fifth is the lowest note.

After the first two beats of bar 10, I quickly leap up to the high A note on the first string's 17th fret. I did this because I wanted to hear that note on the downbeat of beat three. The switch here is that, where I previously used triad shapes, I am now using a four-note, seventh chord arpeggio—A C♯ E G—to outline A7. This allows for double pull-offs on the high E and A strings, as the root note, A, and the dominant seventh, G, are only a whole step, and two frets, apart.

I'll be back next month with part two of this piece. In the meantime, strive to get part one memorized and under your fingers. See you then.

—reprinted from *Guitar World*, September 2010

FIGURE 1

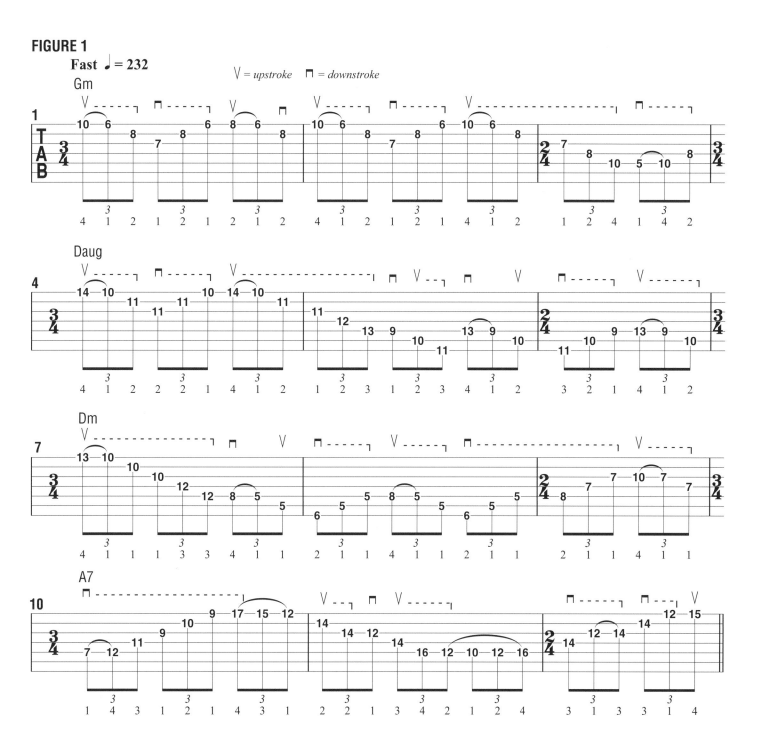

Altered Awareness, Part 2

More of examining altered chords through arpeggiated sequences.

In last month's column, I debuted an original composition that I wrote specifically to address the many technically challenging aspects of performing swept, arpeggiated altered chords, as applied to a wide variety of voicings and fretboard positions. In addition, I incorporated different inversions of regular minor and major arpeggios. Hopefully you've gotten a handle on part one of this composition and are now ready for part two. The techniques used for both sections of the piece are the same.

We finished up part one with an A dominant seven chord that occurred roughly halfway through the piece. This chord set up a shift to the E♭ major arpeggios that begin **FIGURE 1**. I start with the index finger on the fifth of E♭, B♭ (fifth string, 13th fret), and immediately hammer-on with the pinkie up to E♭ at the 18th fret of the same string, then *downsweep* through the notes of an E♭ major triad (E♭ G B♭) in 15th position. As this arpeggiated sequence starts on the *fifth* of the chord, I think of it as a *second inversion* arpeggio; a *first inversion* arpeggio begins on the *third* of the chord.

On beat one of bar 2, I quickly jump to 18th position and then back down to 15th position. On beat three of bar 2, I instill some melodic interest by inserting the ♭5 (flatted fifth), A natural, into the sequence.

The move to E♭ can be analyzed a couple different ways. Since we are coming from A7, one can think of it as a shift to the ♭5 (E♭ is the ♭5 of A), which is known as a *tritone substitution*. Another way to look at it is as an interim step in the resolution from A7 to Dm, as we take a brief detour from A7 to the ♭2 (flatted second) of our intended root chord, Dm, which is E♭. A useful rule of thumb to remember is that the ♭5 of the V (five) chord also functions as the ♭2 of the root chord.

Bars 4 and 5 present a series of D minor arpeggios, but here I switch things up rhythmically by transitioning from eighth-note triplets to 16th notes, which makes the execution of these lines that much trickier. Also, I didn't want to put this shift right on the downbeat at the beginning of a bar; I wanted it to be less obvious, so this rhythmic shift to 16ths occurs on beat two in bar 5 and carries though the entirety of bars 5 and 6, after which, in bar 7, I return to eighth-note triplets. As you play through this section, you'll see that I've included subtle use of additional pitches—such as E, the ninth of D—in order to provide more varied melodic content.

The piece continues with a whole-step shift down to Cm, a two-whole-step shift down to A♭7 (again functioning as a ♭2 dominant chord, or *tritone substitution*) and then wraps up with a return to our "home" key, G minor, and a series of G minor sweeps that cover all seven strings.

When playing a piece this difficult and complex, I try to keep both hands completely relaxed. Some of the sweep arpeggios move across the majority of the strings, such as the Cm arpeggio in bars 6 and 7, the A♭7 in bar 8 and the Gm in bars 11–13. When executing these long sweeps, be sure to keep the pick-hand wrist loose; any stiffness will impede the movement of the pick across the strings, resulting in uneven articulation. Easier said than done, I might add!

—reprinted from *Guitar World*, October 2010

FIGURE 1

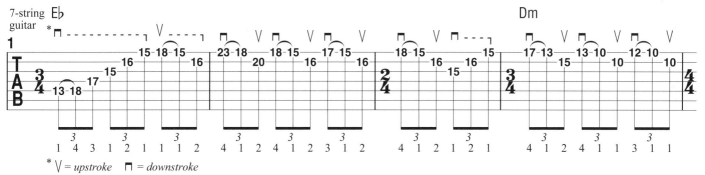

* V = *upstroke*   ⊓ = *downstroke*

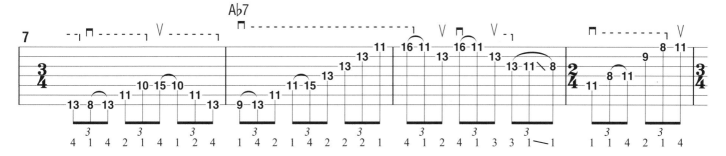

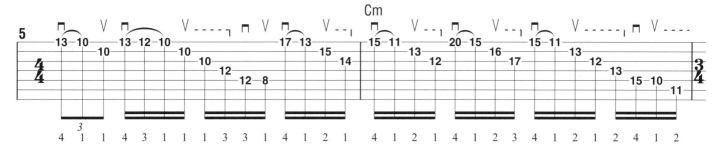

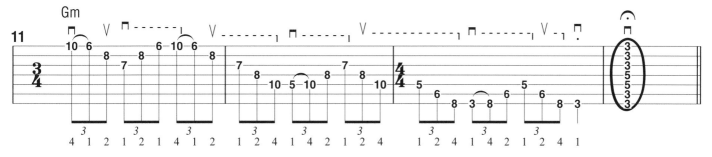

THRASH COURSE

by Dave Davidson of Revocation

Mode-rn Science

Building heavy riffs and unusual chords from the modes

One of my favorite ways to explore new riffs, chord patterns and melodic figures is to take one of the seven *fundamental modes* and use its structure as a guideline. In doing so, I often discover new chord shapes or melodic ideas that I may not have otherwise come across. Using this modal approach also offers a systematic way to take existing riffs or chordal ideas and tweak them in new and different harmonic directions.

The seven fundamental modes are built from the major scale, also known as the Ionian mode, which is spelled, intervallically, one (the root), major second, major third, perfect fourth, perfect fifth, major sixth, major seventh. Starting on each successive note, or degree, of the major scale and ascending one octave through that same set of notes forms a different, unique mode. A♯ a kid, I found this very confusing. I thought, If all of these modes are made up of the same seven notes, what makes each of them different from one another? What I discovered is that one has to think of each starting note as the new root note, or tonal center, which reorients the intervallic structure of the other notes around it and establishes the formation of the "root chord" of each mode.

As an example, let's look at the G major scale, illustrated in **FIGURE 1**. The notes of G major are G A B C D E F♯ and, intervallically, the sequence is 1 (root), maj2, maj3, 4, 5 maj6, maj7, 8 (octave). The next mode—the second mode—is found by starting on the second degree of the scale, A, and playing through the same series of notes up to A, one octave higher; this forms the A Dorian mode: A B C D E F♯ G, intervallically spelled 1 (root), maj2, ♭3, 4, 5, maj6, ♭7, relative to the root note A.

If we move up to the fourth note of the G major scale, C, and do the same thing, we get what's called the C Lydian mode, illustrated in **FIGURE 2**. The note pattern is C D E F♯ G A B, and, if we think of C as the new root, this note sequence is intervallically spelled 1 (root) maj2, maj3, ♯4 (sharp four), 5, maj6, maj7. A♯ it is built from the fourth degree of the G major scale, C Lydian is considered that scale's fourth mode.

The only difference, structurally, or intervallically, between Ionian and Lydian, is the fourth scale degree: in Ionian, it is a *perfect fourth*; in Lydian, it is *augmented*, or "sharp-ed." The ♯4 (in this case F♯) is the *characteristic* interval that distinguishes the Lydian mode from its Ionian counterpart, which in this case would be C Ionian: C D E F G A B.

Tune guitar down one half step (low to high: E♭ A♭ D♭ G♭ B♭ E♭).

FIGURE 1   G Ionian mode

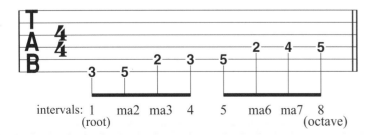

intervals: 1   ma2 ma3   4   5   ma6 ma7   8
(root)   (octave)

FIGURE 2   C Lydian mode

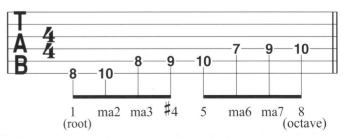

1   ma2 ma3 ♯4   5   ma6 ma7   8
(root)   (octave)

FIGURE 3 is a single-note riff designed to emphasize the Lydian mode's augmented fourth. Bouncing off a low C root note, I play a melodic line on the A string centered around F#, highlighting that note as the riff's "signature" note.

FIGURE 4 applies this same concept to a chordal idea, as I strum a syncopated pattern that shifts from C major triads to Cadd#4 shapes by simply moving the note G (B string, eighth fret) down one fret, to F#. In **FIGURE 5**, I apply this concept to a lead phrase. Using a C major triad (C E G) in three octaves as a basis, I move in each octave from the fifth, G, to the augmented fourth, F#, emphasizing a Lydian modality.

—reprinted from *Guitar World*, March 2014

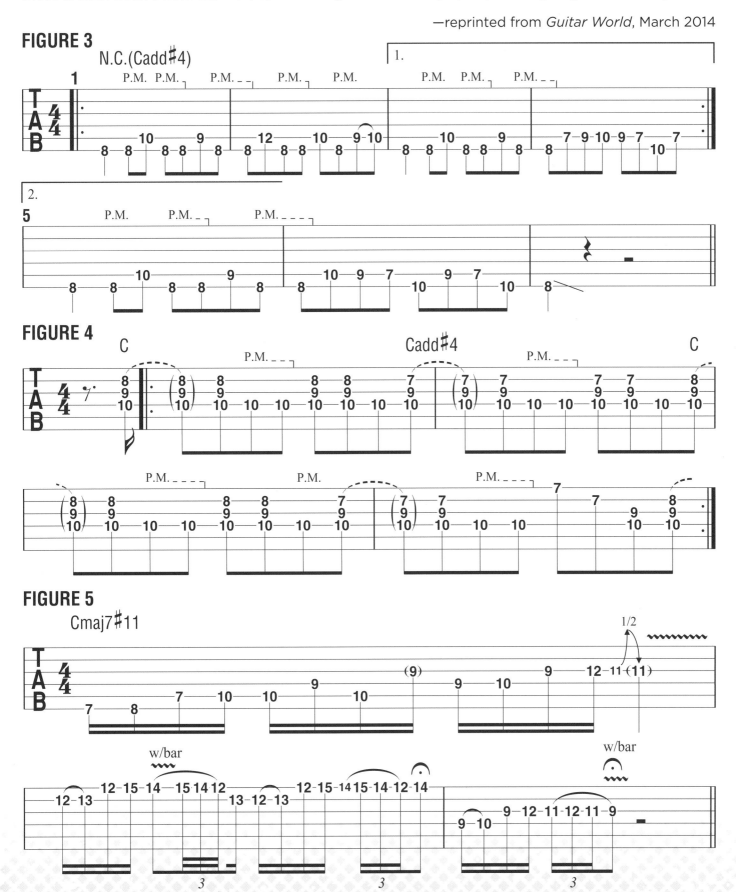

Minor Disturbance

Comparing the fundamental minor modes.

In my last column, I went over the differences and similarities between the major scale, also known as the Ionian mode, and another fundamental major mode, Lydian. This month, I'd like to take the same approach to comparing two fundamental minor modes: Aeolian, also known as the natural minor scale, and Dorian.

In our examination of Ionian versus Lydian, I pointed out the notes within each mode that I feel give it its characteristic quality, such as the major third and major seventh in Ionian, and the augmented, or "sharp-ed," fourth (#4) in Lydian. In composing songs, riffs or solos, I like to emphasize these characteristic tones so that the listener gets a clear picture, harmonically speaking, of the music they're hearing. Let's now take a look at what I consider to be the characteristic tones of Aeolian and Dorian.

As I mentioned last month, the seven fundamental modes are essentially different orientations of the major scale, with each degree of the scale used as a new starting point, or *tonic*, for each different mode. Aeolian is built from the major scale's sixth degree. If we look at the G major scale (G A B C D E F#), its sixth degree is E. If we start from that note and think of that as our new tonic, we get E Aeolian (E F# G A B C D; see **FIGURE 1**). In terms of intervals, or scale degrees, the Aeolian mode's formula is 1 (the root), 2 (the major second), ♭3 (the minor, or "flat," third, 4 (the perfect fourth), 5 (the perfect fifth), ♭6 (the minor sixth) and ♭7 (the minor seventh). To me, the note that most characterizes Aeolian is the minor sixth (♭6). In the key of E minor, that note is C.

Now, if we take these same seven notes and make A the root note, we get the A Dorian mode (A B C D E F# G; see **FIGURE 2**). The intervallic structure, or formula, is now 1, 2, ♭3, 4, 5, 6 (the *major* sixth) and ♭7. To me, the major sixth is the note that best characterizes the unique sound of the Dorian mode, which has a "warmer," or "lighter," quality than Aeolian. Focusing on that characteristic sound is a very useful

Tune guitar down one half step (low to high: E♭ A♭ D♭ G♭ B♭ E♭)

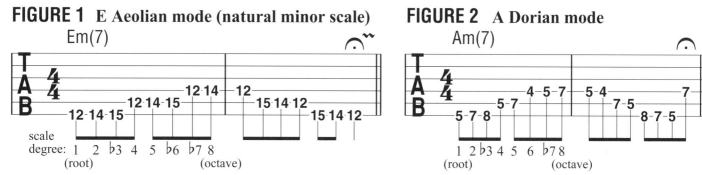

FIGURE 1   E Aeolian mode (natural minor scale)

FIGURE 2   A Dorian mode

thing to do when putting riffs together. **FIGURE 3** offers an example of a metal-style rhythm part that emphasizes the major sixth of A, F♯, throughout to create the sound of D7/A. For comparison, if I were to substitute the *minor* sixth of A, F, in this same riff, the result would be along the lines of **FIGURE 4**.

It's also very cool to put the modes side by side, as I do in **FIGURE 5**, wherein I play a similar melodic line against both E and A pedal tones. I can then use this approach for riff writing. In **FIGURE 6**, I alternate between E and A pedal tones while repeating a *static*, or unchanging, melodic line, thus making the difference between the two *modalities* more pronounced.

—reprinted from *Guitar World*, April 2014

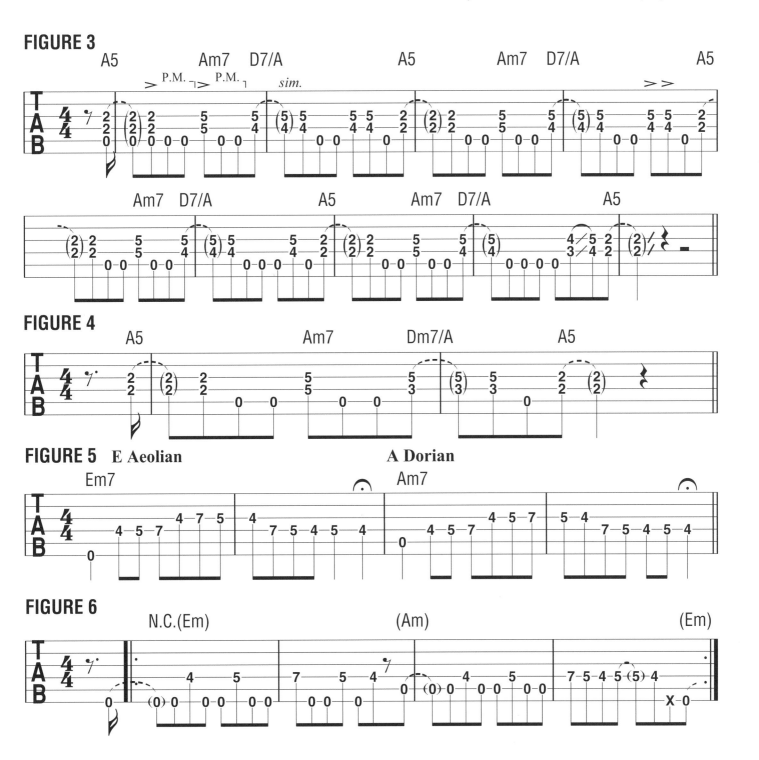

FIGURE 3

FIGURE 4

FIGURE 5   E Aeolian   A Dorian

FIGURE 6

Pentatonic Twists

Varying and applying a common guitar scale in interesting, unusual ways.

The pentatonic scale is the one scale that just about every rock, metal, blues, jazz and country guitar player is well familiar with. These five-tone scales—both the minor and major forms—sound great and fall easily on the fretboard, earning them their prevalence in all popular guitar-driven musical forms. One of my favorite things to do when writing riffs or soloing is to take a pentatonic form in one key and superimpose it over another. The result is often a sound that combines the familiarity of the melodic shapes and patterns with the ambiguity or unusual harmony created by this twist on the conventional approach to using pentatonic scales.

FIGURE 1 is based on E minor pentatonic (E G A B D) played in 9th/10th position. A♯ I ascend through the scale in steady 16th notes, I switch from a four-note pattern, played on beat one, to four consecutive ascending five-note patterns that carry through to the end of the phrase (plus a repeat of the last three notes of the final five-note pattern). You can either alternate pick through this entire phrase (down, up, down, up, etc.) or use economy, or "rest-stroke," picking, as I do. Economy picking involves using the same picking direction when crossing from one string to another. When moving from a lower string to a higher string, two consecutive downstrokes are employed. Conversely, when moving from a higher to a lower string, two consecutive upstrokes are used.

A standard way to spice up a pentatonic lick is to include the flatted fifth (♭5). When adding the ♭5 to minor pentatonic, the resulting scale is known as the blues scale. In the key of E, the blues scale would be spelled E G A B♭ B D. **FIGURE 2** is a lick that ascends through the E blues scale in a manner similar to **FIGURE 1**. Notice that, on the top two strings, I eliminate the fifth, B, altogether, so in effect I end up with a five-note "minor pentatonic flat-five scale," spelled E G A B♭ D.

Now that you have the idea, try experimenting with different ways to ascend through the E blues scale while accentuating the flatted fifth, as I demonstrate in **FIGURE 3**. At the beginning of the pattern, a diminished quality is formed by the use of three consecutive notes that are one and a half whole steps

7-string gtr. arranged for 6-string gtr. Tune down one half step (low to high: E♭ A♭ D♭ G♭ B♭ E♭).

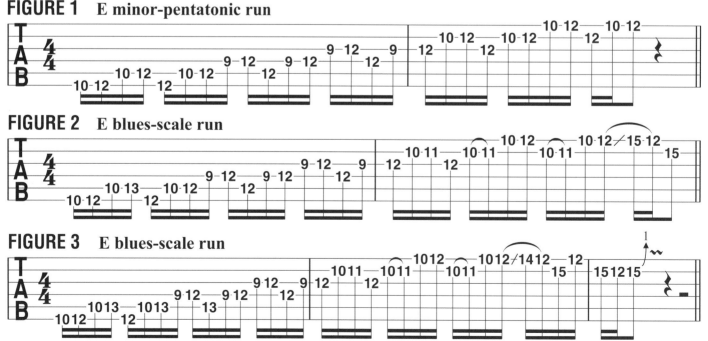

FIGURE 1   E minor-pentatonic run

FIGURE 2   E blues-scale run

FIGURE 3   E blues-scale run

apart: E, G and B♭. Adding the flatted third and flatted fifth to the root note in this way creates what is known as a diminished triad. **FIGURE 4** offers another lick based on this idea, ending in the last two bars with more conventional E blues scale–style licks.

When playing over an E major chord, a cool twist is to play E♭ minor pentatonic licks, as shown in **FIGURE 5**. In this example, I ascend as I did previously, switching from four- to five-note patterns. The notes of E♭ minor pentatonic are E♭ G♭ A♭ B♭ D♭. If we alternatively think of the scale as D♯ minor pentatonic, the notes are D♯ F♯ G♯ A♯ C♯. When played over E, these notes create an E Lydian sound, as they all live within that mode (E F♯ G♯ A♯ B C♯ D♯). A neat twist here would be to incorporate fretboard tapping, as I do in **FIGURE 6**.

Another great technique is to play minor pentatonic shapes off Gs, which is the major third of E. G♯ pentatonic minor is spelled G♯ B C♯ D♯ F♯, and these notes are included in the E major scale (E F♯ G♯ A B C♯ D♯). **FIGURE 7** offers an example of moving through G♯ minor pentatonic over an E pedal tone.

—reprinted from *Guitar World*, July 2014

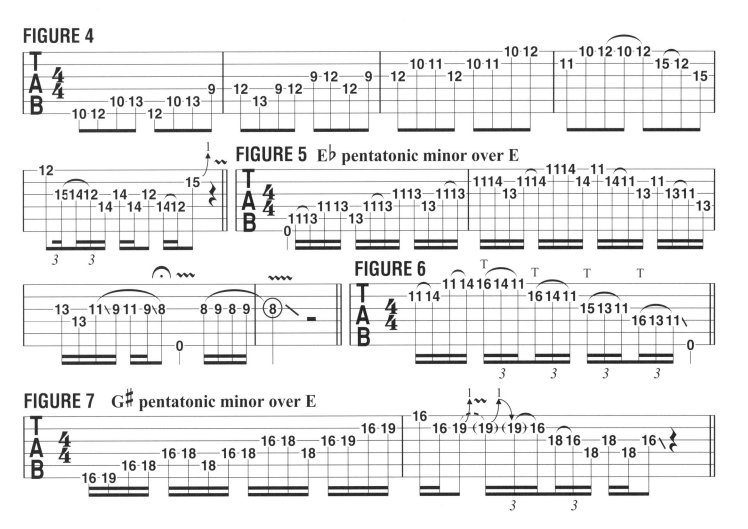

FIGURE 4

FIGURE 5 E♭ pentatonic minor over E

FIGURE 6

FIGURE 7 G♯ pentatonic minor over E

Half-Diminished Schemes

Using minor-seven flat-five chords in metal.

One of my prime objectives when writing music for my band Revocation is to try to push the envelope and come up with sounds, ideas, chord patterns, progressions and riffs that have been rarely explored within the thrash metal genre. A good way to do this is to use *seventh chords*, which are rarely heard in metal. This month, I'd like to demonstrate a few cool ways one can use one particularly cool- and tense-sounding seventh chord in heavy, thrash-style riffs.

Of the different types of seventh chords—major-seven, dominant-seven, minor-seven and what have you—the one that appeals to me most is *minor-seven-flat-five* (m7♭5), also known as *half-diminished-seven*. If you are unfamiliar with this chord type, it's helpful to start with a regular minor-seven chord, like the Cm7 voicing shown in **FIGURE 1**, then alter it. First, strum the entire chord, then pick out each note individually. In the Cm7 voicing illustrated here, the chord tones are, low to high, C, the root; G, the fifth; B♭, the minor, or "flat," seventh (♭7); and E♭, the minor, or "flat" third (♭3). If we lower the fifth, G, by one half step, to G♭ (or F♯), we get the Cm7♭5 voicing depicted in **FIGURE 2**. Again, pick the notes of the chord individually, then strum them together. Our chord-tone "stack" is now, low to high, C, the root; G♭, the diminished, or "flat," fifth (♭5); B♭, the minor, or "flat," seventh (♭7); and E♭, the minor, or "flat" third (♭3). You'll notice that this chord sounds much more tense than Cm7.

The "flat-five" sound has been a staple of metal from the very beginning, a prime example being the intro to the song "Black Sabbath," the opening track on Black Sabbath's debut album. Tony Iommi plays a G octave followed by a trilled D♭, which is the flatted fifth, or "flat five," of G. The root/flat-five interval, by the way, is formally known as a *tritone*, so called because flatted fifth is three whole tones above or below the root.

Now that we're familiar with a standard Cm7♭5 voicing, the next thing to do is to move up the fretboard and rearrange the order, or "stacking," of the chord tones to generate what's known as the next *inversion*. In **FIGURE 3**, a different voicing of Cm7♭5 is played using the notes, low to high, E♭, B♭, C and G♭. Now the chord's third, E♭, is on the bottom, or "in the bass," as they say, which makes this a *first-inversion* voicing. The ♭5 is now on top of the voicing, which gives it more emphasis and lends the voicing a more jarring quality. **FIGURE 4** illustrates a thrash-type rhythm part built from this voicing. In bar 1, I strum the full

Seven-string guitar arr. for six-string
Tune down one half step (low to high: B♭ E♭ A♭ D♭ G♭ B♭ E♭).
All music sounds one half step lower than written.

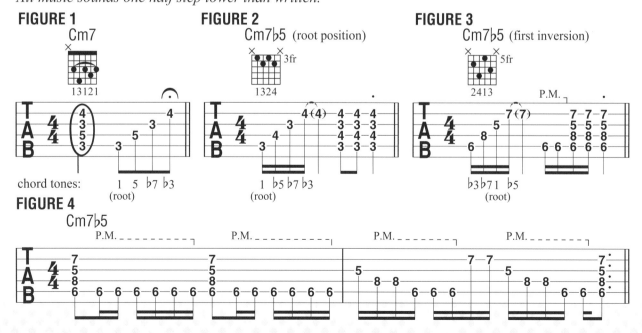

chord then repeatedly pick the bottom note with palm muting, and in bar 2, I *arpeggiate* the chord—play the notes individually, in succession—and double-pick some of them.

FIGURE 5 offers another rhythm approach using arpeggiation. And **FIGURE 6** illustrates a riff built entirely from double-picked arpeggios.

If we move up to the next inversion, placing the ♭5, G♭, on the bottom of the stack, we get the Cm7♭5 voicing shown in **FIGURE 7**. This is known as a *second-inversion* voicing, because the fifth is now in the bass. **FIGURE 8** offers a thrash-type pattern using this voicing.

We can move up one more time and place the ♭7, B♭, in the bass, resulting in the *third-inversion* voicing shown in **FIGURE 9**. **FIGURE 10** places all of the different voicings in ascending order so you can easily compare and memorize their sounds and fingerings.

—reprinted from *Guitar World*, August 2014

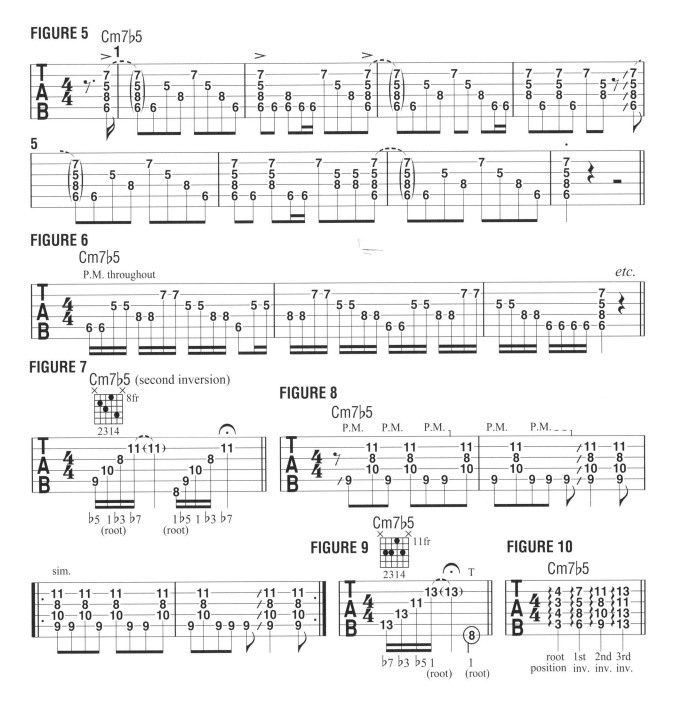

Dark Shadows

Using minor-seven flat-five chords in metal, part 2.

Last month I introduced the dark-sounding *minor-seven flat-five* (m7♭5) chord and demonstrated a few ways guitarists can incorporate it into the writing of thrash-metal rhythm-guitar riffs and ideas. This month, I'd like to continue with more examples of how to use this unusual sound in a variety of cool, effective ways within thrash metal.

To review, let's start with a normal minor-seven chord, such as the Cm7 shown in **FIGURE 1**. Play each note individually, starting with the root, C, then the fifth, G, the minor, or "flat," seventh, (♭7), B♭, and then the minor, or "flat," third (♭3), E♭. Then strum the entire chord, making sure all the notes ring clearly. Let's now lower, or "flat," the fifth, G, (D string, fifth fret), down one half step, to F♯ (fourth fret). The result is Cm7♭5, as shown in **FIGURE 2**. Again, pick out the notes individually, then strum them together. The intervallic structure of this chord voicing is, low to high: root (C), ♭5 (G♭), ♭7 (B♭), ♭3 (E♭). The sound of the ♭5 creates a really cool kind of tension that is fun to explore within metal music.

A great way to find alternate voicings for a given chord up and down the fretboard is to go through all of its *inversions*. This is done by placing a different chord tone on the bottom of a note stack, or "in the bass." When the root note, or *tonic*, is in the bass, as it is with this first voicing of Cm7♭5, the voicing is known as root position. One can easily find other voicings for Cm7♭5 (or any chord) by moving each note in the voicing up to the next higher chord tone on the same string. Cm7♭5 is built from four notes, so there are four different voicings to be found, as illustrated in **FIGURE 3**. I begin with the root-position Cm7♭5, and then move up the fretboard on the fifth string in order to sound the next chord tone, E♭, the minor third. A voicing that has the third in the bass (minor or major) is called a *first-inversion* voicing.

We can also place the fifth as the lowest note, in this case the ♭5, shown as the next chord voicing in **FIGURE 3**. This is known as a *second-inversion* voicing. Lastly, we can sound the seventh as the lowest

7-string gtr. arranged for 6-string gtr. Tune down one half step (low to high: E♭ A♭ D♭ G♭ B♭ E♭).
All music sounds one half step lower than written.

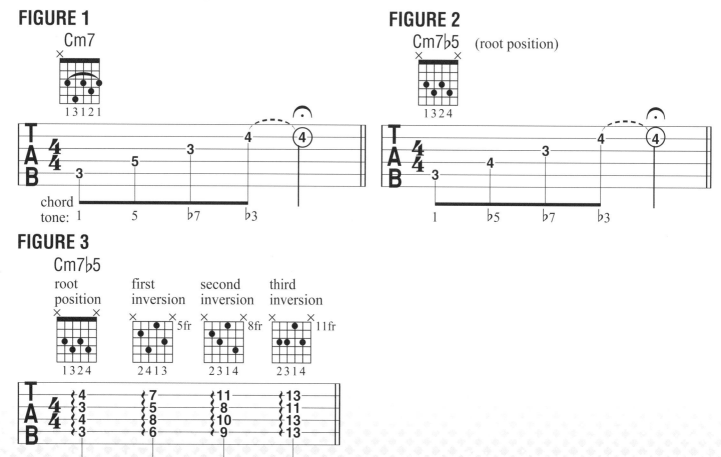

note, in this case, the ♭7, also shown in **FIGURE 3**, and this is known as a *third-inversion* voicing. Memorize each of these chord shapes, or "grips," while also acknowledging the difference in the chord quality as you move from voicing to voicing.

FIGURE 4 presents some cool licks derived from these voicings. I'm simply arpeggiating each voicing, starting with the third-inversion Cm7♭5, and then moving down through the lower inversions, using my whammy bar to dip or shake the top note of each voicing. Another approach is to use the arpeggio as the jumping-off point for fast, repeating licks, as shown in **FIGURES 5** and **6**. I play the arpeggiated notes of the chord in alternating ascending and descending manner using hammer-ons and pull-offs, first demonstrating the idea in 16th notes and then in 16th-note triplets.

Once you become familiar with these shapes, try doing the same thing on other string groups and in other keys, and with other chord types as well.

This is my final column for the time being. I hope the ideas I've shared have been helpful and useful. See you out on the road.

FIGURE 4

—reprinted from *Guitar World*, September 2014

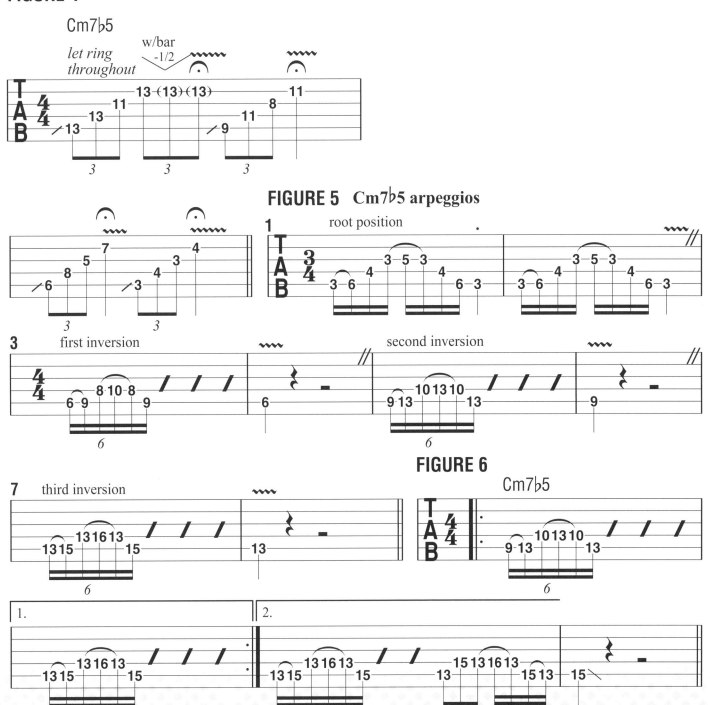

Symphony of Instruction

by Dave Mustaine

It's All in the Hands

Pick-hand anchoring, varying degrees of muting and "cheating at chords."

Hi everyone, Dave Mustaine here. Welcome to my first-ever attempt at writing a guitar column. We're about to embark on a mysterious guitar journey together—and since I really don't know what I'm doing, it should be an interesting one!

I've read other players' columns in the past and always hoped that someday I'd be able to do something similar. But being self-taught, I had to wonder what I could possibly teach anybody, since I have no real idea what I'm doing when it comes to talking about scales and music theory. For me, the exciting thing about writing my first instructional column with *Guitar World* is that it's so much better than creating one of those home videos where you demonstrate how to play stuff and then some butt-wipe speeds it up, dubs another voice over it and posts it on YouTube!

My hands are the most important part of my sound and playing style; they make all the difference in the world. Of course, my Dean guitars, Marshall amps and effect pedals are extremely important to my tone, but because I'm always using my hands, I can pick up pretty much any guitar plugged into any amp and still sound like me. My sound is a result of how I use the flesh of my pick hand to damp or mute the strings on one side and the way I fret the strings on the other side. I also do a lot of muting with my fret hand, which might come as a surprise to most people.

FRET-HAND MUTING

I look at the guitar as being both a percussive and melodic instrument, because it can be played either way. Sometimes I'll choke the strings with my fret hand while I'm picking or strumming, which creates a hollow, pitchless and percussive chu-ka sound. The sound is similar to that of a guiro, a ribbed wooden Latin percussion instrument whose surface you scrape with a stick.

FIGURE 1 is a simple example that demonstrates what I'm talking about. All I do is strum the strings while lightly laying my fret-hand fingers across them, without pushing them down against the frets. In this example I'm muting with more than one finger. I do this so that I don't inadvertently sound harmonic chimes, something that can happen if you use one finger to mute the strings and touch them at one of the harmonic node points, such as directly over the 12th, seventh or fifths frets. Keep in mind that distortion accentuates harmonics, so this issue becomes more acute the more gain you dial in. Mind you, there are times when you may want to induce those chiming sounds, but in this particular case we don't want to.

You can hear me play the guitar in this percussive way on "Train of Consequences." Looking back, I think got into this technique by learning the UFO song "Mother Mary," where it's an integral part of the main riff.

FIGURE 1

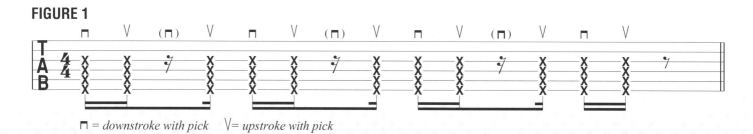

⊓ = *downstroke with pick*   V = *upstroke with pick*

PHOTO A

PHOTO B

PHOTO C

PHOTO D

PALM MUTING

Muting with the picking hand is a major part of my playing style. Palm muting involves pressing the fleshy heel of your picking hand's palm against the strings. The positioning of the hand is critical in order to mute the strings whenever and wherever you choose. Some players will let their palm literally float over the strings, but I cheat (and I think a lot of metal players do the same exact thing): I curl my pinkie around the plastic pickup ring that frames the bridge pickup and let the heel of my hand roll across the string saddles on the bridge (see **PHOTO A**). I think I developed this habit when I started playing guitar. I was attempting to perform simple

PHOTO E

fingerpicking patterns from Beatles songs with a pick, and I figured that anchoring my pinkie in a stationary position would develop muscle memory and allow me to jump to the right string without looking.

Positioning the heel of my picking hand in this way allows me to apply varying layers or degrees of damping (palm muting) as I literally roll my palm over the bridge in either direction. **PHOTOS B-E** illustrate a few of the degrees of damping that you can attain: from none (**PHOTO B**) to a little (**PHOTO C**) to a lot (**PHOTO E**). To hear the differences, try applying them to **FIGURE 2**, which is a rhythm pattern similar to the intro riff from "Sleepwalker" (*United Abominations*), the song we've been opening our live set with lately. As you can see in the tab, the riff comprises only one note—the open low E—and allows you to focus your attention on what your pick hand is doing. As you can also see and hear, doing this not only "chokes up" the string in varying degrees but also produces a weird, but cool, sound as you move the palm down the string to where it's positioned directly over the rear pickup's pole pieces.

"CHEATING" AT CHORDS

Often when I'm playing chords, I'll pull off another cheat by playing only a couple of the notes. For example, instead of playing a full open E chord (see Diagram 1 below **FIGURE 2**), I'll play just the two notes at the second fret on the A and D strings, which are the fifth, B and the octave of the root note, E (see Diagram 2). Like I said earlier, I don't really know what I'm doing or what this is called, but the guys at *Guitar World* tell me that the result is an *inverted power chord*. Whatever it is, I use it a lot! And the cool thing about doing this in this particular key is that it enables me to pedal a palm-muted open low E note between chord stabs, as demonstrated in **FIGURE 3**.

As I just mentioned, I do this in a lot of songs, one of them being "Reckoning Day" (*Youthanasia*). In this song, while pedaling on the palm-muted open low E note, I play inverted power chords that climb up the neck chromatically (one fret at a time). Specifically, I'm playing inverted G5, G#5 and A5 chords against the pedaled E note, which builds tension. As I sound each of these two-note chords, the bassist plays the corresponding root note down low. The combination of my distorted, two-note, inverted power chord voicings and the low, clean-tone bass notes sounds really full and clear because the frequency map isn't cluttered. In this case, *not* playing the low root note on the guitar gives the chords more air and punch.

That's it for my first column. I hope it all made sense to you. Dissecting what I do and then trying to put it into words has already taught me a thing or two, and I think it's going to help make me a better player. This is totally new territory for me, and I'm having a blast exploring it with you. Here's to the "old dog learning some new tricks." See you next month.

—reprinted from *Guitar World*, January 2008

FIGURE 2 rhythm pattern, à la "Sleepwalker"

Diagram 1: E   Diagram 2: E5/B
                    (inverted E5 diad)

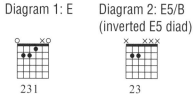

FIGURE 3

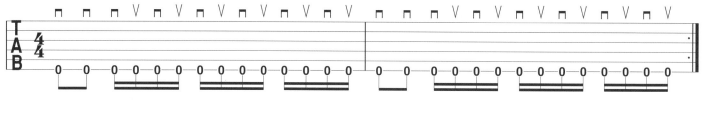

FIGURE 4 "Reckoning Day" main riff, played backwards

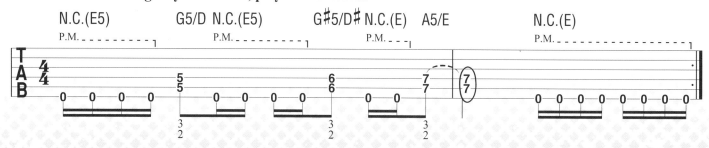

Nit Picking

Getting the most out of your pick.

Hi, and welcome to *Symphony of Instruction* #2, which I'm writing in the "land down under," as Megadeth are currently headlining the Australian leg of *Gigantour* with Static-X, DevilDriver, Lacuna Coil and a new band called Bring Me the Horizon. Last month, in my debut installment of this column, I discussed pick-hand anchoring, palm muting and a "chord-cheating" fingering technique. This month I'm going to zone in on picking.

First, let's start with the pick itself. Some guitarists prefer a really thick, rigid pick. Brian May of Queen, for example, uses an old English coin called a sixpence that's about the size of a dime. I like a pick that has some flexibility to it, where I can alter its rigidity depending on how I hold it. I use a Tortex pick that's .73mm thick. I prefer Tortex because the surface of the material has a certain texture to it that's not as smooth and slippery as regular plastic picks. I find that Tortex picks are easier to hold onto than normal picks, which can be a big issue onstage when your hands get sweaty in the heat of battle.

I basically have two ways of holding the pick. When I'm pedaling a note—and pedaling for me is controlled by palm muting—I'll hold the pick near the tip with a firm grip, as shown in **PHOTO A**. The faster I'm pedaling, the more I tend to tighten my grip on the pick and hold it closer to the tip, as doing this effectively makes the pick more rigid. This, in turn, helps me pick with greater precision and consistency.

If I'm playing something that's more percussive, like the intro to "Train of Consequences" or the chorus of "Washington Is Next," I'll loosen my grip on the pick and hold it a little further away from the tip, as shown in **PHOTO B**. Doing so makes the pick a bit more flexible. **FIGURE 1** is an example of a percussive part I'd play using this picking technique in conjunction with completely damping the strings with my fret hand. **FIGURE 2**, by contrast, is a palm-muted pedal riff for which I'd really "choke up" on the pick in order to play with precision.

PHOTO A

PHOTO B

FIGURE 1   ⊓ = *downstroke with pick*   ∨ = *upstroke with pick*

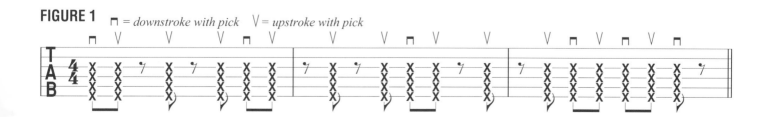

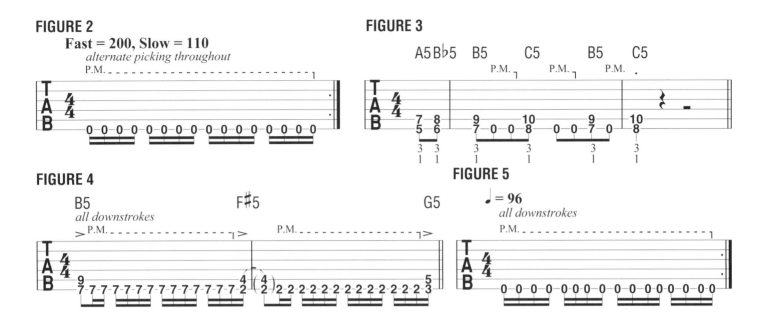

For many of my riffs I down-pick exclusively in order to make them sound precise, consistent and aggressive. For example, the riff shown in **FIGURE 3**, which is similar to one in "Wake Up Dead," just doesn't sound as clean when played with alternate (down-up) picking. Try picking it both ways—entirely with downstrokes and then with alternate picking—and compare the two. You'll immediately hear what I mean. Do the same with **FIGURE 4**, which is not unlike one of the riffs in "Tornado of Souls."

It seems to me that down-picking is an art form that many of today's players overlook or miss completely. Performing this technique cleanly requires a lot of precision and concentration. I've noticed that some players tend to pick in a circular fashion when they're picking fast, but that tends to result in the pick slicing the string at an angle (**PHOTO C**). When I pick, and especially when I down-pick, I always try to keep the plane of the pick as parallel to the string as possible (**PHOTO D**). I do this because it shortens the amount of time the pick is in contact with the string. This results in a more "plucked" sound as opposed to the "rubbed" sound that occurs when the flat side of the pick is turned at an angle to the string. You can hear this effect when you really dig in on a riff like **FIGURE 5,** which is similar to one in "Gears of War."

Another discovery I've made when attempting to down-pick quickly is to avoid letting your fingers fan out, as shown in **PHOTO E**, because the additional momentum produced by extending the fingers slows you down. It helps to keep your fingers in (**PHOTO F**), kind of like an airplane when it needs to haul ass.

—reprinted from *Guitar World*, February 2008

PHOTO C

PHOTO D

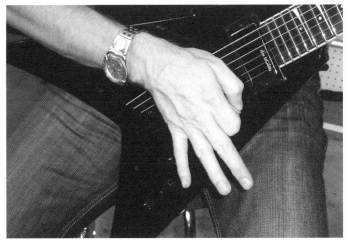

PHOTO E

PHOTO F

Spider-man

Using unconventional fingerings for maximum fretboard economy.

One thing I try to do in my playing is economize hand movement as much as possible. More often than not, I'm singing and trying to have a visual dialog with the audience while also playing rhythm guitar, which limits my ability to look down at my hands and control my instrument. I've seen some great players like Robert Fripp literally fly all over the neck effortlessly, but I don't have that much time to watch what I'm doing, and even when I'm not singing I still try and minimize my fret-hand movement.

Years back, I noticed that many of my songs incorporate a progression where a root/fifth chord shape played on the A and D strings, like the E5 in **DIAGRAM 1**, is followed by a chord played one fret higher and one pair of strings lower, like the C5 in **DIAGRAM 2**. When using heavy distortion, as I tend to do, it can be difficult to move back and forth between these two chords quickly and smoothly with the conventional index-ring fingering shown in **FIGURE 1**. If it's a fast-moving riff, your timing is going to be a little off, and there'll be some unwelcome string noise. If, however, you finger the E5 chord with your index and ring fingers (see **PHOTO A**) and then fret the C5 chord with your middle finger and pinkie (see **DIAGRAM 3** and **PHOTO B**), you can quickly and easily alternate between the two shapes with barely any movement and noise—and, just as importantly, without having to look down at your fingers! **DIAGRAM 4** presents a composite view of both fingerings.

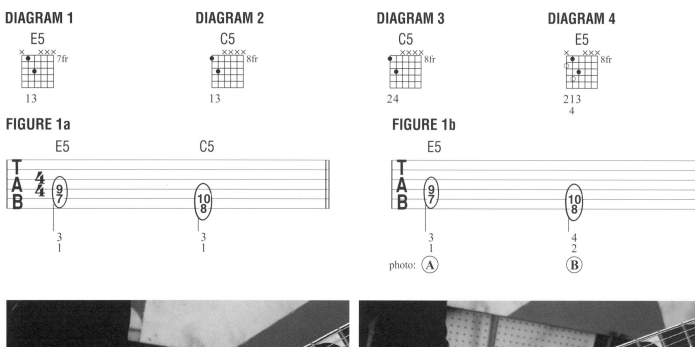

FIGURE 1a

FIGURE 1b

photo: Ⓐ   Ⓑ

PHOTO A

PHOTO B

I had used this "spider chord" technique in my previous band, but I can't really remember what I played with those guys! So instead I'm going to show you how I use it in a riff similar to one I play in "Wake Up Dead" (*Peace Sells...But Who's Buying?*) (**FIGURE 2**). The correct spider chord fingering is indicated below the tab. For the sake of comparison, **FIGURE 3** shows the same part played with conventional fingering. When you compare the two fingerings you'll definitely hear and feel the difference right away. If you've been trying to master this riff you've probably had a tough time until now because you didn't know how I'd been "cheating" like this! **FIGURE 4** shows a more complete version of the riff, with my fingerings included.

I'd love to give you a great story about how I came up with this fingering idea in an incredible moment of Zen-like clarity, but in reality I just did it and realized what I was doing later on. Back in my teens I would be playing and writing fast riffs and fretting root/fifth power chords on the A and D strings with my first and third fingers, and my second and fourth fingers would be twitching because I was playing so fast. And it just so happened that the guitar and fingers kind of serendipitously collided. It was kind of like, "Wow, you stuck your peanut butter in my chocolate."

I named this technique "spider chord" fingering because it kind of looks like a spider crawling across your fretboard. Try using it in some of your own riffs.

—reprinted from *Guitar World*, March 2008

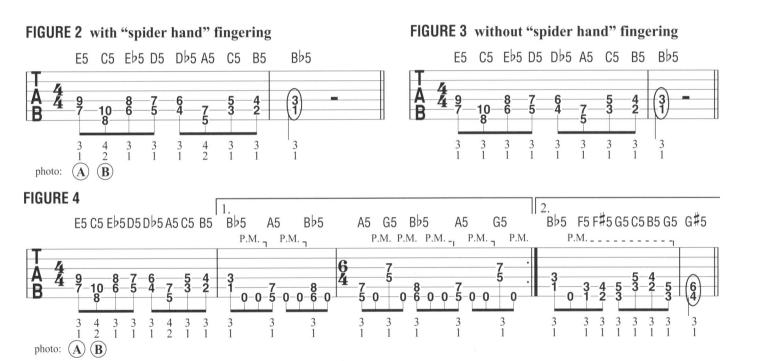

Scratches, Scrapes and "Upside-Down" Strumming
More "spider chord" fingerings, plus pick scrapes and upstroke chord strums.

First off, I'd like to say a big "thank you" to everyone who voted *United Abominations* the "Best Metal Album" in the 2008 *Guitar World* Reader's Poll. That's incredibly flattering, and I'm extremely grateful. Thanks also for voting for me in the "Best Metal Guitarist" category. Coming in second right behind Tony Iommi? I'll take that! Cheers!

Last month I talked about a technique I call "spider chord" fingering, and the specific example we looked at involved moving from a power chord on the A and D strings to one located one fret higher on the low E and A strings. You can also use this same fingering technique to quickly and efficiently alternate between two power chords that are one fret apart on the same pair of strings, as demonstrated in **FIGURES 1a** and **1b**. It also works well when shifting from an open E5 chord to F5 at the first fret (**FIGURE 1c**), as I do in "Symphony of Destruction" (*Countdown to Extinction*), or from an open A5 to B♭5 (**FIGURE 1d**). Some of the faster songs in Megadeth's catalog require economy of movement with hand shapes, and that's where this approach really proves useful.

ODE TO GENE SIMMONS

I love adding pick scratches and scrapes to my guitar lines. The only trouble is they "eat" Tortex picks alive! A typical pick scrape starts near the bridge and descends the neck toward the nut. You can also do it in the opposite direction, which changes the "note" or pitch of the scratch. I got into this technique as a kid by listening to Kiss—Gene Simmons would often do a quick finger slide up and down the low string of his bass with his fret hand at the start of what seemed like every single measure. Pick scrapes essentially create the same vibe as a finger slide.

I usually perform pick scrapes on a single string because it's easier to control the pitch of the scratch—I rarely go for ones that involve two strings. I rotate the pick at a slight angle to the string so it creates almost a skipping sound instead of just a "rubbing" sound. What I'm doing is effectively pushing, as opposed to dragging, the pick along the length of the string; this results in a much more aggressive and pronounced attack because of the way the edge of the pick is hitting the ridges on a wound string. To me, pushing the pick is similar to pushing a putty knife or a scraper to get some crap off of a wall. If I'm doing a scrape toward the nut, the edge of the pick that's actually involved in creating the scraping sound is in front of the hand that's pushing it.

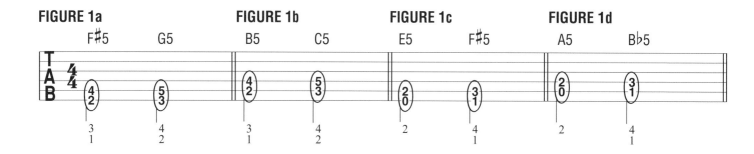

CREATIVE AND CREEPY SCRATCHING

Rather than just performing the obvious type of pick scratches, I like to be as creative as possible with the technique. One song that has some interesting pick scratching in it is "Bad Omen" (*Peace Sells… But Who's Buying?*). **FIGURE 2** shows a riff that's similar to it. A♯ you can see from the tablature, in that teeny little "breathing space" between the E5 and B♭5 chords, I do a "stuttering," three-step pick scrape, specifically on the low E string, which is really creepy sounding.

I also do something like this in "Skin O' My Teeth" (*Countdown to Extinction*). When the band rebuilds the tension after the guitar solo, the riff stops for a second and I play a series of very short pick scratches that kind of sound like a man scratching his stubbly face [**FIGURE 3**].

Hopefully these two short examples illustrate that there's a bunch of really interesting and creative things you can do with your pick without even having to fret a note at the other end of the guitar.

STRUMMING CHORDS UPSIDE-DOWN

Normally, when you strum a chord you do so with a downstroke of your pick, hitting the lower notes first. To me, hearing the low note first is kind of like having a fat person in your house: there's not much you can do once that note takes over because there's no room left. Usually, that's okay, but on occasion strumming a chord "upside-down"—by picking the higher notes first—sounds better because you can hear the whole chord. This is especially true when your sound is heavily distorted. Play the Em chord in **FIGURE 4** with a downstroke and then with an upstroke and you'll hear exactly what I'm talking about. Ditto the riff shown in **FIGURE 5**.

—reprinted from *Guitar World*, April 2008

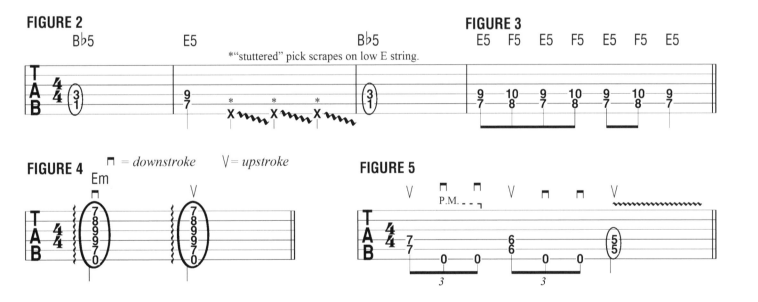

Spooky Chords

Exotic voicings, major and minor dyads, and more on picking chords "upside-down."

I'm writing this column while in Europe, where we're currently on tour. A# you've probably already heard, we have a new guitarist, Chris Broderick [Nevermore, Jag Panzer]. Chris is heavily influenced by Marty Friedman, which is great, because Megadeth play more music from that era of the band than any other and I've always liked that particular style. I look at Chris as raw talent. He sounds just like Marty, and with him in the band we have a new lease on life. Glen Drover, who recently left the band, endorsed Chris as his replacement, and Chris has come in and kicked everything up to a whole new level.

Last time out, in the April 2008 column, I touched upon the technique of picking chords upside down, meaning with an upstroke strum. This month I'm going to continue with this topic and give you some examples of how to use this move to good musical effect. **DIAGRAMS 1–3** show three somewhat unusual chord-voicings where, if you strum them upside down, you get the high notes sounding before the low ones have a chance to eat them up.

During the earliest days of Megadeth, even before David Ellefson was on bass, I jammed with a strange guitarist a few times, but we never played a gig together. He played a lot of really weird, cool chords, like those that George Lynch and Warren DiMartini used sometimes. I watched what he did, took several of those chords that I liked and worked them into a progression that I thought was pretty scary sounding. **FIGURE 1** shows what I came up with, which is similar to something I do in "Looking Down the Cross." As you can see, I used the chords from **DIAGRAMS 1** and **2**, and they're picked upside down.

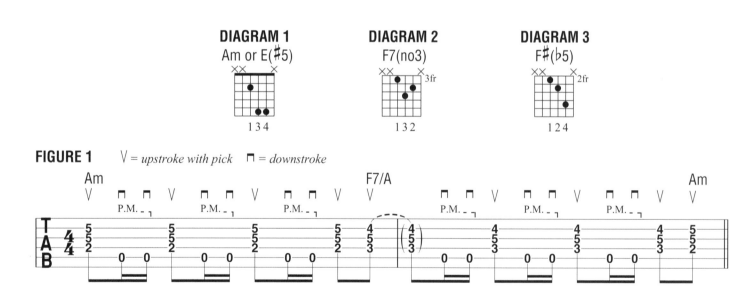

FIGURE 7 is a progression similar to one I play in "Holy Wars...The Punishment Due," and **FIGURES 2–6** show this part broken down into five small, simplified sections. I'm using upside-down picking for all the chords, most of which are major or minor diads. All I'm doing with these chords is playing a root note and a major or minor third above it, instead of the more typical root/fifth power chords. There's no mathematical reason for me doing this; it was merely for the colorful sound of the chords. I was listening to a lot of Mercyful Fate and Diamond Head at the time, two bands that have a lot of really great riffs built around these same kinds of two-note major- and minor-chord voicings, and I found myself really enjoying their songs. To truly appreciate how much color these kinds of major and minor diads add to a riff, try playing **FIGURE 7** again, this time substituting a root/fifth power chord for every chord. You'll hear the difference immediately.

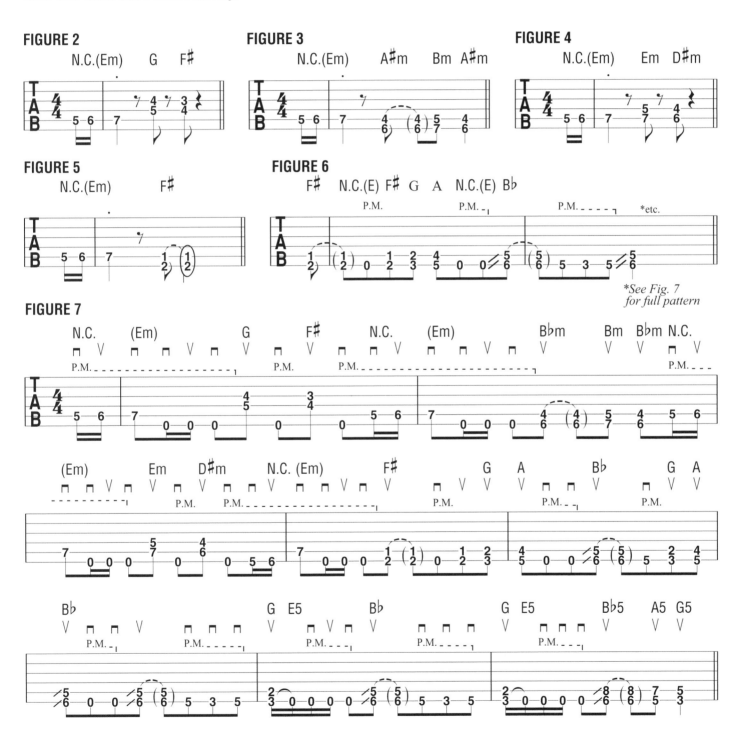

FIGURE 2

FIGURE 3

FIGURE 4

FIGURE 5

FIGURE 6

FIGURE 7

The Groan Zone

Using chord slides to add aggression to a riff.

By the time you read this month's column, the U.S. leg of *Gigantour 2008* will have started. I'm really stoked about the bill. Once again it consists of exciting bands, amazing guitarists and great overall musicianship. There's no bullshit bands, just a bunch of talented people who are itching to work and will really deliver the goods to the fans.

Over the past few columns we've looked at subtle rhythm nuances that can really make a huge difference in the sound and impact of a riff, and this month we're going to examine another such technique: *chord sliding*. At some point you begin to realize that rhythm guitar is a completely different animal than lead guitar, though people often don't give it the attention it deserves. One of the greatest rhythm players I've ever heard is Malcolm Young of AC/DC, who I believe is almost criminally underrated and overlooked. I learned a hell of a lot about playing rhythm from listening to him when I was growing up. Malcolm has amazing timing, is able to hold things down and is great at pedaling one note while the rest of the song goes off in other directions. Malcolm opened up my world to the idea that a simple and well-executed rhythm idea can make a huge impact on even the simplest chord progression.

Chord sliding involves fretting a chord and sliding it into the next position. The effect is like a groaning sound. The guitar takes on a guttural voice that's really overwhelming.

I first used my chord-sliding technique when I was in Metallica. **FIGURE 1** shows a riff that's similar to one I did with them and that they still play. To hear how chord sliding changes the sound of a riff, compare **FIGURES 2a** and **2b**. **FIGURE 2a** is nowhere near as heavy as **FIGURE 2b**.

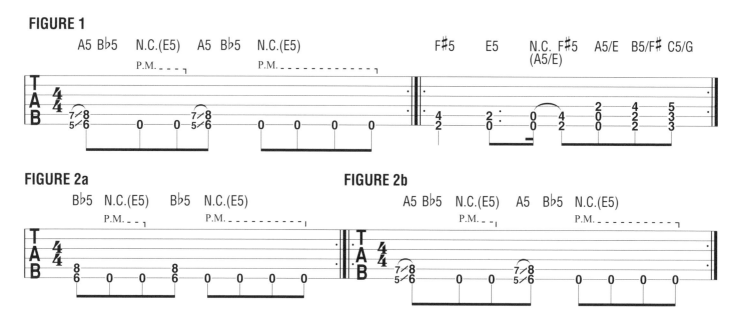

FIGURE 3 is a riff not unlike the intro to "Ashes in Your Mouth." As you can see, I go from an open E5 power chord to sliding an inverted, one-fingered shape from the first fret up to the third and play C5 before moving to G5 in the same position. The whole thing sounds a little odd when played slowly, but it sounds pretty cool when played at tempo in the indicated rhythm. Near the end of "Hook in Mouth" I play slides that are even more exaggerated in a simple B♭-A-G power-chord progression. It really accentuates the groaning sound. **FIGURE 4** is based on a similar idea.

Try incorporating some chord-slide "groans" into your own riffs. A♯ always, I recommend that you employ these ideas sparingly and tastefully. I strongly advise against overusing any technique for that matter. A♯ the old saying goes, "familiarity breeds contempt."

—reprinted from *Guitar World*, July 2008

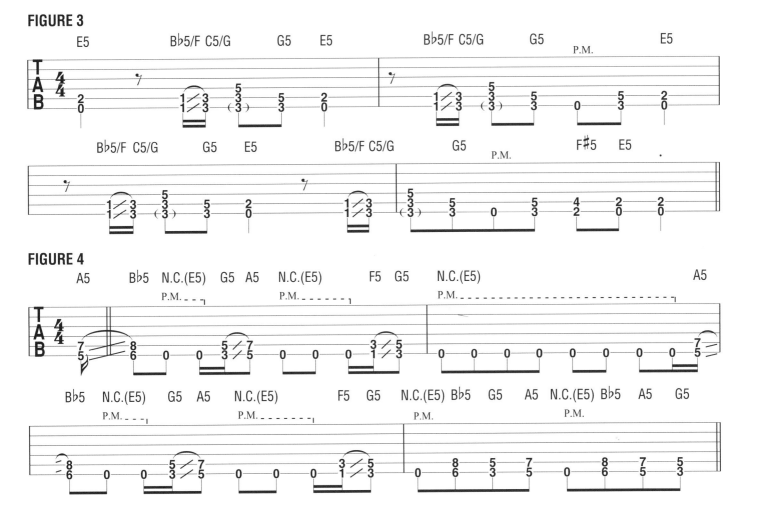

FIGURE 3

FIGURE 4

Thumb's Up!

Wide-stretch drone licks, plus the "over-the-top thumb trick."

Hey, what's up? Before we get into this month's topic I'd like to say a quick but sincere "thank you!" to the many thousands of you that have already come out to support Gigantour. Even though it's only just started, the turnout at all the shows has been incredible, and I love the fact that even the critics are saying nice things about it! In fact, they've been proclaiming this year's bill as the best and most diverse lineup yet, which is quite an accolade as both of the previous Gigantour lineups have had great bands. It looks like Gigantour is fast becoming a franchise in its own right without being correlated with Megadeth or myself, which is exciting too.

This month we're going to look at a few wide-stretch licks that have become something of my trademark. The first one under the microscope is an F♯ minor blues lick (**FIGURE 1**) similar to one I play in the song that opens our current set, "Sleepwalker." For all intents and purposes the lick I'm playing is basically an Ace Frehley–type pentatonic lick like the one shown in **FIGURE 2**, but with a subtle twist to it.

In **FIGURE 1** I barre the top four strings at the 14th fret with my index finger and then leave it there throughout the lick. What I'm effectively doing here is using my first finger as a capo. I could easily play this phrase without doing that, but I'd lose the advantage of having the strings that aren't played ringing sympathetically underneath the ones that are, which creates a drone-y, almost sitar-like effect.

FIGURE 4 is similar to what's probably my most well known wide-stretch lick, the one I do toward the very end of "Holy Wars." What I'm doing here is playing the wide-stretch, pull-off lick on the B and G strings shown in **FIGURE 3** and shifting it up the neck, one fret at a time. To play this lick, I barre the top three strings with my index finger even though I don't use the high E string. I do this because, once again, this allows the unused barred string to resonate in the background, which to me sounds pretty interesting.

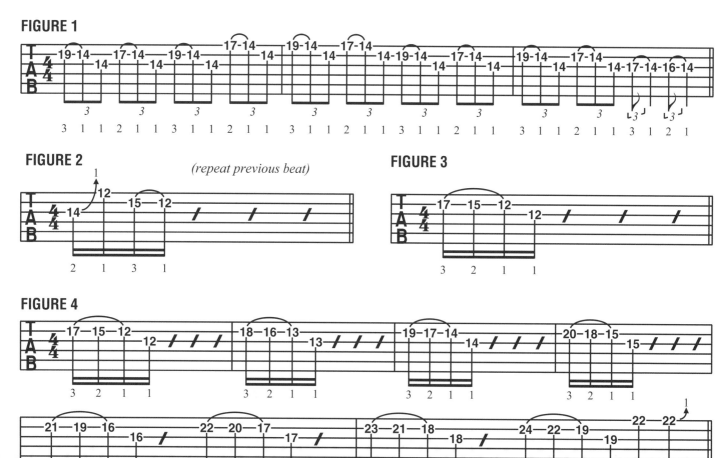

FIGURE 1

FIGURE 2

FIGURE 3

FIGURE 4

The final wide-stretch lick I'm going to show you is one from "Washington Is Next!" I start off with a typical chicken-pickin' pull-off lick in **FIGURE 5** and then expand it into **FIGURE 6** by quickly bringing my fret-hand thumb around to the front of the fretboard and capo-ing the high E and B strings with it. This "over-the-top thumb trick" not only looks pretty cool, it also increases the span of your fretting hand considerably—from about seven frets to an entire octave (12 frets). **FIGURE 7** is another wide-interval lick that I play using this same technique.

—reprinted from *Guitar World*, August 2008

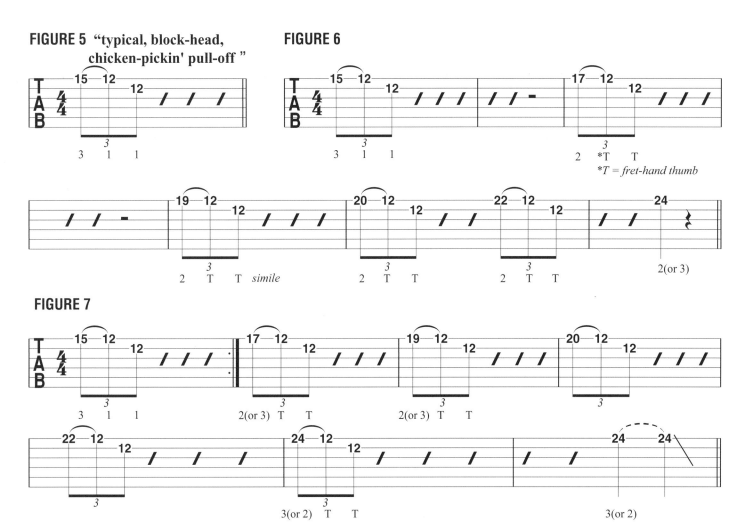

Questions, Questions, Questions

Answers to some of the many reader queries I've received.

Hi there. Greetings once again from Gigantour. This month I figured it was time to answer a few of the numerous playing-related questions many of you have been sending me. Some of them are really worthwhile, so please keep 'em coming.

You've got great rhythm and lead chops. Do you have any special practice or warm-up exercises?
—Ben Smith

I firmly believe that all guitar players who are serious about their craft should practice. That said, I have a terrible practice regimen! I know I should do it a great deal more, and that I'd be a better player if I did, but unfortunately I have a lot of other career- and band-related business to tend to during the day that takes up a lot of my time.

I'm ultimately a songwriter, so whenever I pick up the guitar I want to write. As a result, my practicing consists mainly of coming up with and developing song and riff ideas. I'd rather not sit around and work on scales I've stumbled upon because I'd much prefer to write music.

Regarding warming up; when I'm in the dressing room before a show I make sure that both my hands are thoroughly loose and relaxed. Due to the fast pedaling that occurs in many of the guitar parts in our songs, I can develop cramping and congestion in the muscles of my right (picking) forearm if I don't limber up properly before I hit the stage. I know some guys like to crack their knuckles and things like that prior to performing—if that floats your boat then go for it, but that's not for me. Instead I'll do some of the exercises I showed you in one of my earlier columns, and then I'll basically just plink around.

Also, as weird as it may sound, one of the things I almost always do prior to a show is just hold the guitar for a while so it becomes part of who I am. I start to bond with the guitar, feel it and let it make sense with my body.

Many of your songs contain multiple riffs and parts. How do you remember them all when you're writing?
—Ed Proctor

I'd love to say that I have a great memory when it comes to remembering exactly how I played a riff or part I wrote, but if I did I'd be lying! I can't come up with something, walk away from it and then come back and play it exactly the same way again. There are too many nuances in my playing, such as all the damping and picking I do with my right hand, and the slurring subtleties with my left. For example, if a single chord or note in a riff is phrased a fraction of a second earlier or later, it changes things. To give you an idea, let's look at a riff similar to the chorus in "Skin O' My Teeth," wherein the phrasing of every other note is vital. If you play it straight, like this (see **FIGURE 1**), it sounds pretty cool, but that's not how it was written. As I told the band when we were rehearsing that song, the rhythm is more like someone

FIGURE 1

running with a short leg. Check out **FIGURE 2** to hear what I'm talking about. Just that subtlety of forcing the second note out quicker makes all the difference in the world...and also makes the riff very Led Zeppelin-esque.

The only way I can remember subtleties and riff variations is by recording myself, as I don't write things out on paper. That's basically how I remember the stuff I come up with, and for this reason I carry a micro-cassette recorder wherever I go.

To keep a riff from becoming monotonous and to make it more interesting I'll sometimes throw in little runs and licks. **FIGURE 3**, which is similar to "99 Ways to Die," is a good example of what I'm talking about, as it has some funky little background stuff in it. To keep the basic riff (bar 1) interesting I'll throw in pentatonic fills (bars 3 and 6) and also the little Stevie Ray Vaughan, AC/DC bit in bar 4. That came from me listening to Robin Trower and hearing a chord progression I loved in one of his songs. So choose your influences wisely because they'll help you come up with weird little bits to throw into your own original songs!

FIGURE 4 is based on the chromatic riff in "Reckoning Day." As you can see, it modulates up twice and makes for a very predictable progression. In order to keep the song from getting boring I turned that final modulation upside down and inside out, as shown in **FIGURE 5**.

—reprinted from *Guitar World*, September 2008

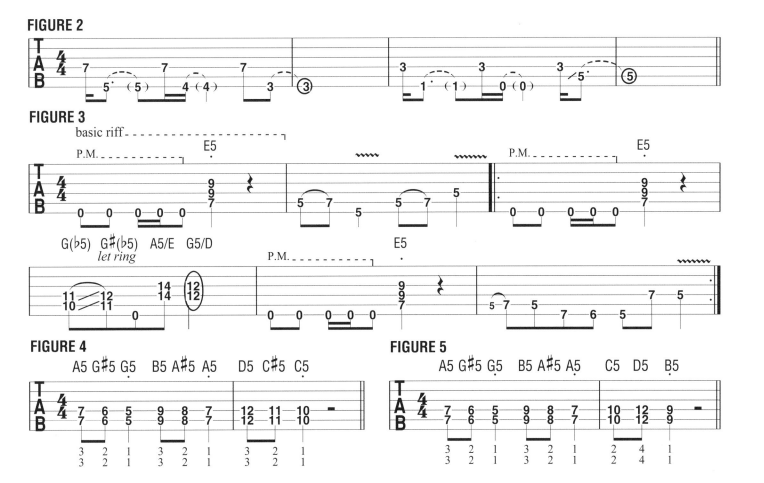

Reckoning Day
Answers to more reader questions.

Your column about using your fret-hand thumb to fret notes on the top two strings and achieve otherwise impossibly wide stretches blew my mind and opened up new playing ideas. Thank you! Do you ever use your fret-hand thumb in any other non-standard ways?   —Kenny Wilson

I sometimes use my thumb to fret notes while riffing or playing chords, a good example being the main riff in "Reckoning Day," similar to **FIGURE 1**. Here I'm pedaling on the palm-muted open low-E string, but then I modulate from E to F♯ (**FIGURE 2**) and do a similar thing, except now I'm pedaling on the second fret on that string. I initially fret that F♯ note with my index finger (bar 1 of **FIGURE 2**), but then I hook my thumb over the top of the neck and use it to fret the note for the remainder of the passage (see **PHOTO A**).

FIGURE 1

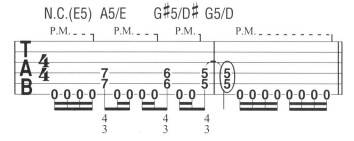

FIGURE 2

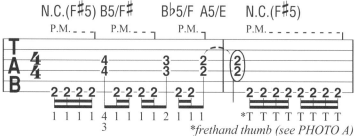

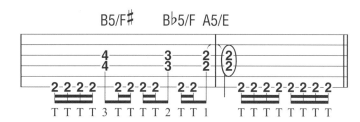

PHOTO A

I'm a huge fan of not only your rhythm work but also your soloing, especially melodic solos like the one you play in "Reckoning Day." Could you please dedicate some space in the column to your thoughts on lead playing?

—Jon Fuente

When soloing, I find that if you really listen to the song, it will tell you what it needs. Solos are so important to songs, but they have to fit the mood. For example, the solo in the Beastie Boys' "(You Gotta) Fight for Your Right (To Party!)" is perfect for that particular track—it's a party solo for a party song. David Gilmore also achieves this kind of thing with his solos on numerous Pink Floyd tracks. And he does it with just a few notes. It blows my mind.

A solo's structure is very important as well. I like to give a solo an explosive beginning. A good example of that is in "Wake Up Dead," where I grab the G string at the sixth fret and pick the note really fast while bending and releasing it (**FIGURE 3**). A lot of the guitar players I've had in Megadeth over the years play with a lot of love, but I'm the exact opposite—I tend to play with hate! They like to make the guitar sing, whereas I like to punch it in the stomach and make it squeal like a little girl. Hee-hee.

I also feel that if you're going to play the guitar, you should use every bit of it. It's important not to get stuck in one position. For example, in "Reckoning Day," I introduce and establish a melody with the listener and then, in order to make the solo climax, I do the same thing an octave higher with a slight, subtle change, as shown in **FIGURE 4** It's not a wank-fest solo, and the simple approach of revisiting a melody line an octave higher makes it both climactic and memorable.

—reprinted from *Guitar World*, November 2008

FIGURE 3 **gradual bend and release**

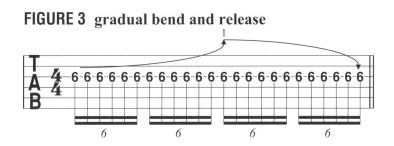

FIGURE 4 **(freely)**

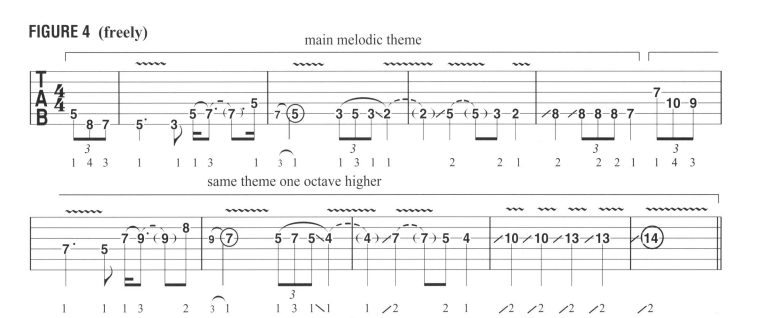

RIFTER MADNESS

By Dimebag Darrell

Stretching Out

Wide left-hand stretches, symmetrical runs and more!

Hey pops, I'm back! This month we're gonna shoot the shit about learning from others; wide-assed left-hand stretches; symmetrical runs, and the importance of your pinkie.

Some dudes tend to get intimidated whenever they come across a guy who really rips on guitar, but not me, man; I get inspired. As far as I'm concerned, playing ain't a competition. Hearing someone smoke always lights my fire and makes me try out new ideas and learn new shit. I don't sit down with a pile of records and try to cop licks, though. What I'm into is checking the dude's overall playing vibe and learning from that. Use your ears and learn all that you can from anything. Listen!

When I first started out, one of my biggest influences was Eddie Van Halen—the stuff he did on the first two Van Halen albums was so aggressive and ballsy-sounding it still gives me chills. Anyway, I kept seeing pictures in *Guitar World* of him doing big-assed left-hand finger stretches, and that inspired me to start dicking around with some wide-stretch ideas of my own—like the two E minor licks shown in **FIGURES 1** and **2**. Another thing I learned from studying those pictures was the importance of my little finger. It's there, so use it—it definitely gives you more reach!

AWKWARDLY COOL RUNS

As I got to know my guitar neck better, I realized that there was an E note at the 19th fret on the A string—how 'bout that! Then, when I was jamming around one day I thought to myself, Hey! I know some wide-stretch E minor licks on the high E string that start on the E note at the 12th fret and also use the 19th fret. So, why don't I try moving one of these fingering pattern ideas across each string in turn until I finish up on the E note at the 19th fret on the A string? **FIGURE 3** shows me applying this concept to the lick we looked at in **FIGURE 2**.

Since the fingering pattern in **FIGURE 3** is exactly the same on each string, a lot of guys call this kind of thing a symmetrical run. It's simple, but cool. To be honest with you, I have no idea what the hell scales this run uses because I'm not a cat that's heavy on theory. All I know is that it sounds awkwardly cool in the key of E minor and that's all that matters. Listen closely and let your ears decide what notes are right or wrong! Anyhow, because this idea worked I got into futzing around with symmetrical runs in a major way.

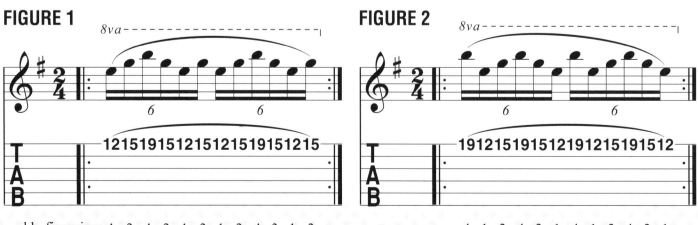

FIGURE 1

l.h. fingering: 1 2 4 2 1 2 1 2 1 2 4 2 1 2

FIGURE 2

4 1 2 4 2 1 4 1 2 4 2 1

Another example of a wide-stretch, symmetrical run in E minor is one I do near the start of my "Cowboys from Hell" (*Cowboys from Hell*) solo. **FIGURE 4** shows a similar run. How I came up with this ascending passage was real simple: I was messing around with a wide-stretch lick on the low E string (indicated as the "initial lick" in **FIGURE 4**) and figured, Hey, let's see what happens if I take this pattern right across the neck and end up on the high E string. I tried it, it sounded cool as shit, and so I used is in my "Cowboys" lead. Once again, I have absolutely no clue what's happening, scale-wise: to me it's just a ripping E minor run that works.

Try creating some wide-stretch symmetrical runs of your own, and never be afraid to try something out—just go for it, dude. Hell, if what you come up with sucks, just C-section it and move onto something else! I know the idea behind these runs is simple, but who gives a shit—as we've just seen in **FIGURES 3** and **4**, the results can sound bad-assed! Until next time, keep on jamming and stay hard, damn it! Timbale!

Warning: If you're not used to using your pinkie a lot or doing these kinds of wide-stretch runs, then please do yourself a favor—always warm up your fingers before you go for broke. If you don't, you could tool your hands off—and that would suck big-time!

—reprinted from *Guitar World*, July 1993

FIGURE 3

FIGURE 4

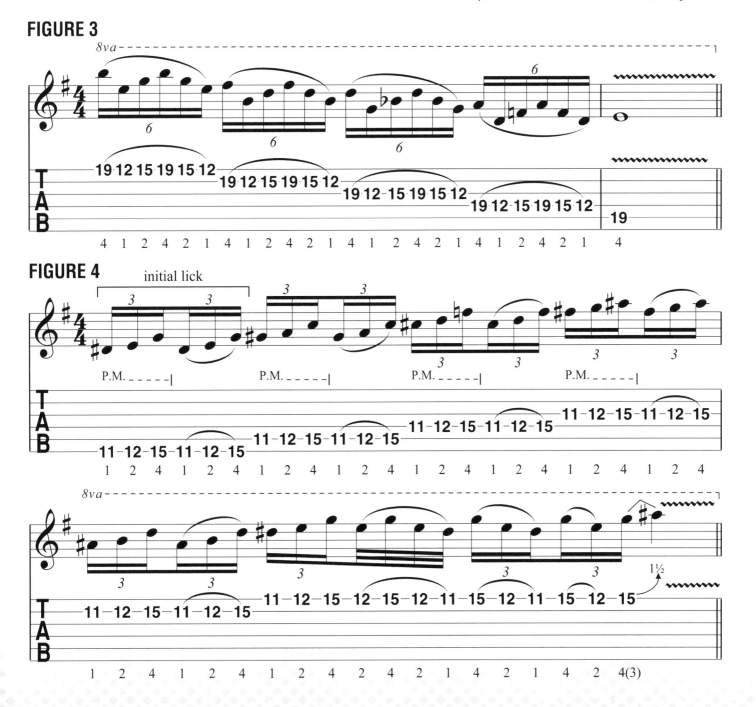

Hell's Bells

Harmonics Pt. 1.

This month we're gonna talk about harmonics—how to get 'em, where you can find 'em and what you do with 'em. There are a number of different ways you can make harmonics happen. You can induce 'em with your pick (pinch harmonics), you can tap 'em like Eddie Van Halen does sometimes (tap or touch harmonics) or you can get 'em by lightly resting one of your left-hand fingers on a string and then picking it. The last type are called natural harmonics, and they're the suckers we're gonna be dicking with.

The easiest place to get a natural harmonic on any string is at the 12th fret. All you do is lightly rest one of your left-hand fingers on a string directly above that fret and then pick it. Don't let the string touch the fret, though, or it won't work, dad! When you do this right you'll hear a bell-like note that's exactly one octave higher than the open-string note. To help make harmonics easier to get, use your lead (bridge) pickup and a lot of gain. When I first started experimenting with harmonics, I'd sometimes hook up two distortion boxes just to get my strings "frying," which helped bring out the harmonics. Also, once you've chimed the harmonic it's not necessary to leave your finger on the string—in fact, if you let go of the string immediately after you pick it the harmonic will ring twice as well.

You can also get harmonics happening above other frets like the 7th, 5th and 4th. Some dudes seem to think that these are the only points where harmonics happen but, as far as I'm concerned, there is literally a harmonic to be found at any place on any string. Check this out and you'll hear what I'm saying: rest your left-hand bird (middle) finger lightly over the highest fret of your fat E string. Then start chugging out a groove on that string with your pick. While you're doing that, keep your left-hand finger resting lightly on the string and start moving it slowly toward the nut. You should hear a shit-load of different harmonics all over the string!

Some of my favorite harmonics are located between frets. There are two really cool ones between the 2nd and the 3rd frets that I use a lot. One is at about a quarter of the way between the 2nd and 3rd frets and the other is at about three quarters of the way. They're pretty hard to get, so once you find 'em make a mental note of exactly where they are.

I use some pretty radical harmonics at the beginning of "Heresy" (*Cowboys from Hell*). **FIGURE 1** shows a riff similar to the one I'm talking about and, as you can see, it uses harmonics on the low E string. The best way to make sure you're playing this right is to listen to the record real carefully and then find the exact spots where all the harmonics are. Use your ears and your eyes, man—look and listen!

TO BAR OR NOT TO BAR

A lot of guitarists tend to only use harmonics when they want to make weird noises with their whammy bars. That's cool but, as **FIGURE 1** shows, you don't need a tremolo arm to make harmonics wail. Two of my favorite players, Edward Van Halen and Randy Rhoads, both did some real happening things with harmonics without reaching for their bars! **FIGURE 2** is similar to the verse riff of "Mouth for War" (*Vulgar Display of Power*). In bar 4 I play a simple little fill using harmonics a quarter of the way between the 2nd and 3rd frets on the G and B strings to create a high-pitched percussive sound that gives the riff an extra dimension. And, once again, no whammy shit is going on.

Harmonics are cool to screw around with, so don't be afraid to experiment with 'em. As long as you remember to look and listen you'll do just fine. Next month I'll tell ya all about how I get my trademark harmonic screams, like the ones at the end of "Cemetery Gates" (Cowboys from Hell). Until then...try, fail, live, learn—and die happy trying!

—reprinted from *Guitar World*, September 1993

FIGURE 1

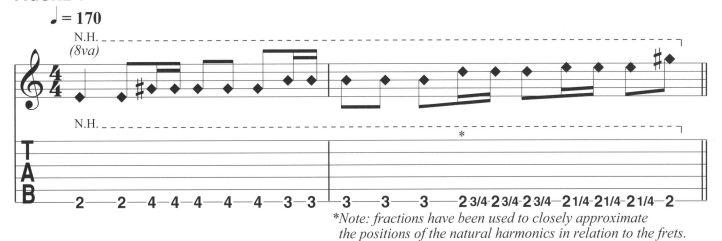

*Note: fractions have been used to closely approximate
the positions of the natural harmonics in relation to the frets.*

FIGURE 2

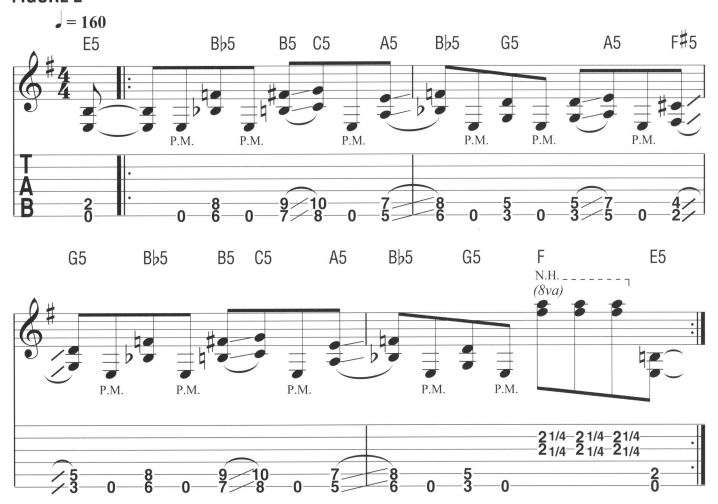

Hell's Bells, Part 2

Harmonic screams

What's shakin', tough guy? Like I promised at the end of last month's column, this time I'm gonna light you up on how to do "harmonic squeals," like the ones at the end of "Cemetery Gates" (*Cowboys from Hell*). A bunch of you have written in asking about this technique. Thanks for all your letters; keep 'em coming, man!

To get "harmonic screams" (same shit, different term) happening, you need a whammy bar. So, if your ax doesn't have one, then you're gonna have to sit this lesson out—sorry, dude! Also, just so you know, we're gonna be doing some pretty brutal dives that will definitely knock a non-locking tremolo system way out of tune. So a locking one, like a Floyd Rose–type, is kind of essential.

In case you're not exactly sure what I mean by a harmonic scream, there's a long, slow one in "This Love" (*Vulgar Display of Power*) which starts at 6:21 and runs to the very end of the track. You can also hear me doing a bunch of them in "Cemetery Gates," between 6:14 and the end, where I imitate Phil's [*Anselmo, Pantera's vocalist*] screams. I love that sort of vocal stuff, but there's no way in hell I can do it in my voice—I don't have that kinda range! So, harmonic screams are my way of "singing out," using my guitar instead of my throat—that's why I really dig this technique.

I stumbled on harmonic squeals when I was dicking around one day. A lot of people think I use a harmonizer or a DigiTech Whammy Pedal to do them, but I don't; all I use is my bar and some natural harmonics. To make harmonics scream, I first dump my Floyd Rose real quick, hit a harmonic with my left hand while the string is still flapping, and then use the bar to pull it up to the pitch I wanna hit.

If this sounds kinda complex to you, don't schitz; it's actually a pretty simple thing to do once you've got the technique down. So, let's learn how to do a real basic harmonic scream in "slow motion" by breaking the idea down into four easy steps. Let's use the harmonic that's directly above the 5th fret on the G string ('cause it's a pretty easy one to nail) and make it "scream" up to its original pitch of G. First though, dial up a distorted sound (remember, gain helps harmonics happen) and switch to your lead (bridge) pickup.

Step 1: Position your left hand so you're ready to hit the 5th-fret harmonic on the G string with your bird (middle) finger. Then mute the high E and B strings with your left-hand index finger, and the low E, A and D with your thumb by wrapping it around the top of neck.

Step 2: Flick the G string with your bird finger and dump the bar down to the pitch you want the scream to start at. You can take the bar down as little or as far as you want; just don't take it down too far or the string will die of shock and the harmonic won't happen.

Step 3: A♯ soon as the bar is dumped, sound the harmonic by lightly tapping the G string directly above the 5th fret with your bird finger. While you're doing this, make sure you're still keeping the other strings quiet with your thumb and index finger.

Step 4: A♯ soon as you've hit the harmonic, release pressure on the bar and let the G string return back up to pitch. A♯ long as you've sounded the harmonic properly, it'll "scream" up to G (as shown in **FIGURE 1**).

The first few times you do this you're gonna hear the open G string "growl" before the scream starts happening. This is just because you're doing everything in slow motion. Once you've got this technique down, though, you won't hear the growl because you'll be doing the first three steps so quickly they'll almost be simultaneous. If it takes you some time to get these squeals happening, don't skid—it took me a while too.

Work on this technique until you can nail **FIGURE 1** no problem, then move onto **FIGURE 2**. This one stays on the G string but has you "screaming" a bunch of different harmonics up to pitch. The last one can be a bitch to hit, but stick with it 'cause it sounds real cool when you nail it. Once you get this one down, try doing the same thing on the other five strings.

—reprinted from *Guitar World*, October 1993

FIGURE 1

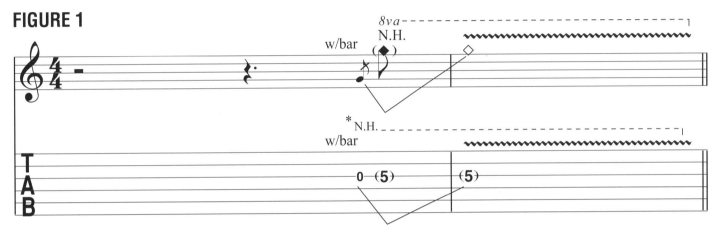

*Sound open note, drop bar, hit harmonic indicated
and then return to pitch with bar, as indicated.*

FIGURE 2

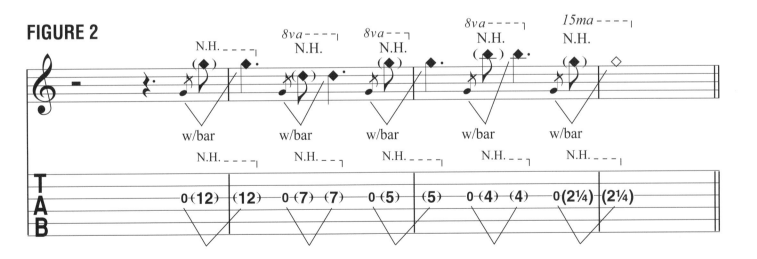

Dear Dime

Answers to some cool "Feedback Sack" questions

Goddamn! I just got done reading every one of the more than 500 letters you've sent in to my "Feedback Sack." Thanks for all the cool things you said about the column. The special packages we made up for the beer receipt winners have just hit the mail so by the time you read this you'll know whether you pulled a top 50 luck-out spot. Good luck!

Over the last 19 months, we've covered a hell of a lot of techniques, ideas, riffs and licks. Now, because a bunch of your letters contained some really good questions, I'm gonna spend the next few columns answering some of 'em. The most common question of all was about my gear and how I get my tone, so let's kick off with that one.

What's up Dimebag? I really dig your column, it's got mega gonads! How about some advice on getting a ripping sound like yours? I'd also like to know exactly what pickups, strings, amps, pedals and rack gear you use.
—Matt Leone, Syracuse, NY

I'm more than happy to let everybody know exactly what I've got going in my rig but I'm not gonna tell you how I've got it wired up! The order in which you put your shit in line definitely makes a big difference and that's something you should dick around with for yourself. For example, if you run your wah before all your forms of gain, it'll sound different than if you place it after a distortion or EQ pedal—it won't be as ferocious or effective. It also makes a big difference if you put certain units in front of your amp instead of in its effects loop and vice-versa. For example, my bud Kirk Windstein from Crowbar uses basically the exact same rig as I do but he wires it up in a completely different way and he's got an awesome sound! So I suggest that you take some time and try to wire up your shit in all the ways you can think of until you get the tone you dig best.

Another thing I recommend you dick with is using different forms of gain. There are very few amps that can get as distorted as you want 'em to be by themselves, so you've usually gotta heat 'em up a little bit with a pedal of some kind. Anyway, even if your amp has all the gain you need right out of the box, or you put another form of gain in front of it then you'll get a completely different type of crunch or distortion. It doesn't have to be a distortion unit either; anything that you can use to get more gain is cool—like a graphic EQ or a boost pedal.

I use a little blue MXR 6-band EQ pedal I got from a pawn shop for some of my gain. The cool thing about using a graphic EQ as a form of gain is you can decide what frequencies you want to add crunch to by pushing those particular EQ points up more. With a distortion or overdrive box though, the overall tone tends to get distorted. That's why I prefer to use gain units rather than distortion pedals. Altogether I run three types of gain before I even hit the amp—a hot pickup (a Bill Lawrence XL500; humbucker lead); my MXR graphic and a Furman PQ-4, which I use for EQ and gain. Because I've got all this gain going on, my Rocktron Guitar Silencer is very important to me. I gotta have something that'll shut my shit down or there's too much hiss and uncontrollable feedback—kinda like my "feedback sack!"

Anyways, in addition to the stuff I've already mentioned here's what I use: modified Dean ML guitars; Randall Century 200 125-watt solid state heads; Randall [412JB] straight 4X12 cabinets loaded with 80-watt Jaguar speakers for my dirty sound and Randall [412CB] straight 4x12 cabinets loaded with 70-watt Celestion speakers for clean; DR strings [.009, .011, .016, .026, .036, .046 (high to low) for regular and dropped-D tunings; .009, .011, .016, .028, .038, .050 (high to low) for guitars tuned down a whole step]; an MXR flanger/doubler rack unit; two DigiTech Whammy Pedals—one onstage, one off—and a Vox Wah. I also use a Yamaha SPX 90 and a Korg G3 for my clean shit.

Just so you know, even if you get all the gear I use and wire it up the same way I do, it won't be my sound exactly. Having said that, the rig's there and it's definitely doing something! The bottom line is this: try to emulate your favorite player's sound only as a basis to help you find your own tone. And don't be afraid to experiment with different amps, pickups, effects, wirings, axes, etc. Try anything and everything—give it all a chance. Most important of all, get your rig rigged the way *you* want you to sound.

> *How in the hell do you make that high pitched sound in "Becoming"? I've heard you use some sort of pedal but I wanna know exactly what you do. Are you using natural harmonics as well as a pedal?*
>
> —Kasey Weirich, Torrance, CA

I use my DigiTech Whammy Pedal set on two octaves up to get that sound. What I do is push the pedal down real quickly on the second beat of each bar of the riff. I'm not hitting any harmonics when I make the squeal happen either; all I'm playing are the octave C notes at the 3rd fret on the A string and the 5th fret of the G string. The whole riff is shown in **FIGURE 1**. When you try it, just move the pedal exactly the way the rig sounds. You may think, Oh man, that's all he's doing? But just remember, simple can be lethal.

> *Dime, my man, I thought you used a pedal to get that high squeal during the main riff in "Becoming" but when I saw you play the song live you weren't stepping on anything. What's the trick bro!?*
>
> —Ken "Z Man" Zemanek, Chicago, IL

The trick is to have a bad-assed guitar tech like Grady Champion and let him work his Whammy Pedal back there for you so you can dance and jam to the groove instead of being strapped to a pedal! That riff smokes, man, and there's no way I could just stand still onstage in one place while I play it. Grady, if you're reading this, you #%&*in' rule 88 bud! (Jimmy Johnson! Plus DDS pushing 12 with your name on it! Right back at ya).

—reprinted from *Guitar World*, November 1994

FIGURE 1   **Tune down one whole step (low to high, D G C F A D)**

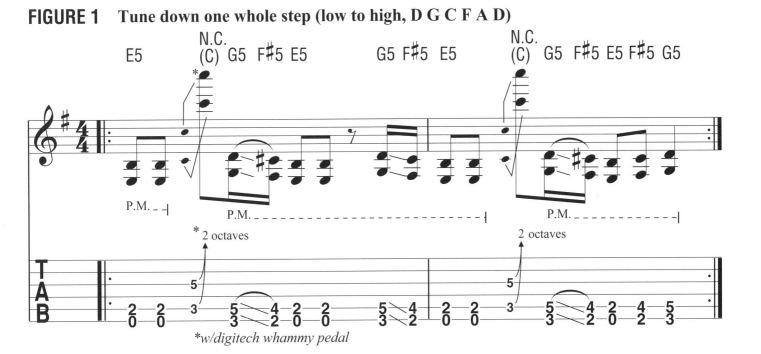

*w/digitech whammy pedal

Dear Dime

More answers to your questions

What the hell is the weird-assed sounding chord you play at the end of the "25 Years" riff that starts with a string scrape? I can't suss it out, bro. Please help me!

—Ken Doyle
Los Angeles, CA

It's just a two-note D5 root/fifth power chord played on the low E and A strings at the 5th fret. [**FIGURE 1**. Because the fifth (A) is lower than the root (D) it's called an inverted power chord [*written D5/A*]. The reason it sounds kinda weird is that as soon as I hit the chord I bend it by pulling both strings down toward the floor. To do the pick scrape that starts the riff, I jam the sharp end of my pick between the E and A strings near the bridge and then head for the nut. To make sure there's not a gap between the scrape and the power chord, I just pop the pick upward and out from between the strings at the end of each scrape—by doing this I sound the chord. **FIGURE 2** shows the complete riff. Once again,. it's real simple shit, but who cares? It crushes.

Just so you know, when I doubled this riff in the studio I did the pick scrape up on the high strings to fatten up the sound of the scrape.

Hey dude, how did you make the cool sounding chirping noise that ends your "Hard Line, Sunken Cheeks" solo?
—Tom Gillis, Seattle, WA

What I'm doing there is bending the D note at the 15th fret on the high E string and then tapping the string at the 22nd fret with the edge of my pick while gradually releasing the bend. I start off making a straight up and down motion with my pick that gets smaller and smaller as the "chop" gets faster and faster. Then, once I'm "chopping" as quick as I can, I start going back and forth with my pick—kinda like I'm sawing the string. If your pick is beat up a little bit and has some small grooves in it, that'll help too. To make the trill jump out a hair more on the album I overdubbed a harmony part to it on another track.

I think it's great how you use parts of your songs to make points in your lesson. After listening to "This Love," I'm curious how you control such wide bends. I tried to figure it out but was unsuccessful.
—Jake Kouns, Centreville, VA

To be accurate when you're doing big-assed string bends like the ones in "This Love," you've gotta use your ears, man—it's all a matter of pitch. Another thing that'll help give you more control over your bending is using more than one finger to do the bend. For example, when I bend a note with my pinkie, I help it out with my other four fingers. The guys at *Guitar World* tell me that the correct term for this technique is *reinforced bending*.

I think it would be cool in future columns if you talked about how Pantera make it work as a band on and off stage. It would help other bands stay together if they know how you guys do it.
—Jim Hagerman, Warenton, VA

Man! That's a hard question to answer 'cause there are a whole bunch of factors you've gotta take into consideration. Basically, a band is just like a family. You gotta make space for each other and understand and respect what the other guys are into 'cause we're not all exactly the same, y'know. Probably the most important thing of all, though, is this: you've all gotta have an honest love for what you're doing if you even want it to halfway happen. Also, if each member of the band doesn't share the same vision to start with, then you'll probably have problems down the road because your goals are gonna be different.

The way it works with us is that each person kinda plays a different role within the band. It wasn't planned out, though; nobody said, "Okay, I'm gonna be the 'business man,' you be the 'mediator,' you be the whatever." No one put us in those spots; that's just the way it worked out with us. We always try to help each other rather than go against each other. I guess you could say that being in a band is kinda like a marriage except you've got more than one wife!

If you've got any tips on getting a record deal or anything else to do with making it in the business, I'd be grateful.
              —Jason Tousignant, Corinth, NY

Two words, man—*time* and *endurance*. That's what it takes to get anywhere in this business. We were jamming together for eight or nine years before we got signed. So hang tough and give your shit to as many people as you can. The main thing is to have your own style and that kinda thing doesn't happen overnight. Hell, it took us nearly eight years to find ourselves and get our "Cowboys from Hell" identity together. It *is* possible to get a deal though, I swear—I'm living proof.

—reprinted from *Guitar World*, January 1995

FIGURE 1 D5/A

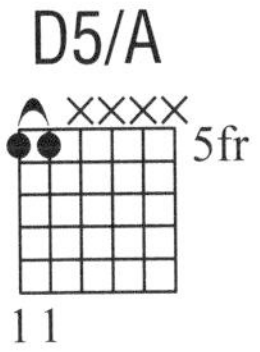

FIGURE 2

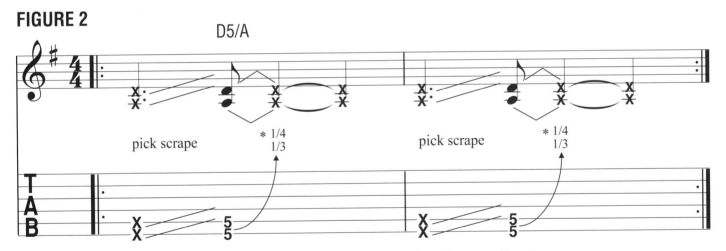

listen to CD for exact pitch and timing of bends

PRACTICE WHAT YOU PREACH

by Eric Peterson of Testament

Fleshing It Out

Downpicking versus alternate picking.

Hi, and welcome to my new column for *Guitar World*. Over the next few months we're going to crunch away on various aspects of the important art of playing rhythm guitar. I'm really excited to be doing this column, and I think it will be a good addition to the columns already here. It seems like the majority of them are concerned with playing lead and the virtuoso side of guitar playing, whereas I'm more of a riffer and rhythm player. I think this column will really help you concentrate on riffing, arranging songs and stuff like that.

I tune my guitar down one half step (low to high: E♭ A♭ Df G♭ B♭ E♭). I prefer this tuning because it gives me a slightly darker, heavier tone, but it still has the tightness to get crunchy chords and keep the strings from becoming too floppy.

In this first column I'm going to talk about playing riffs using only downpicking, rather than alternate (down-up) picking. They're both great techniques, but as you can hear by comparing the alternate-picked **FIGURE 1a** with the downpicked-only **FIGURE 1b**, the latter approach definitely gives you a more solid, consistent and aggressive sound. As another example, if you were to play a riff similar to the one in Diamond Head's "Am I Evil" and make the same comparison (see FIGURES 2a and 2b), you can immediately hear that down picking gives more of a driving crunch tone.

A lot of thrash metal guitarists prefer to downpick riffs, especially midtempo riffs, for this very reason. There comes a point, however, when you're playing at such a fast tempo that it becomes impossible to downpick consecutive notes or chords, no matter how good you are. I mean, there's no way you could play **FIGURE 3** beyond, say, 130 beats per minute using only downstrokes. In this case, you need to switch to alternate picking, interrupted here and there by pull-offs.

In addition to being more consistent and aggressive, downpicking a riff also produces a certain harmonic overtone that you don't get when alternate picking. I've never really analyzed how this occurs until now, but by looking closely at how I downpick, I see that it's caused by the fact that I'm not only hitting the string with the pick but also with the tip of my pick-hand index finger and thumb. The first thing that hits the string is my index finger, followed by the pick and then the thumb. My index finger is pretty worn from all the contact!

For the really fast, alternate-picked stuff like **FIGURE 3**, it's primarily the pick that's hitting the strings, both on the downstroke and the upstroke. It's just on the midtempo, crunchy stuff where the flesh comes into play, and I can't see letting just the pick hit the string on a downstroke-only riff. You might think that's what you should do, but it doesn't quite cut it in this aggressive style of rhythm playing.

FIGURES 4 and **5** are really good examples of midtempo riffs that benefit hugely from this downpicking technique. As you can hear, they noticeably lose that crunchy drive and sound a little sloppier when played with alternate picking.

—reprinted from *Guitar World*, July 2008

Guitar tuned down one-half step (low to high: E♭ A♭ D♭ G♭ B♭ E♭).

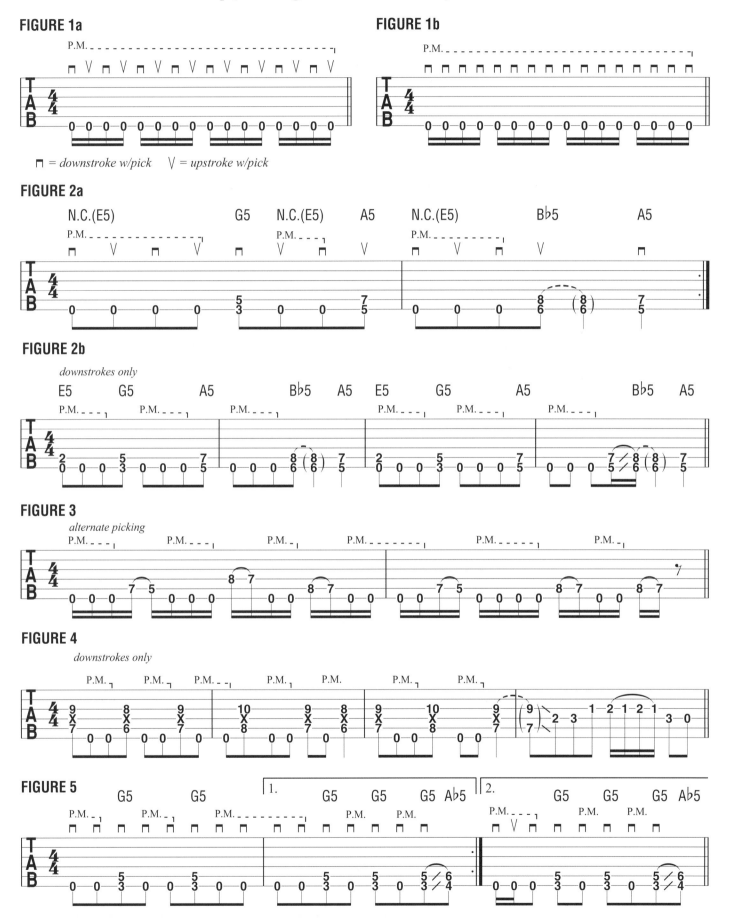

Death-Metal Diads

Percussive picking exercises, and using minor and major diads to add darkness and mystery to a riff.

Last month we got into the importance of downpicking when playing rhythm. This month we're going to start off with a few warm-up exercises that really zone in on your picking hand. **FIGURE 1** is a simple warm-up that has you chugging on an open E5 power chord and single E notes using downstrokes only. Start off slowly and gradually build up speed. This drill is very basic, but it effectively gets the job done, as it really zones in on your downpicking precision and stamina.

FIGURE 2 builds on this 16th-note rhythm pattern by adding some "gallops" (pairs of 32nd notes). To perform each gallop you'll have to use a down-up combination of pick strokes, as indicated above the tab. You'll notice that, in addition to the picking change on each gallop, I also strum the A string, fretted at the second fret and momentarily suspend the right-hand palm muting, which lets the sound "open up" a little bit. This adds more saturation to the gallop and almost gives me that accented, snare drum–to-tom sound. This kind of playing is very percussive, and I think like a drummer when I'm doing this sort of thing. I've noticed that a lot of lead-oriented guitarists don't really get this aspect of rhythm guitar. They'll play something like this with correct timing, but they'll miss the pick-hand feel.

FIGURE 3 is a similar kind of percussive, warm-up gallop idea, but here I add a few fretted power chords and chord slides to the mix so that the fret-hand gets into the action, too.

DARK-SOUNDING DIADS

One thing I really like to do is incorporate major and minor diads (two-note chords; see **DIAGRAMS 2** and **3**) into a riff instead of using just single notes and root/fifth power chord shapes (**DIAGRAM 1**). Switching things around like this gives a riff more of a European death metal sound.

FIGURE 4 is an example of what I'm talking about; it's a power chord riff with muted, open low E notes pedaled between root-fifth chords. Now check out **FIGURE 5**, which is the same riff but with some of the root/fifth chords replaced by major and minor diads. Hear the difference in the character of the riff?

I didn't get into doing this until I heard Emperor's *Anthems to the Welkin at Dusk* in 1997. That album has a lot of those kinds of chords in there, and it really opened my mind to getting more of a darker, mysterious sound. I really started injecting those influences and elements into my own riff writing with Testament on 1999's *The Gathering*. You can hear something like this on the chorus of "D.N.R."

—reprinted from *Guitar World*, August 2008

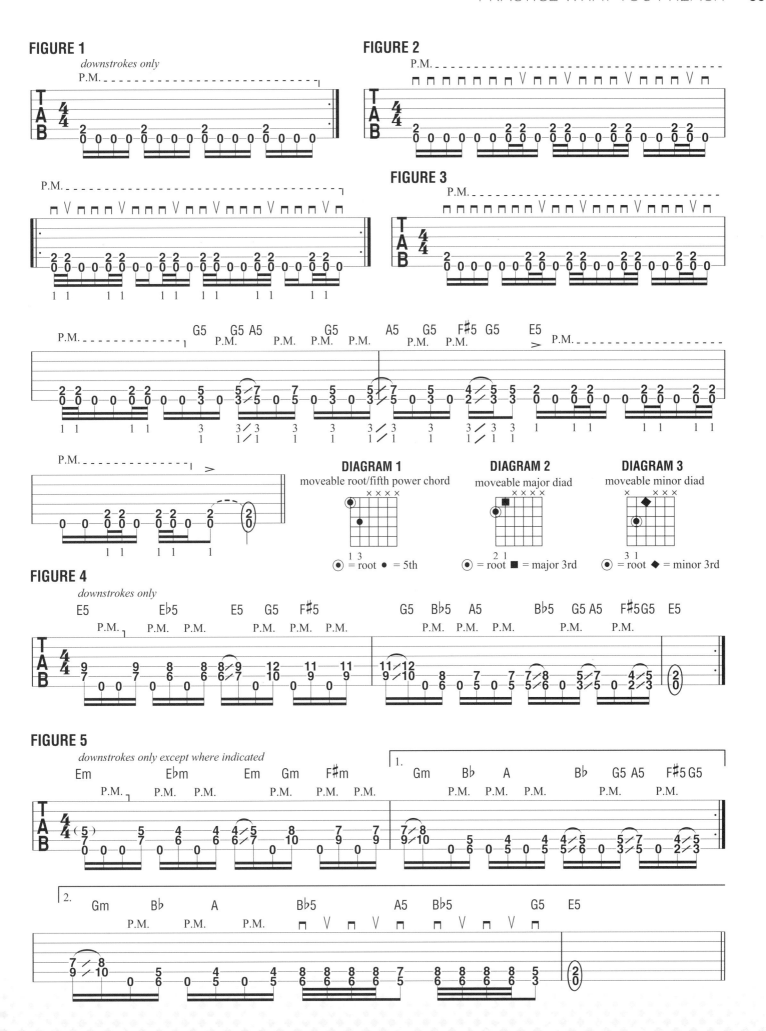

Ominous Octaves

Using strummed octaves to create a haunting vibe.

Hi, there. I'm writing this month's column in an airport in Serbia, on my way to a Testament gig in Belgrade. It looks like our luggage didn't make it, but at least our gear did!

Last month I showed you how to give a riff a more "European death metal" sound, by replacing regular root/fifth power chords (see **DIAGRAM 1**) with minor and major diads (see **DIAGRAMS 2** and **3**, respectively). This month we're going to look at replacing basic power chords with octaves (see **DIAGRAM 4** and **PHOTO A**), which is something we like to do in Testament, especially on crunchy riffs that have a lot of palm-muted, open low E pedaling going on.

FIGURE 1 is a riff in E with power chords played on the A and D strings between low E chugs. **FIGURE 2** shows the same riff but with all the power chords replaced by strummed octaves played on the A and G strings. As you can hear when you play the two versions of the riff back-to-back, there's a pretty big difference. To me, substituting the octaves gives the riff a thicker, brighter, yet darker, sound, especially when the riff is doubled by another guitar. The octaves definitely leap out at you more and give the riff a more ominous vibe.

One thing I sometimes like to do is apply finger vibrato to an octave by shaking the strings. You can shake a root/fifth power chord but, as you can hear in **FIGURE 3a**, doing that tends to sound kind of messy. When you shake an octave, however (**FIGURE 3b**), you get a really cool sound because it's almost like you're adding vibrato to one note and then overdubbing (recording) the other one on top. And because you're playing the same note one octave apart, the slight differences in the vibrato modulations add thickness to the overall sound. **FIGURE 4** shows the riff from **FIGURE 2** with vibrato applied to the G notes in bar 5. As you can hear, the vibrato-ed octave works really well in this context.

When playing a strummed octave, it's crucial that you mute the unused string between the two that you're fretting. Until I started writing this column I'd never really thought about muting like this—it was just something I did instinctively. In the examples I've demonstrated here, the unused string would be the D string. You can finger an octave with your index and ring fingers, or with the index finger and pinkie (see **PHOTO A**). I do both, but as my hands are fairly small, I tend to use index-pinkie because it's a more comfortable shape to form, especially in the lower positions. Either way, I use my fret-hand index finger to mute the D string by angling the finger so that it lightly touches the string and prevents it from ringing. Then I just strum the octave on the A and G strings with a single pick stroke.

FIGURE 5 is a good riff to play to check if you're doing this correctly while applying vibrato to both the A and G strings. Your ears will tell you if you're muting correctly.

—reprinted from *Guitar World*, September 2008

PHOTO A

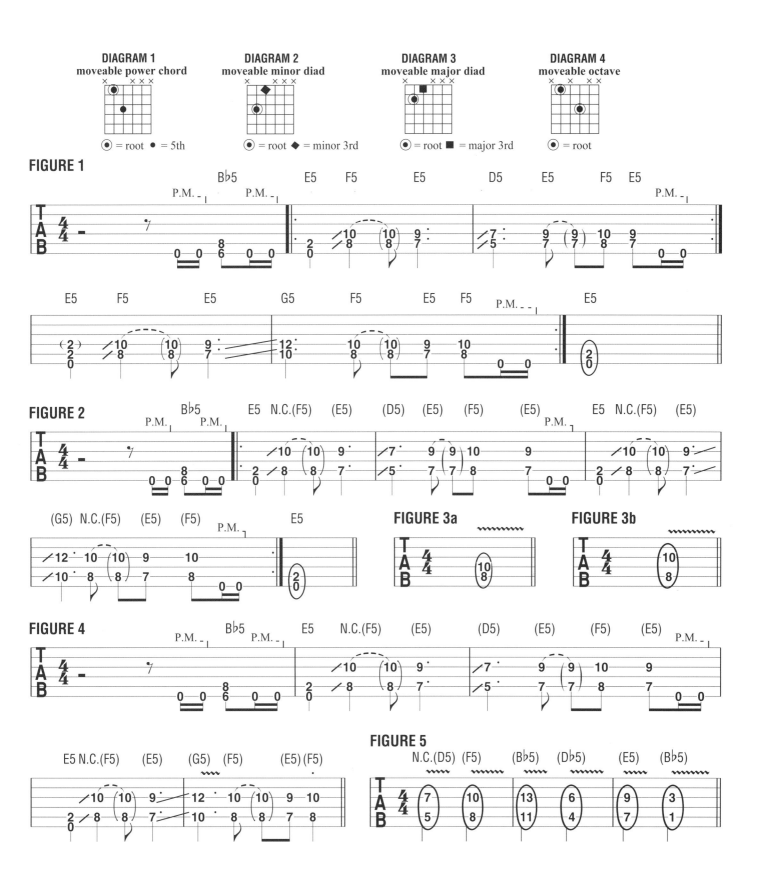

Stay Single
Using single notes in a heavy riff.

In the last two columns, we looked at a few different ways to add a dark, ominous vibe to an already heavy power chord riff. We began by substituting major and minor diads for standard root/fifth power chords, and then we looked at using strummed octaves to add a thicker, yet brighter sound to a progression. Now we're going to check out another idea I think is important to playing heavy metal: using single notes within a heavy riff.

Older metal tunes, like Judas Priest's "Breaking the Law," UFO's "Rock Bottom" and Def Leppard's "Wasted" are built on classic riffs that feature single notes played with a crunch tone. **FIGURE 1** is an "old-school" style riff similar to the one heard in "Wasted." As you can see and hear, it combines single notes and power chords, along with a palm-muted open low E pedal tone, for a very cool effect. **FIGURE 2** is another example in E minor that incorporates the use of a palm-muted open low E note, in this case with a somewhat "busier" riff. The line is similar to the one Michael Schenker plays in "Rock Bottom" and, as you can hear, the single-string stuff works really well. It involves a fair bit of string skipping and some neat half-step moves that give it a bluesy edge.

To make this kind of riff jump out more and sound even cooler, you'll want to try and get a slight pick, or "pinch," harmonic happening on the fretted notes. You can achieve this by choking up on the pick with your thumb and index finger so that only the very tip is exposed, and "digging in" as you pick a downstroke so that the tip of the thumb grazes the string as you pick it. In order to sound a harmonic, however, the thumb needs to touch the string at one of the harmonic nodes—they're different for each fret position, so you'll need to experiment by picking the string at different points to find them. **FIGURE 3** is a simple riff in E that you can use to work on this idea.

Another thing I like to do that can sound really cool is alternate between muting certain notes and getting a little bit of a harmonic happening. I do this in the Testament song "Burnt Offerings" (*The Legacy*), in a riff similar to **FIGURE 4**. As you can hear, it's another E minor line, except it has more of an Egyptian vibe to it due to the chromatic notes in the runs between the open low-E gallops.

When playing the little run in bar 2 of **FIGURE 4**, you can add pick harmonics on the way up and then palm mute the notes as you climb back down, as shown in **FIGURE 5**. **FIGURE 6** shows this idea being incorporated in the first half of the riff. As you can hear, going back and forth between muting and harmonics like this works well and sounds *very* metal!

—reprinted from *Guitar World*, October 2008

Tune down one half-step (low to high, E♭ A♭ D♭ G♭ B♭ E♭).

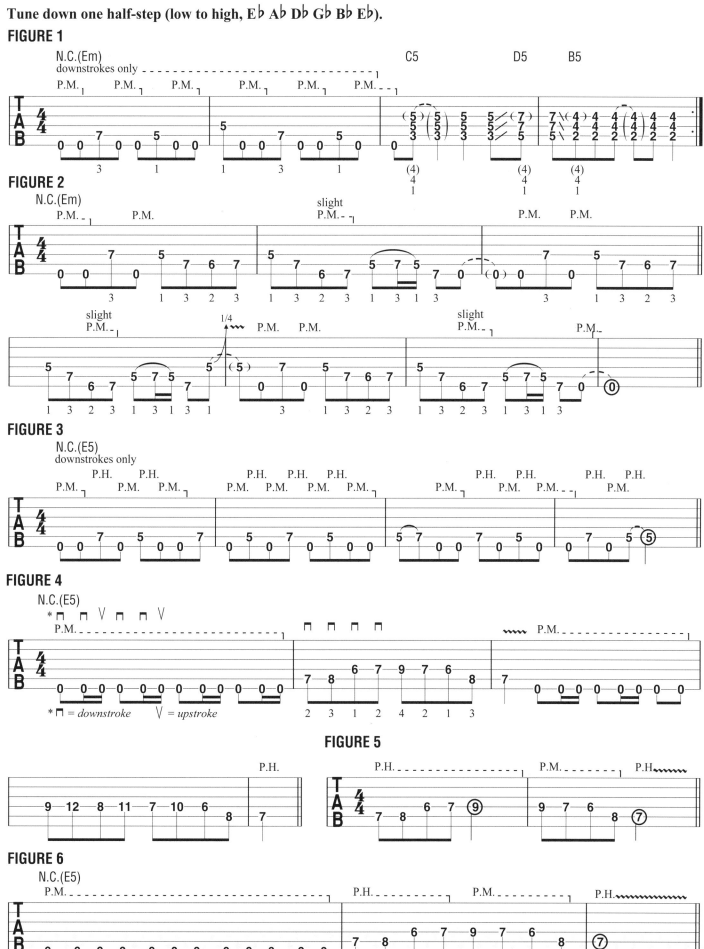

Chug It!

Alternate picking, palm muting, inverted power chords and more on pick harmonics.

This month we're going to look at a some key metal rhythm techniques and strategies: alternate picking; the importance of palm-muting (P.M.) to the sound of a riff; inverted, one-finger power chords; and using pick harmonics with chords.

Let's start with alternate picking. When playing faster, busier thrash riffs, it isn't always possible to use downpicking exclusively, and that's when alternate (down-up) picking comes into play. An example of where I'd use alternate picking is the verse riff to Testament's "Over the Wall," which features some gallop rhythms and sliding power chords. When galloping like this, it's really important to apply palm muting; if you don't, the 16th notes will ring into each other and sound loose and messy. The key to playing thrash metal riffs tightly is to mute the strings with the heel of your picking hand at the bridge. The resulting sound is highly percussive—what guitarists refer to as the "chug."

To help you appreciate just how important palm muting is, I'm going to demonstrate a gallop pattern similar to the one heard in the verse of "Over the Wall." **FIGURE 1** is the pattern performed with palm muting, and **FIGURE 2** is the same thing, minus the muting. As you can hear, **FIGURE 1** sounds tight, punchy and percussive, whereas **FIGURE 2** is an indistinguishable, grungy mess, and you don't want that—at least not in thrash metal!

FIGURE 3 is the riff pattern applied to the song's chord progression. In this example I'm employing the pick harmonic technique we talked about last month on the sliding chords, which makes them jump out a little more. This provides a musically effective contrast to the percussive gallops. Another possibility here would be to replace the root/fifth power chords with strummed octaves, a technique we looked at in a previous column (see **FIGURE 4**).

Another cool variation is to take a full root-fifth-octave power chord voicing (see DIAGRAM 1) and eliminate the low root note so that you're only hitting the fifth and octave (DIAGRAM 2). This is something the guitarists in Judas Priest, K.K. Downing and Glenn Tipton, often do. This voicing, with the fifth on the bottom, is called an *inverted power chord*. **FIGURE 5** is a riff similar to Priest's "Grinder" (*British Steel*) played with full power chords, while **FIGURE 6** is the same thing played with inverted voicings, which sound a little darker and also allow you to get more of that pick harmonic sound happening. I like to do this sort of thing in Testament, and **FIGURE 7** is a good example of that. Once again, if I played the same riff with full power chords, as demonstrated in **FIGURE 8**, I wouldn't be able to get the pick harmonics on the chords to pop out as much.

Next month we're going to look at harmony guitar parts. See you then!

—reprinted from *Guitar World*, November 2008

Tune down one half-step (low to high, E♭ A♭ D♭ G♭ B♭ E♭)

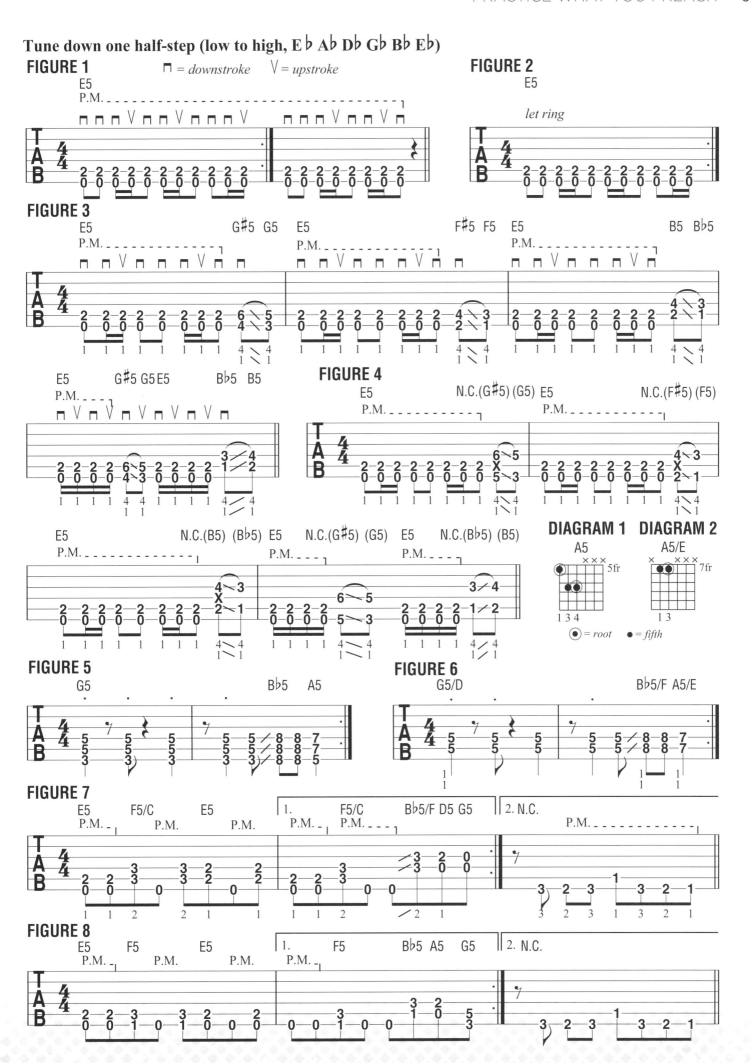

Haunting Harmonies

Creating cool harmony lines with minor and major thirds.

As promised last month, we're going to take a look at crafting two-guitar harmony lines, which is something I do totally by ear. A lot of the guitar harmonies that Testament uses are based on thirds because they give us that really cool, Egyptian vibe that's become part of our sound. This means that the harmony notes are either a minor third or major third above the primary melody notes. A minor third is three frets, or one and a half steps, higher, and a major third is for four frets, two whole steps, higher. We often switch between major and minor thirds as we see fit in order to get the harmony sound we're looking for.

FIGURE 1 shows the riff I presented at the end of last month's column. Let's harmonize the single-note line in the final bar. In this case, I prefer to go with a harmony line that's totally major (see **FIGURE 2**), with each note being four frets above its corresponding primary melody note, because that's what sounds best to me. The two guitar lines together create parallel major thirds (**FIGURE 3**), which, in this particular instance, sounds cooler to me than octaves (**FIGURE 4**) or a straight unison double (**FIGURE 5**).

Next up is a harmonized riff similar to that in "The Haunting" (**FIGURE 6**), which features a mix of both minor and major thirds in the harmony line (Gtr. 2 part). This gives it that really cool, Mercyful Fate kind of sound, which is what we were shooting for on this particular song. These harmonies are a lot of fun to play. A♯ you can see, the main riff (Gtr. 1 part) is a 12-note pattern that repeats in different positions on the neck. The same is true of the harmony line (Gtr.2), which is another 12-note pattern repeated at different frets.

Now that I've given you a couple of examples, here's an easy approach you can use to work out a harmony line. First, come up with a cool, single-note theme or phrase that you want to harmonize. Then record it and experiment by playing different harmony-line ideas along with the playback. What I do is this: I record the main run performed really slow, then I play it back and play the same exact phrase three frets higher, in parallel minor thirds, to hear what it sounds like. Invariably, a note or two in the harmony line won't sound right to me, so I'll just move those notes up one fret to make it a major third. So, I start minor and then correct up to major on the harmony line notes that sound like they need fixing. Easy.

Not all runs need a harmony line, but try using the above method on some of your own lines. Good luck, and have fun! See you next month.

—reprinted from *Guitar World*, December 2008

Tune down one half-step (low to high, E♭ A♭ D♭ G♭ B♭ E♭)

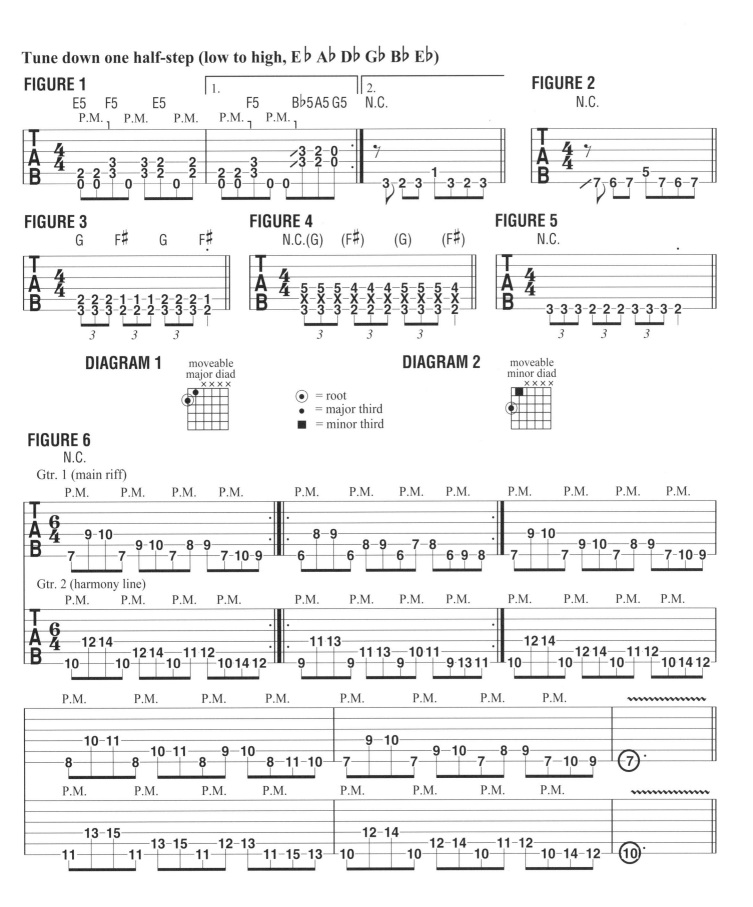

DIAGRAM 1 — moveable major diad

DIAGRAM 2 — moveable minor diad

⊙ = root
● = major third
■ = minor third

Theme Song

Playing a simple, melodic and catchy solo over a clean rhythm track.

This month's column is coming to you from the Metal Masters tour, on which we're performing with Judas Priest, Heaven and Hell and Motörhead. It's a real honor to have been picked by three bands that have influenced so many genres. Priest's *Unleashed in the East* and Sabbath's *Heaven and Hell* were my top records in seventh and eighth grade, so being on tour with those guys and seeing them every day really trips me out!

This month I'd like to talk about soloing. A lot of lead guitar players, including my bandmate Alex Skolnick, like to shred when they solo. They'll play really fast licks and runs, exotic scales, sweep-picked arpeggios and complicated things like that. When it comes to leads, however, I like to come up with a simple, bluesy single-note theme, which I think helps strike a balance with Alex's style. To demonstrate the sort of soloing approach I'm talking about, I'm going to illustrate a clean chord progression and then put a lead on top of it.

FIGURE 1 shows a repeating, four-bar rhythm pattern. It's fairly straightforward, played with a clean tone and, as you can see, includes a lot of open-string notes. There's a fair amount of single-string picking and notes ringing together as long as possible. In addition to using a clean sound to play **FIGURE 1**, I've added some chorus and reverb to sweeten my tone. The chord progression is in the key of A natural minor—A B C D E F G—so that's the scale I'll be using when I play a lead over the top of it.

FIGURE 2 is the lead I've come up with to play over **FIGURE 1**. For the lead, I've dialed in a pretty thick, distorted tone, which gives me a really nice sustain and also helps give my lines more of a singing quality. As you can see, for the vast majority of the lead—the first six bars in fact—I play all the notes on the G string. I do this because staying on the same string enables me to use expressive finger slides, hammer-ons and pull-offs to link quite a few notes together without having to pick them, which adds to the smooth, vocal-like vibe I was striving for. The distortion and reverb in my tone definitely helps in that regard, too.

As you've probably noticed, I start the lead by playing a melody in bars 1 and 2 that I revisit again in the second half of the solo, beginning in bar 5. The second time through the phrase, I keep the timing of the notes the same but climb higher up the neck (bars 6 and 7 of **FIGURE 2**) instead of going back down, so the melody is familiar but slightly different at the end. This is something singers often do.

This lead is pretty basic, but because of the melodic theme it gets stuck in your head rather quickly. The trickiest part of it is the last note, which I play by tapping the B string with the middle finger of my picking hand (**PHOTO A**) at the 22nd fret. This produces an A note that sounds an octave (12 frets) higher than the previous one at the 10th fret on the same string.

Try coming up with and recording a simple rhythm pattern of your own and inventing a melodic lead to play over it. Have fun with it!

—reprinted from *Guitar World*, Holiday 2008

All guitars tuned down one half step (low to high: E♭ A♭ D♭ G♭ B♭ E♭).

FIGURE 1 rhythm part

w/clean tone, chorus and reverb
let ring

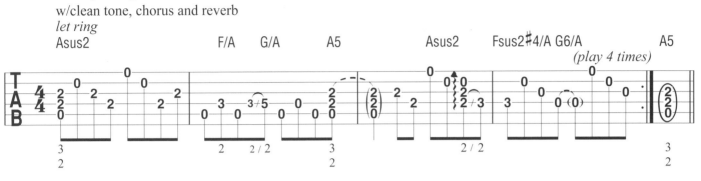

FIGURE 2 lead guitar part

w/distortion and delay

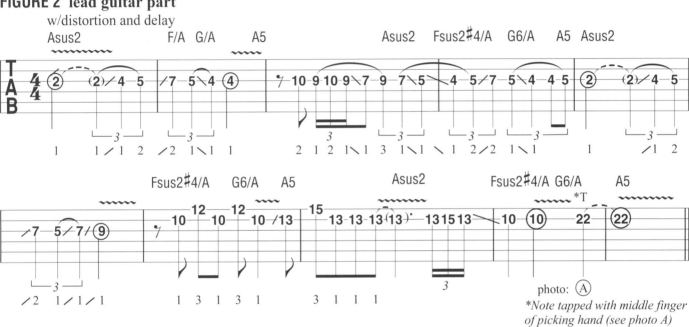

photo: Ⓐ

Note tapped with middle finger
of picking hand (see photo A)

PHOTO A

"Vocalizing" Your Solo
How to play a lead that really sings.

I'm writing this column while we're getting ready for a four-show run opening for Judas Priest in Mexico. Alex [*Skolnick*] is tied up doing the Trans-Siberian Orchestra tour, so Glen Drover, ex–King Diamond and Megadeth lead guitarist, is filling in for these few shows. Alex is really particular about who stands in for him, but as soon as I mentioned Glen, he immediately gave me the thumbs-up. Glen's a cool guy and a great player, and he really impressed us in rehearsals because he has the material totally down.

This month I'd like to discuss the idea of thinking like a vocalist, rather than a guitarist, when playing a lead melody. To demonstrate this concept, I'm going to play over a really simple two-chord sequence (**FIGURE 1**). Here I'm using a clean tone for both parts so they'll blend and complement each other really well. I've got a little bit of phase-shifting on the backing part (Gtr. 1), and I'm using the neck pickup for both parts because I prefer its warmer, denser sound for clean stuff.

"Castle Shadow Grey"
Tune down one half step (low to high: E♭ A♭ D♭ G♭ B♭ E♭).

FIGURE 1 accompaniment

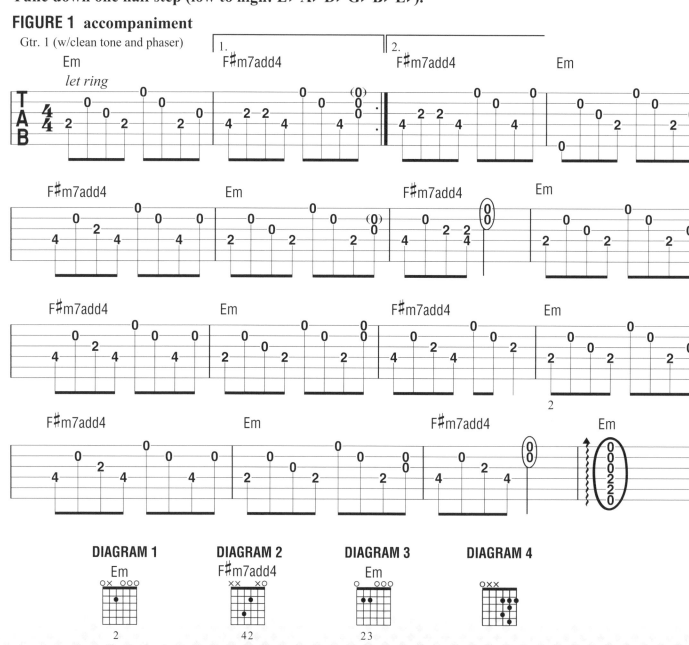

DIAGRAMS 1 and 2 show the two arpeggiated chord shapes in FIGURE 1. A♯ you can see, they're both pretty easy to play, especially the first shape, as it only requires one finger. A♯ you can also see, other than the Em chord I play at the very end (DIAGRAM 3), I'm only using the top four strings. Both chords incorporate ringing, open strings and are what I call "folk chords," as opposed to barre chords. These kinds of open chords sound really full, especially when played with a clean tone, and the open, ringing strings give the progression a nice dirge-y, somber sound.

I came up with the melody line shown in FIGURE 2 by imagining what a vocalist might sing over FIGURE 1. If you approach this kind of situation like an instrumentalist, you immediately start thinking in terms of scales and licks, but thinking like a singer can lead you to something memorable and unique. You can even conjure a specific singer: For example, thinking of Iron Maiden's Bruce Dickinson might have led me to something very note-y and "operatic." When I came up with FIGURE 2 I was thinking of the simple, cool phrasing used by the Scorpions' Klaus Meine. As a result, I ended up playing only the five notes (E F♯ A B C♯) shown in DIAGRAM 4.

Try coming up with a simple, two-chord progression of your own and then playing what you think a certain vocalist would sing on top of it. The result might really surprise you.

By the way, I've named this piece "Castle Shadow Grey" and have already copyrighted it. So don't rip it off!

—reprinted from *Guitar World*, January 2009

FIGURE 2 melody

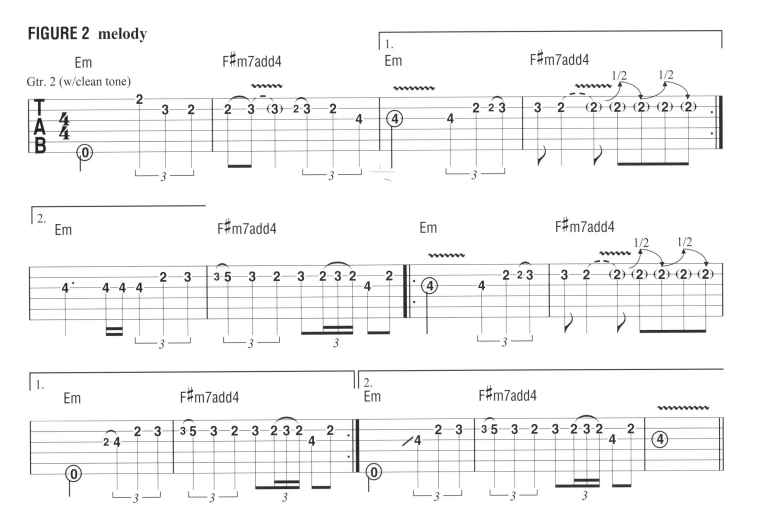

Last Will and Testament

Signing off with a fast picking idea and a $350 warm-up exercise.

I'm writing this month's column from home, in between tours with Testament. We have a couple months off before we head out on the road again, this time to Europe with Judas Priest and Megadeth on the Priest Feast tour, which we're really looking forward to. During our brief autumn break we're going to start working on some new material for our next album, which we'd like to begin recording before the end of '09. I've also got a signature Dean Flying V guitar coming out in January. I designed some of the artwork for the body, and it's pretty metal looking, so I'm really excited about that, too.

For my last column I'd like to talk about something that is incredibly important but also often overlooked: stretching. Taking time to warm up before you play is something I've touched on before, but one thing I didn't talk about is stretching. This is very important, because when you play the kind of fast music Testament does your hands can not only cramp up if you're not properly warmed up but you can also develop tendonitis, also known as "tennis elbow." Both of these conditions are painful, and if you get either one you probably won't be able to play guitar for a while. And the last thing you want is for your bandmates to have to get another guitar player to replace you for gigs.

That said, before a Testament gig I like to do some physical stretches in addition to playing exercises. One of these is a four-step process:

Step 1: Stretch both arms out straight in front of you with your palms facing up toward the ceiling. Make a fist with each hand and bend your wrists upward and toward you, as far as you can, and hold that position for 10 seconds.

Step 2: Bring your hands back down, open your fists and bend your wrists downward as far as you can so your fingers are pointing toward the floor. Hold that position for 10 seconds.

Step 3: Leave your wrists bent backward, but bend your elbows upward so that your fingers end up horizontal and your palms are facing the ceiling, as if you're "holding up the pyramids" like in one of those old Egyptian drawings, or carrying a tray of food like a waiter. Again, hold that position for 10 seconds.

Step 4: Shake out your arms and hands and relax.

Performing this four-step process before you play will help to stretch your muscles. It's a little like getting a hydrocortisone shot: it's really effective, especially if you're cold or don't have much time before going onstage.

I'd love to tell you I came up with this stretching routine myself, but the truth is this lesson cost me $350. A while back I started to get a tingling feeling from my elbow down, and it got to the point where it would be physically painful to do a hammer-on or a wide stretch. I went to the doctor and described my symptoms, and he sent me to a therapist. I was signed up for six sessions, but as soon as I got the bill for the first 45-minute session I stopped going because it was so expensive. But that $350 exercise stuck with me, and it works, so I'm giving it to you for free.

The other thought I'm going to leave you with is a fast-picking technique that I had no idea I was doing until someone pointed it out. When picking fast, many guitarists tend to play from the wrist, but I've found that I can pick even faster and with less effort by making a rotating motion with my thumb and index finger. This is a personal thing that might not work for everybody, but it's worth trying.

This is my last column for now, and I'm going to sign-off by answering another one of your questions:

Your tone on the new Testament album is killer, and so is your live sound. What equipment did you use in the studio, and is it different from your live rig? Great column too! Thanks! —John Lewis

Thanks. I've been tone searching for a while, and by accident I stumbled onto the new EVH 5150III head and ended up using it to record The Formation of Damnation. In my opinion, the amp has all the tonal characteristics of Eddie's sound on the first Van Halen record: a nice top end, plus endless presence and gain. Live, I'm using the new Marshall JVM head because it has those same characteristics I love in an amp: sharp top with a bite, plus a decent clean tone. I use the two-channel version of the head because it gives me exactly what I want: good clean and crunch tones, plus a lead boost for soloing. I suggest using Celestion Vintage 30 speakers or even 25-watt Greenbacks. Celestion Greenback speakers have an awesome tone, but be careful with them. If you're only using a single 4x12 cab with a 100-watt head, they're easy to blow up.

Let me finish by saying it's been a blast writing this column. Many thanks to *Guitar World* for the opportunity. A♯ I said from the outset, my intent with this column was to discuss some points that I thought would appeal to the intermediate player. But judging by some of the emails and letters I've received, it looks like it has impacted some more advanced players too, and that's really flattering. Thanks for reading.

—reprinted from *Guitar World*, February 2009

SOUTH OF HEAVEN

by Kerry King of Slayer

Wrist Watch

Wrist placement, muting, warming up and developing a right-hand technique from hell.

As you may remember, in last month's column I told you that my "right wrist sits on the bridge and effectively works like a little pivot." Well, guess what? That's fucking wrong! Although I do use my wrist as a pivot, that's not where it sits. How I described it to you last month isn't how I play, it's just how I assumed I play! I didn't realize this until several days later when I was actually thinking about the column as I was playing and went, Oh shit, I told them wrong. That's not how my hand sits at all! Here's what I actually do with my picking hand.

Instead of my right wrist sitting on the bridge like I told you, it actually sits above the bridge. To be exact, when I'm playing my Flying V my wrist actually sits on the top bevel of the top wing of the guitar. And even when I'm playing my [B.C. Rich] Warlocks the wrist of my picking hand is still probably a good two inches above the bridge. There's a lifeline, loveline or whatever-the-fuck-line it is on my palm, and that's the part of my hand that actually sits on the bridge, not my wrist. The line I'm talking about is a crease that starts about half an inch below my right pinkie knuckle and then goes across my palm before curving up toward my middle finger. Like I've just said, that's the part of my picking hand that rests on the bridge and is also what I use to palm mute the strings.

As a rule, when I palm mute it's normally only one string, the low E or A, unless I'm muting a two- or three-note power chord. Either way, it's all about applying pressure against the strings in certain places, but not enough pressure to where you throw a floating tremolo bridge out of tune. The place you actually rest on the string is important too; if you go too far back over the bridge then the string will just ring open, and if you go too far forward you'll end up muting the string so much that you won't be able to tell what note or chord you're playing because you'll have killed the string(s) dead. Where I do my muting is right where the string goes over the bridge, or maybe just a tiny fraction of an inch—and I literally do mean a tiny fraction—in front of that point. You can hear when you're doing it right, and after a while it becomes second nature and you don't even think about it.

The way I use my picking hand probably evolved from playing Flying Vs for so long and isn't exactly commonplace, so I won't recommend copying it, unless it feels right, of course. The best thing for you to do is find a place to rest your right wrist that feels comfortable to you and then stick with it. The same goes for where exactly you do your palm muting. Anyway, now that I've fixed my fuck-up, let's get back to working on your picking speed.

Last month we talked about how building up picking speed was kind of like bodybuilding—you don't start off by trying to curl 150 pounds unless you're a total fucking moron! Instead you work up to it. Also, like any sport, even when you get good at it, you don't just go for broke right off the bat. Hell, when a runner goes to a track meet he always prepares himself for his first race by warming up. If he doesn't, then he's runs a much higher risk of getting hurt, not to mention the fact that he won't perform as well. And, to me, playing guitar is the same kinda deal. So, when we're playing a show and we're opening with something fast like "War Ensemble," I never go up onstage "cold turkey." I warm up backstage, starting off slowly and then increasing the speed until it's right.

FIGURE 1 is a typical picking warm up exercise that I might do. It involves some palm-muting and focuses predominantly on my right hand, which is the most important one when it comes to fast, tight picking. So, I'll start off by playing it slowly and then build up speed as I get warmed up.

FIGURE 2 is another good warm-up exercise that gets your left (fretboard) hand a little more involved and will help you with coordinating both hands when picking. Once again, start off slowly and build up speed at your own pace. The last warm up idea I'm gonna show you, **FIGURE 3**, is a chromatic bitch that uses all four of your left hand fingers. This one will really test and improve the coordination of your left and right hands.

—reprinted from *Guitar World*, October 2002

FIGURE 1 warm-up exercise

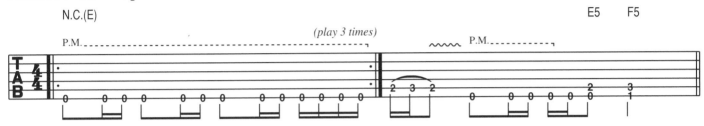

FIGURE 2 warm-up exercise

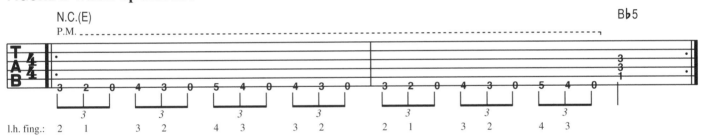

FIGURE 3 warm-up exercise

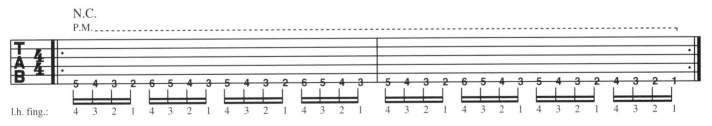

Hand of Doom

Achieving a pronounced "chunk"; using a triangular pick.

I'm a big fan of your rhythm "chunk," which always sounds heavier than hell, especially on slow, chuggy riffs like in "Divine Intervention," "Expendable Youth" and "Jesus Saves." I know you're palm-muting the low open E string notes on these riffs, but even when I do that, it just doesn't sound that "chunky" or heavy. What am I doing wrong? Is it my tone, my palm-muting technique, the strength of my picking (or lack of it!), or all of the above? Also, I'd love to know how you set up your Marshall head. You've told us all about the settings on your 10-band graphic EQ but not on your amp. Help!

—Sam Chappell

That's a tough one to answer because, not being able to hear or see exactly what you're doing, I have no idea what's going on. So, the reason for the lack of balls in your tone could be one, two or even all three of the things you've just mentioned! From my experience, though, I would say that the biggest reason for this sort of problem starts and probably ends with the tone you've got coming from your amp. In fact, I'd say that nine times out of 10 it's probably that.

I've already discussed palm muting in this column and, to be honest, it's a pretty easy technique to do once you've gotten it down. Also, palm muting won't miraculously add nuts to a weak tone. You can only do so much with your hand, and there's no super, secret palm muting spot that'll change that. When it comes to palm muting there's a sweet spot for everybody, and once you've found that spot it's not going to get any better or any worse. That's your sweet spot, as far as I'm concerned.

As far as picking goes, I'd say that picking harder isn't going to make that much of a difference, especially if you're playing a hot, juiced-up rig like I do. And, once again, picking harder certainly isn't going to add balls to a sound that has none to begin with. In fact, when I'm recording, I intentionally try not to play too hard because, the harder you play, the more chance you have of throwing the strings out of tune, especially when you're using a low tuning. So, when we're in the studio I play as lightly as possible while still achieving the sound I want. In the intensity and adrenaline rush of playing live, though, all bets are off. In fact, Jeff [Hanneman] and I dig in so hard when we're on tour that the nails on our index fingers become flat—they're not round anymore because they've been filed down by the strings!

As I told you in the very first *South of Heaven* column, down-picking a riff is always chunkier-sounding and has more attitude than alternate (down, up, down, up, etc.) picking, especially when you're palm muting. To add even more balls when I'm chugging on the open low E string, a lot of times I'll hit two notes, as opposed to just one. Instead of merely picking the low string by itself, as demonstrated in **FIGURE 1**, I'll add the fifth and play a power chord, as shown in **FIGURE 2**. Whenever I do this, I'll always use consecutive downstrokes because using alternate picking on a palm-muted open E5 chord just doesn't sound right.

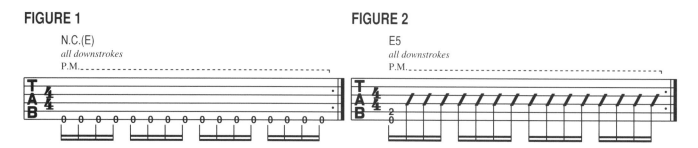

FIGURE 1

N.C.(E)
all downstrokes
P.M.

FIGURE 2

E5
all downstrokes
P.M.

So, as I told you at the beginning of this answer, to get more balls happening in your sound, I suggest you zone in on the tone of your amp. As you know from one of my recent columns, I set my Boss 10-band graphic EQ to have a mid-curve that goes up rather than down because that's what works best for me. That doesn't necessarily mean it will work for you, though. In fact, you may prefer the exact opposite—

"scooping" out the mids, as they say. I use EMG 81 pickups, which are pretty beefy sounding, and always have the Gain control on my Marshall JCM800 head cranked all the way to 10. As far as all the controls on my amp go, my settings are typically this: Volume on 4 or more; Gain on 10; Middle on 8; Treble 7–9; Presence on 7 or more (to add some high "cut") and Bass somewhere between 5 and 8. Where I set my bass control depends on a number of things, like how new my tubes are and the stage I'm on. Before every show, I'll invariably tweak my sound to the stage we're playing on and make sure I'm totally happy with it myself before I even consider hitting one note in front of an audience. Hollow, wooden stages sound the best, but sometimes you get on a stage that's made of scaffolding with a big, plastic top. Those are really bright-sounding and have no chance of making your nuts shake. In fact, the sound you get depends on a bunch of factors, including several that you might not even think of, such as what your cabinet is actually sitting on. Wood, carpet, concrete, tile—each surface has a big effect on your sound. So, my advice is to crank the gain up, pay attention to the environment you're playing in and always take the time to fine tune your tone to it. Good luck!

> *I've noticed that you use a triangular-shaped guitar pick, as opposed to the standard "teardrop"*
> *pick. What is the reason for this, and how did you find out that you prefer this shape to the other?*
> —Robert Strack

Well, first off, for anybody that doesn't know, I don't use those silly, big triangular picks—they make better Frisbees than anything else! The ones I use are actually kinda circular and triangular, if that description makes any sense. **PHOTO A** shows one of my picks together with a regular "teardrop" pick, or whatever they're called, and also a penny to provide a sense of scale. My picks are made by D'Andrea. They're medium-gauge, and the main reason I use them is their numerous sides. My pick essentially has six useable sides whereas a conventional pick only has, on its best day, two. So, when we're playing live, if I put a rut in the side of my pick by doing a pick scrape, all I have to do is rotate it or flip it over and I'm immediately on a fresh, useable side!

Another pretty cool thing about the picks I use is that they're not as pointy as the teardrop ones. So, as far as picking technique goes, it stands to reason that it's easier to play with this type of pick because you're less likely to dig in too far with it, as you don't have as much of a point. I don't remember exactly how I discovered this particular shape; I don't think anyone said, "Hey, check this out." I think I just tried one out one day, thought about it and decided it made sense to me. Plus, on a side note, in the midst of a sweaty thrash-fest, it's a hell of a lot easier to hang onto!

—reprinted from *Guitar World*, June 2003

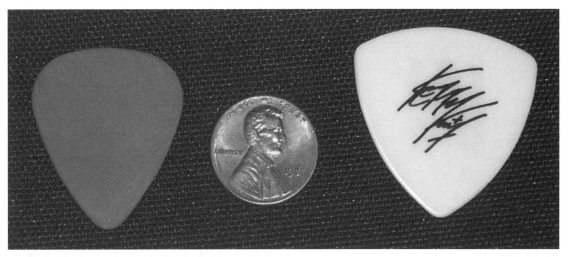

PHOTO A

THE SOUND AND THE FURY

By Kirk Hammett of Metallica

Stevie Wonder

How to play like the great bluesman Stevie Ray Vaughan.

As you probably know, Stevie Ray Vaughan is one of my all-time favorite guitarists. Ironically, I never had a chance to spend much time with his music while he was alive. Shortly after he died, I got hold of a video of him playing a live show, and I was totally blown away by his timing, tone, feel, vibrato, phrasing—everything. Some people are just born to play guitar, and Stevie was absolutely one of them.

It's nearly impossible to emulate Stevie's tone, because his hands and soul had a lot to do with his sound. Of course, you can approximate the tone of your favorite players by using the same gear that they do. If you want to get a sound similar to Stevie's, use a Fender Stratocaster. [Fender makes the Stevie Ray Vaughan Stratocaster, which is based on his legendary Number 1 guitar, which had a 1959 body, a 1962 rosewood neck and a left-handed tremolo unit.] You'll get even closer if you get a vintage Strat and a vintage Fender amp, because that's what he used. His effects included an Ibanez Tube Screamer and a Vox wah.

Another factor in Stevie's killer tone was the gauge of his strings and how hard he would play. A lot of people try to get his sound by using a set of .009s, and you just can't do what he did with slinky strings like that. Stevie used really heavy strings—.013 (high E) to .058 or even .060 (low E)—so to get even close, you need to start with at least a set of .011s.

In addition, he was a super-aggressive player, so you'll have to play forcefully to get that big, percussive sound. Stevie didn't just pick from his wrist; he picked with his entire arm, as you can see in videos of him performing. He also used a lot of downstrokes and string raking, which added to his unique rhythm and lead sound.

STRING RAKING

String raking is like percussive sweep picking, and it's a relatively easy way to spice up your lead playing. **FIGURE 1** shows a simple C minor blues lick that starts with a string rake. To play this, mute the A, D and G strings by lightly resting your left-hand index finger across them, and then quickly rake your pick across them using a single, smooth downstroke that ends with the half-step bend at the 10th fret on the B string. Adding this simple move to the lick adds extra emotion, attitude and emphasis. Try playing it without the rake and you'll hear what I mean.

QUARTER-TONE BENDS

Another SRV move that adds bite and bluesy tension to a solo is to bend certain notes just a tad so they end up sitting right between two notes. **FIGURE 2** is an A minor run that features this technique. As you can see, the second-to-last note you play—the C at the 5th fret on the G string—is bent up a quarter step so that it sits right between C and C♯. Great blues players do this kind of thing all the time, and Stevie was especially good at it. He'd even add a quarter-note bend to notes he'd already bent up by one or even two steps. **FIGURE 3** is a Stevie Ray–style, bluesy E minor lick that uses string raking and quarter-tone bends.

VIBRATO

Being able to shake a note in a way that complements both the song and the mood of the solo is a highly expressive art that Stevie perfected. I especially love his vibrato, because it is so wide and muscular. Unfortunately, this technique is almost as difficult to describe as it is to perform. To learn more about this, I recommend that you listen closely to his albums and watch videos of him in action, zoning in on what he does with his left hand. Check out SRV's *Live at the El Mocambo* video. It's a jaw-dropping experience, and if you watch closely, you can learn a lot.

—reprinted from *Guitar World*, April 2000

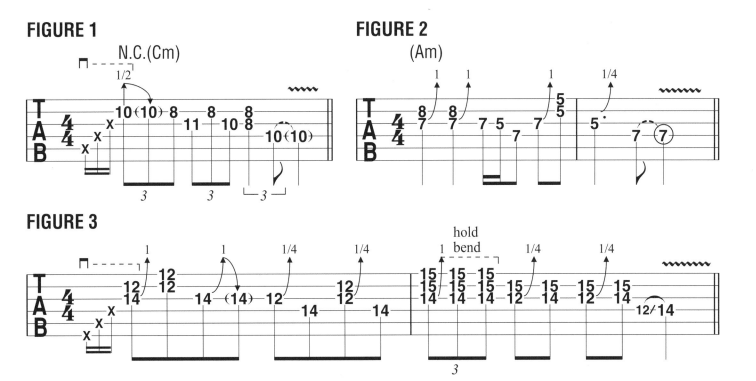

Get the Bends

Answers to more of your letters and emails.
This month's topic: wide string-bends.

I hate to sound like a kiss-ass, but I look forward to your column every month—your playing on Load *is the reason I started playing guitar. At the end of last year, I was lucky enough to attend the concert you guys played with the Orchestra of St. Luke's at Madison Square Garden in New York. What a killer show! Anyway, even though I was in one of the higher sections of the arena, thanks to a pair of binoculars I was able to watch your every move. A bunch of things you did blew me away, but the one thing that really stood out was just how big and accurate your string bends were. Can you explain this a bit? Thanks.*

—Mike Hill, Hoboken, NJ

Looking back, I've had some kind of string-bending fetish for as long as I can remember. Soon after I first started playing, I saw someone bend a string for the very first time and my eyes practically popped out of my head. I ran straight home and immediately started bending the shit out of pretty much every single note I played—and I guess I've never stopped since. As far as I'm concerned, there's no limit to how wide a string bend can be: I mean, I've seen Buddy Guy literally bend notes on the B and high E strings all the way up to the upper edge of his fretboard! Stevie Ray Vaughan was also a master of the big bend, as is another one of my all-time favorites, Gary Moore.

The great thing about wide bends (bends greater than a whole-step, or "full") is that, provided they're done well, they can help add a "vocal" quality to a solo, especially when played in conjunction with a wah pedal. The only drawback of doing a lot of big bends is that you greatly increase your chances of breaking a string. I've always hated changing stings—especially on a guitar with a whammy bar. I guess that's a small price to pay for adding a more lyrical feel to your leads. Like half-step or whole-step bends, though, wide bends have to be performed accurately.

Wide bends really test the accuracy of your string bending, so I'm going to start by giving you a few simple exercises to help you ensure you're doing them right. Before we go any further, though, for maximum strength and control, I recommend that you use a technique called *reinforced bending*, which simply means using more than one finger to do a bend. For example, if you're bending a string by pushing it with your middle finger, use your index finger to help push it, and if you're bending with your ring (third) finger, use your index and middle fingers to help the ring finger push the string. By doing this you can even perform accurate, wide bends using your pinkie. Sure, the pinkie is the weakest finger, but when you support it with the other three it can get quite strong.

Whenever you're doing any bend, wide or small, its important to know what your *target pitch* is because if you overshoot or undershoot it you're gonna sound pretty stupid—unless you deliberately want to do that, of course. **FIGURE 1** is a simple exercise that involves doing three different bends in succession—one whole step, one and one half steps and two whole steps. Before each bend, play the target note as indicated to help fix it in your mind's ear. Don't get frustrated if you don't nail this right away. Like any playing technique worth learning, wide, accurate bending takes time to master.

Once you can perform the bends in **FIGURE 1** consistently, try doing the same exact exercise in different places on the neck, such as closer to the nut (**FIGURE 2**) and higher up the fretboard too (**FIGURE 3**). As you'll quickly find, the closer you get to the 12th fret (the midpoint between the nut and the bridge), the easier the bends become. Once you feel you've gotten the hang of bending the G string, try to execute bends on the other strings, as in **FIGURE 4**. A♯ you'll also quickly discover, how hard (or easy) a particular note is to bend not only depends on how far you want to bend it, but also on what string you're on bend where on the neck you are. The B string is the easiest string to bend because of the ratio between its thickness and pitch.

Keep in mind that, in addition to having a good, reinforced bending technique, you also have to develop your ear if you want to consistently perform wide bends—or small bends for that matter—accurately. This is why I still dedicate a substantial part of my practice and warm-up time to practicing string bends all over the fretboard.

When you feel comfortable doing these bends, try doing them in "slow motion." Then, to make them even more challenging, add some sweet left-hand vibrato on the end of each bend (make sure you used reinforced fingering!). **FIGURE 5** is the slow motion, vibrato version of **FIGURE 1**.

Until next time, keep bending the hell out of those strings!

—reprinted from *Guitar World*, May 2000

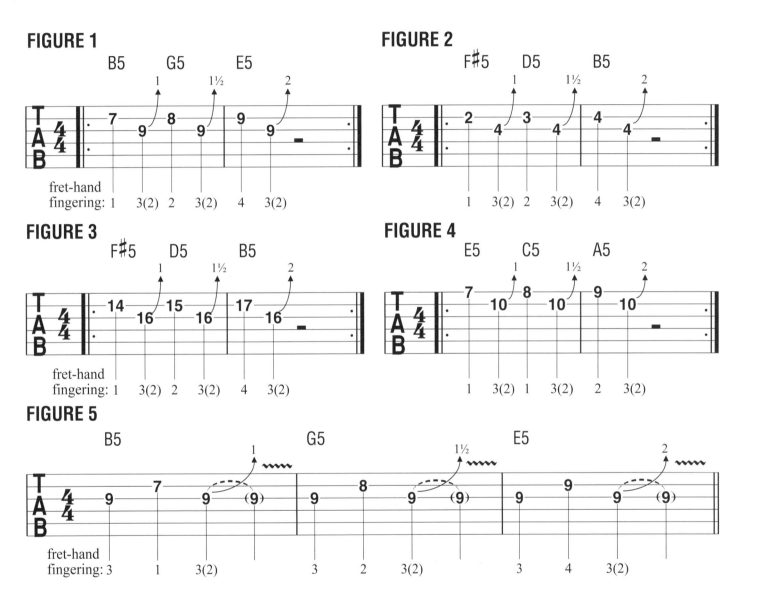

Get Bent
Navigating compound bends

In the May 2000 issue you did a really cool piece on wide string bends and finished the column by saying "next issue we'll take this idea even further and get into a cool-sounding technique called compound bending. Until then, bend the crap out of those strings!" Well, just like you suggested, I've been bending the crap outta my strings ever since. But I'm still waiting to learn about compound string bending because in the last two columns you've been talking about using open-string notes instead.
                                                                    —Hugh Gilmartin, Centerport, NY

Damn, guilty as charged! I *did* end my May 2000 column by saying we'd get into compound bending next time and then spent the next two issues talking about open-string licks instead! Thanks for pointing out my oversight. So here we go:

As you may recall, when we covered wide bends back in the May issue, I recommended that you always do them using a technique called *reinforced bending* which simply means using more than one finger to push the string. We also talked about the importance of knowing what your *target pitch* is before you do any bend, be it big or small. After all, few things on guitar sound shittier than a bad bend.

The reason for this reminder is that both of these things are very important when it comes to compound bending.

So far we've only talked about bending a note up to another note. Let's take this a step further by bending a note up to one pitch and then, without releasing the first bend, bending it up *again* to another note. This is what is known as a *compound bend* (a.k.a. *multiple bend*). If you're not quite sure what I'm talking about here, check out **FIGURE 1A**. In this exercise we're bending the A note on the G string at the 14th fret up a whole step to B, hold it there for two beats and then bending it up an additional half step to C. As you can see, the second bend is done without releasing the first one. So, what you're doing is bending an already bent note even further, a total of one and one half steps.

Compound bends really test the accuracy of your bending technique, which is why using *reinforced fingering* and hearing your *target pitches* is so important. Although these types of bends may look easy on paper, they're pretty hard to do accurately, so don't get mad if you don't nail this example right away. To help you get the sound of the two notes you're aiming for fixed firmly in your head, play **FIGURE 1B**, which mimics the sound of the rising pitch by using regular unbent notes instead of bends.

Once you feel you can play **FIGURE 1A** accurately and consistently, try adding some left-hand finger vibrato to the bends as shown in **FIGURE 2**. This is not an easy technique to master, but make a determined effort to learn how to do it well because the soulfulness the vibrato adds to the bends definitely makes it worth the extra effort. To achieve the desired vibrato effect on the bent notes, you'll need to repeatedly release the bend slightly (by a half step) and then bend back up to the target pitch in a smooth, steady rhythm (not too fast, not too slow).

Here are a couple more examples of compound bends for you to work on. **FIGURE 3** is a half-step bend that is bent up an additional whole step, while **FIGURE 4** is a whole-step bend on top of another whole-step bend. Once you feel you've conquered both of these examples, try adding some vibrato to the bent notes, just like we did with **FIGURE 2**.

FIGURE 5 is a three-stage compound bend that will really challenge you: a whole-step bend, followed by another whole-step bend and then a half-step bend on top of that. Be sure to use two or three fingers to push the string (reinforced bending) for maximum control. Once you feel you can accurately hit the "target" pitches every time, add some vibrato to the bent notes to make them "sing."

Let's say you're playing an A minor pentatonic lead in the 5th position (**FIGURE 6**) and you're gonna bend the G note on the B string at the 8th fret up two whole steps to B. What I'll sometimes do is this: I'll start bending the shit out of that G note and then, when I get the pitch up to around A♯, I'll quickly shift my left-hand fretting finger (the ring finger) up one fret while I'm still holding the bend, pick the string again and then finish the bend off. Doing this sounds similar to a continuous wide bend from G to B except it has a slight pause that almost sounds like you're taking a quick breath just before you get to that final plateau. I got this idea from watching Stevie Ray Vaughan and also Buddy Guy, who does the exact same thing. **FIGURE 7** is an example of what I'm talking about here.

I realize that the examples we've just gone through aren't the most exciting ones on the planet, but check 'em out because mastering these bending techniques will add an exciting new dimension to your playing. So compound-bend the heck out of your strings and we'll talk more next issue.

—reprinted from *Guitar World*, August 2000

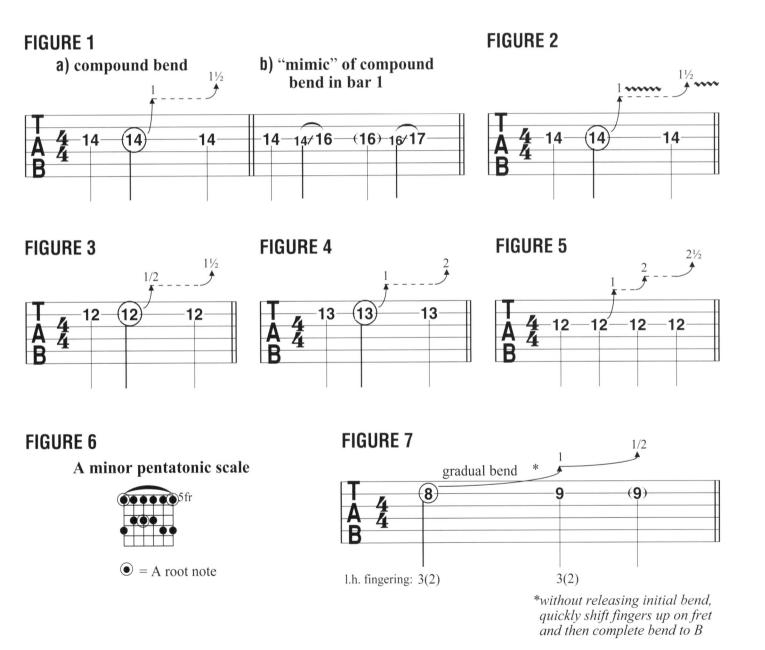

FIGURE 1
a) compound bend
b) "mimic" of compound bend in bar 1

FIGURE 2

FIGURE 3

FIGURE 4

FIGURE 5

FIGURE 6
A minor pentatonic scale
5fr
◉ = A root note

FIGURE 7
gradual bend
l.h. fingering: 3(2)   3(2)

without releasing initial bend, quickly shift fingers up on fret and then complete bend to B

Night in the Ruts

Using phrasing and other simple ideas to make the most of licks and runs you already know.

I started playing guitar after hearing your lead work on Load *a few years back. However, I've gotten into a bit of a rut with my soloing lately because I always seem to play the same old licks and runs. A friend of mine says I've got to learn some new scales. Is this true? Please help!*

—Matt Fox, San Francisco, CA

Some people, like your friend, think that the only way to come up with new soloing ideas is to learn more scales. I definitely don't agree with that. I mean, if that's the case, what happens when you run out of new scales and modes to learn? In my opinion, you don't need to know every exotic scale under the sun to be able to come up with creative and exciting leads. Take, for example, a standard minor-blues box [**FIGURE 1**]; there's only six different notes in there but there's so much you can do with them. I always find myself stumbling across different ways to spice up my well-worn blues licks...ways that are often so simplistic it's unbelievable. In fact, sometimes the thing that makes all the difference is so very basic that if you sat down and deliberately tried to do something different you'd probably never think of it.

For an example of what I'm talking about here, compare FIGURES 2A and 2B. As you can see, they're virtually the same exact A minor-blues scale (A C D E♭ E G) lick, except that in **FIGURE 2**B you bend up to the last note (G) from a half step below (F♯). This simple, subtle nuance gives that final note a completely different type of vibrato sound plus a crying, vocal-like quality that adds emotion to the lick. Now compare FIGURES 3A and 3B. **FIGURE 3**B is basically the same E minor-blues (E G A B♭ B D) lick as the one in **FIGURE 3**A, with just a couple of trills, double-stops and a slide thrown in for extra excitement. Get the picture? As these two examples illustrate, it doesn't take much to breathe new life into a seemingly tired idea.

A really great and effective way of rejuvenating an old lick is to see how many different ways you can *phrase* it. In case you're not 100 percent sure what I'm talking about here, I'll quickly explain: to phrase a run or lick differently, you don't change the order of the notes you're playing; instead you just mess with their timing. Basically, phrasing is all about two things: 1) how you attack each note, and 2) how long before you move onto the next one. Confused? If you are, don't worry—the following example should make this concept crystal clear.

Check out the simple A minor-blues lick shown in **FIGURE 4A**. By keeping the running order of the notes the same and merely changing the timing of each note you can come up with a bunch of variations in no time. **FIGURES 4B–F** are just a few of 'em. Get it? It's real easy to do and those five variations we've just looked at are just the start. There are literally an infinite number of ways this short sequence of notes can be phrased without altering their order or adding extra slurs or passing notes.

So, the next time you find yourself guilty of recycling the same exact licks over and over again, try taking a few of them and seeing how many different ways you can phrase them. I realize that this is an unbelievably basic concept, but then again, most of the great ones are—and for that very reason, are often overlooked. Don't dismiss this one—it could very well save your ass the next time you find yourself caught in a "lick recycling" rut!

—reprinted from *Guitar World*, November 2000

FIGURE 1
moveable minor-blues box

⊙ = root note

FIGURE 2
a) A minor-blues lick

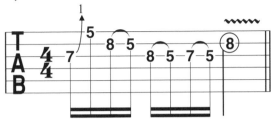

b) same lick w/added bend

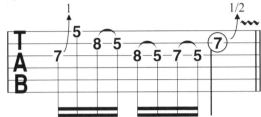

FIGURE 3
a) E minor-blues lick

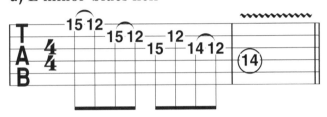

b) variation

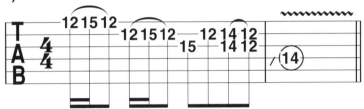

FIGURE 4
a) A minor-blues lick

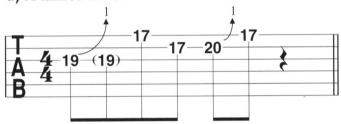

b) phrasing variation 1

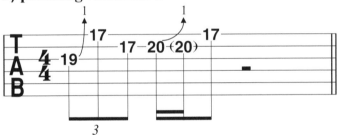

c) phrasing variation 2

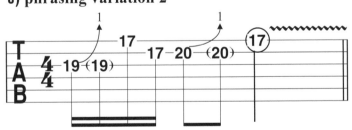

d) phrasing variation 3

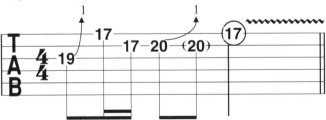

e) phrasing variation 4

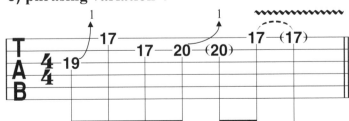

f) phrasing variation 5

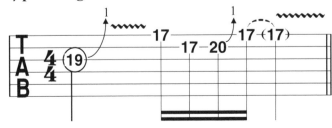

Stuck Mojo

Listening to different music to get out of a rut.

I've been playing guitar for around five years and I love it to death. What's been driving me nuts, though, is that for the last three or four months, every time I jam along with friends or to a CD, I always seem to end up playing the same old shit. I guess I'm stuck in a rut. One of my pals told me that you recommended listening to other types of music to help get out of this sort of thing. Here's hoping you can help!
—Gene Ripley, Denver, CO

When you're serious about your guitar playing, there's nothing worse than getting stuck in a rut. Each of us has what I call a "comfort zone," which is basically a library of well-trodden licks and runs that we turn to out of habit because we know they work. In a nutshell, being caught in a rut means that you're trapped in your comfort zone and can't get out. Whenever this happens, though, don't get too depressed because: 1) it happens to us all from time to time and, 2) There are things you can do to get out of this six-string nightmare. A# I've received quite a few letters on this subject, that's what we're going to address over the next few columns.

To my way of thinking, one of the most obvious ways to get out of a rut is to listen to a style of music you don't normally listen to and then try to learn something from it. You can do this by either trying to learn some of the licks and runs you hear or by merely trying to solo over it. The latter is great because you'll get chords and progressions thrown at you that you aren't used to playing over. Because of this, you'll get so caught up in trying to discover what scales and modes will work that you'll get so disoriented and will forget all about your comfort zone. I often do this when I'm in a bit of a rut and I especially like doing it with jazz music because trying to solo over that stuff always gives me a totally new perspective.

Because doing this type of thing can be really helpful, don't cut yourself off from some potentially great stuff by being narrow-minded. Instead, give everything a chance. For example, if your favorite bands are Fear Factory, Korn and Rage Against the Machine, you might think, Shit, I'm never going to listen to funk or r&b because they're both lightweight and wimpy. Even if you feel this way about a particular genre of music, I urge you to listen to a decent cross-section of it before you write off the whole damn genre! You never know, you might learn something and you might even find something you like. For example, not all country music sounds like Shania Twain. I mean, check out some of Albert Lee's stuff. He's an amazing guitarist in anyone's book. And what about the Allman Brothers? Their unique blend of blues, rock and country is unbelievable, and in my mind, every guitarist can learn something from the late, great Duane Allman.

To illustrate exactly what I'm talking about here, let's take a look at the country-blues phrase in the key of B shown in **FIGURE 1**. This string-skipping lick was inspired by listening to the Allman Brothers' classic album *At Fillmore East* and is worth learning if for no other reason than the double-string bend/release passage at the end, which has a definite pedal-steel vibe to it. This can be a tricky bending technique to master due to the fact you have to bend the note on the G string (F#) up a whole step while bending the high E string up only a semitone (half step). I recommend using the left-hand fingering indicated below the tablature and also employ *hybrid picking* (pick and fingers) with the right hand: hit all the G-string notes with your pick while plucking all the high E string notes with your right middle (or ring) finger. Doing this means you don't have to worry about continually jumping over the B string with your pick after every note. It will also give you a snappier attack on the notes you pluck with the finger.

To get you used to exactly how this double-string *oblique* bend-and-release move should sound, you may want to master **FIGURE 2** first—it's the same basic lick, except it uses hammer-ons and pull-offs to mimic the double-string bend-and-release. It's also in a different position to give you another pattern to explore.

I used a run very similar to this during my live solo in "Wherever I May Roam," which was featured on the *Live Shit: Binge & Purge* box set. I go to the lick immediately after playing some very Eastern-sounding stuff in E minor; the contrast it adds to the solo at that point is really cool.

Think about what we've talked about here today and experiment with hybrid picking and double-stops in your own playing.

—reprinted from *Guitar World*, December 2000

FIGURE 1

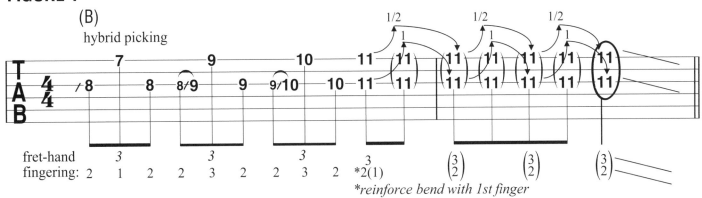

FIGURE 2

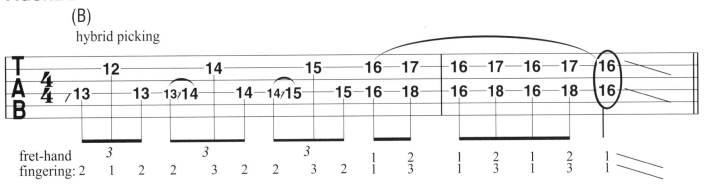

Slide It In

Using finger slides to open up the neck and explore uncharted fretboard territory.

Thanks for writing such a consistently cool column. I look forward to it every month and have gotten some great ideas from it. I've been playing for just over two years and lately I've been getting really bored with my playing. I keep using the same couple of box patterns and, no matter how hard I try, I always end up going back to them. I was lucky to see you guys play at the Experience Music Project opening in Seattle this summer, and I was totally blown away with how you managed to use the whole length of your neck without any pauses or stutters when you moved around. I'd like to be able to do the same thing...please help!

—Larry Manzi, Denver, CO

A great way of making use of the whole neck and getting around it as seamlessly as possible is by using finger slides. A good example of what I'm talking about here is the E minor pentatonic (E G A B D) passage shown in **FIGURE 1**, which is similar to the cool run Kiss guitarist Ace Frehley uses during the breakdown in the middle of "Love Gun." As you can see, in the space of just four bars, it covers quite a lot of fretboard area. It starts at the 10th fret on the low E string and ends up at the 22nd fret on the high E string. And, as you'll hear when you play it, the thing flows very smoothly from start to finish, without any pauses or gaps. And, as you'll also discover, all it took to achieve this was three simple finger slides up the neck. They're pretty short slides too; the first two go up two frets and the third one goes up three.

You can obviously do the same kind of thing going the other way too (descending). **FIGURE 2** shows an E minor run that uses a couple of slides going down the neck (toward the nut).

I've heard quite a few people say that they always slide up the neck using their ring or middle fingers, and down using only their index finger. I generally avoid that kind of thinking because it only causes you to lock into using certain fretboard patterns all the time and that's what we're trying to avoid here. This is why I always try to use all my fingers to slide both up and down the neck. Let me give you an example of why this is a good habit to get into.

Let's say you're playing a lead in E minor and you start out using the blues box shape we all know at the 12th position [**FIGURE 3**]. A real common way of getting out of this box is to slide up the G string from the 14th fret to the 16th using your middle finger, just like we did near the end of the second bar of **FIGURE 1**. By doing this we go from one well-worn box shape [**FIGURE 3**] straight into another equally familiar one [**FIGURE 4**]. All we're doing here is retreading old, familiar ground. So go ahead and try something new...like sliding up the G string from the 12th to the 16th fret using your first finger, as depicted in **FIGURE 5**. By doing this, you force yourself to explore a new area of the neck.

The "new" blues box this slide takes us into is the one illustrated in **FIGURE 6**. And, once we've lingered there for a bit we can slide into another "box," like the one shown in **FIGURE 7**, as demonstrated in the run shown in **FIGURE 8**.

Talking about sliding around the neck with all your fingers, some players seem to avoid doing it with their pinkies at all costs. To me, that's a mistake—it's there, so you should use it. My friend Larry Lalonde of Primus slides with his little finger all the time; in fact, I don't think I've ever seen anyone slide around the neck with their pinkie as much as he does.

—reprinted from *Guitar World*, January 2001

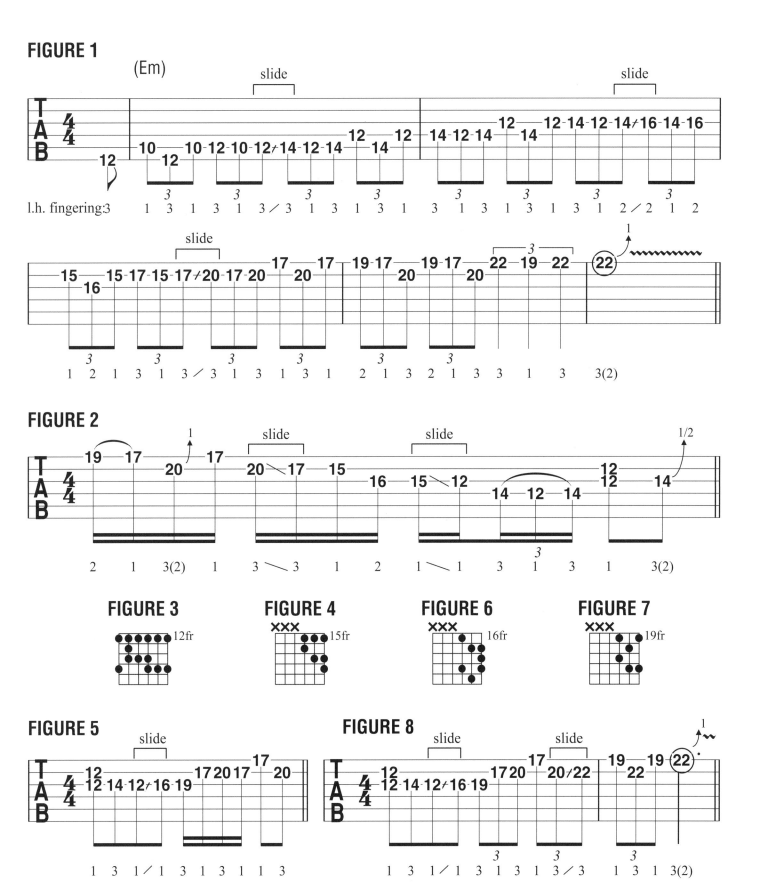

Skip 'Em All

Using string skipping to open up the neck and break out of your "comfort zone."

Greetings! Last month we talked about how wide-stretch licks and runs that make full use of your pinkie can definitely open up new doors in your playing. As you may recall, the last lick we looked at was a cool-sounding Am7 arpeggio that combined wide stretches with string skipping. I ended our last lesson by promising that we'd talk more about these techniques this month, so that's exactly what we're gonna do. Before we get started, though, let's warm up with the wide-stretch exercise shown in **FIGURE 1**. I've only given you the first six bars of the pattern, but the idea is for you to continue it all the way up to the 12th position and back down again.

FIGURE 1 may seem pretty basic, but it's a great exercise because it can really help build up the strength and stamina of your fretboard hand. It also gives your fingers a good stretch, which is always a wise thing to do whenever you're warming up. Also, if you're not used to doing a lot of hammering-on with your pinkie, then you'll probably find this exercise a real mother! In fact, by the time you've played through **FIGURE 1** a few times, it will definitely have done a real number on your fretting hand—especially your pinkie!

FIGURE 2 is another warm-up exercise that incorporates string-skipping. Once again, I've shown you the first few bars of the pattern; to get the most out of it, take it all the way up to the 12th fret and back down again, just like you did with the first exercise.

Learning to string-skip fluently is very useful in that it instantly changes your "normal" horizontal/ vertical outlook on a scale because it automatically gives you a different order of notes...and sometimes that's all you need to add color to a solo or run. For example, let's take a well-worn 12th-position E minor pentatonic scale pattern that we all know (**FIGURE 3**), and apply the simple string-skipping pattern we just used in **FIGURE 2**. The resulting run, shown in **FIGURE 4**, definitely makes that familiar old scale sound new and fresh again.

I'm not saying that string-skipping is something you should do all the time—like any technique, it can be overused. I'm just pointing out the fact that it provides you with a great way of breaking out of your comfort zone. As I've mentioned before in this column, every guitarist has a collection of licks and runs that we know will work in any situation. And, because of this, we all have a natural tendency to head straight for 'em, especially when jamming. As a result, we end up merely regurgitating our library of "safe" licks instead of being creative and fresh. String-skipping is definitely a great way of forcing yourself out of that comfortable rut and into exploring some new playing ideas.

FIGURE 1

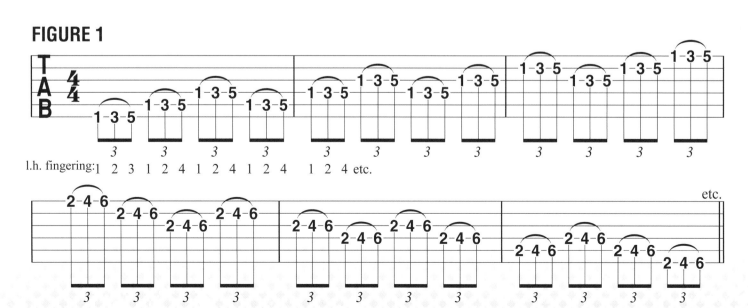

FIGURE 5 is an example of an E minor string-skipping lick that I sometimes play live during my "Of Wolf and Man" [Metallica] solo. Whenever I play it, I always barre the G and B strings at the 12th fret and let them ring. Doing this gives the lick a fatter, more colorful sound and definitely works during an E minor solo because both notes are part of the E minor chord (E G B). Jimi Hendrix crafted a bunch of great-sounding, melodic licks by playing moving lines while allowing other notes to ring out—"Little Wing" is a perfect example of him doing that. FIGURE 5 is basically a simple, melodic E minor idea that Hendrix might have played, but here it's sped-up and placed in an aggressive, heavily distorted setting. It just goes to show that, in music, anything is possible!

—reprinted from *Guitar World*, May 2001

FIGURE 2

FIGURE 3

FIGURE 4

FIGURE 5

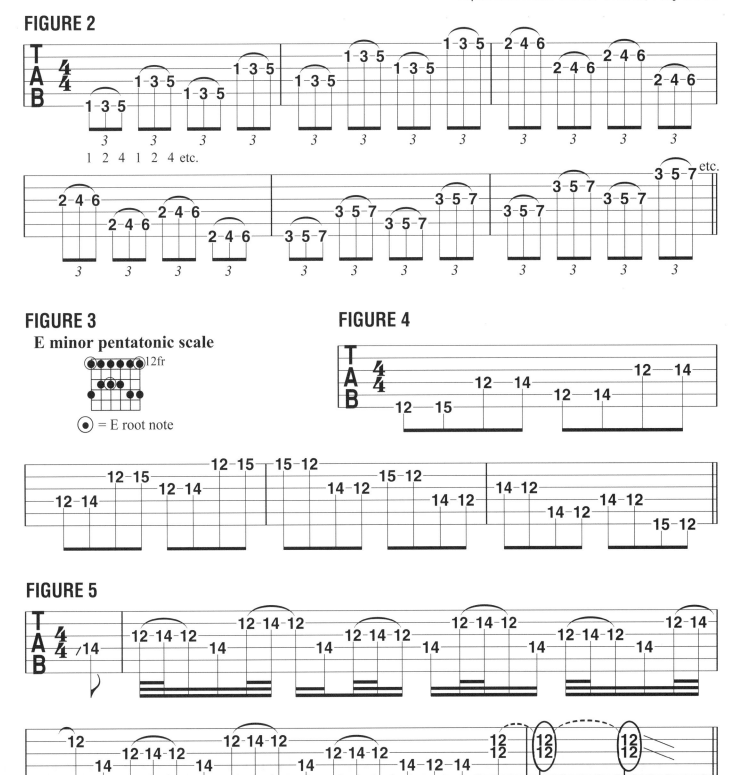

FULL SHRED

by Marty Friedman

Personal Touch

Take licks you've learned from others and make them your own

Hello, and welcome to my new *Guitar World* instructional column. I hope the ideas and concepts I present here in the coming months will give you inspiration and insight into your own path to musical creativity.

The most important thing I can say is that you should always strive to make your own distinct musical statement with what you play on the guitar. Once you've learned from the examples I present in this column, I would like you to completely disregard the examples themselves and retain only the techniques contained within them. As soon as you get the idea of where I'm coming from with a certain lick or phrase, I want you to change it into something of your own invention and tap into your own creative curiosity as quickly and fully as possible.

The overall idea is to try your hardest *not* to sound like everyone else. We all basically play the same stuff, and it is your responsibility to change things around so that you can find your own musical voice. I'm going to start with some basic licks and patterns that everyone knows and plays, and demonstrate a few ways one can add twists and turns in the pursuit of musical phrases that are unpredictable and ultimately unique.

A key concept for me when playing the guitar is to avoid looking at the fretboard as a big block of space across which you need to know dozens of scales and modes. I prefer to view the fretboard in smaller pieces, thinking of just a group of a few frets as a roadmap to little side streets and alleyways, and to concentrate on those little places.

Let me demonstrate this concept for you. **FIGURE 1** illustrates a common lick, based on the A blues scale (A C D E♭ E G), that you'll typically hear in metal, rock, blues, jazz and country. There are about *five billion* different things you can do with just these five notes. **FIGURE 2** represents a lick that we have all heard a million times. There's nothing particularly wrong with the lick, but I'd prefer to make it more interesting and unpredictable by simply changing the order of the notes slightly, as I do in **FIGURE 3**. Notice that I've moved the initial hammer/pull on beat one to the 11th and 12th frets (as opposed to the 10th and 11th) and then, on beat two, I added the 12th-fret high E note to the beginning of the legato phrase to end up with a five-note shape. To my ears, this lick sounds more interesting than the "standard" lick shown in **FIGURE 4**.

We can now easily switch a few notes around and end up with **FIGURE 5**, which is a bit more complex and interesting. If we move the hammer/pull up one fret, we get **FIGURE 6**, another nice variation on the original idea.

Let's look at another example. We can start with a predictable lick like **FIGURE 7** and twist it up to get **FIGURES 8** and **9**. Similarly, **FIGURE 10** presents a standard phrase, and **FIGURES 11** and **12** offer twisted deviations.

As a rule, try to avoid anything you've heard anyone else play before, unless it's something you really like and want to play out of choice. This is how to carve out your own niche when you are creating improvised solos.

—reprinted from *Guitar World*, June 2014

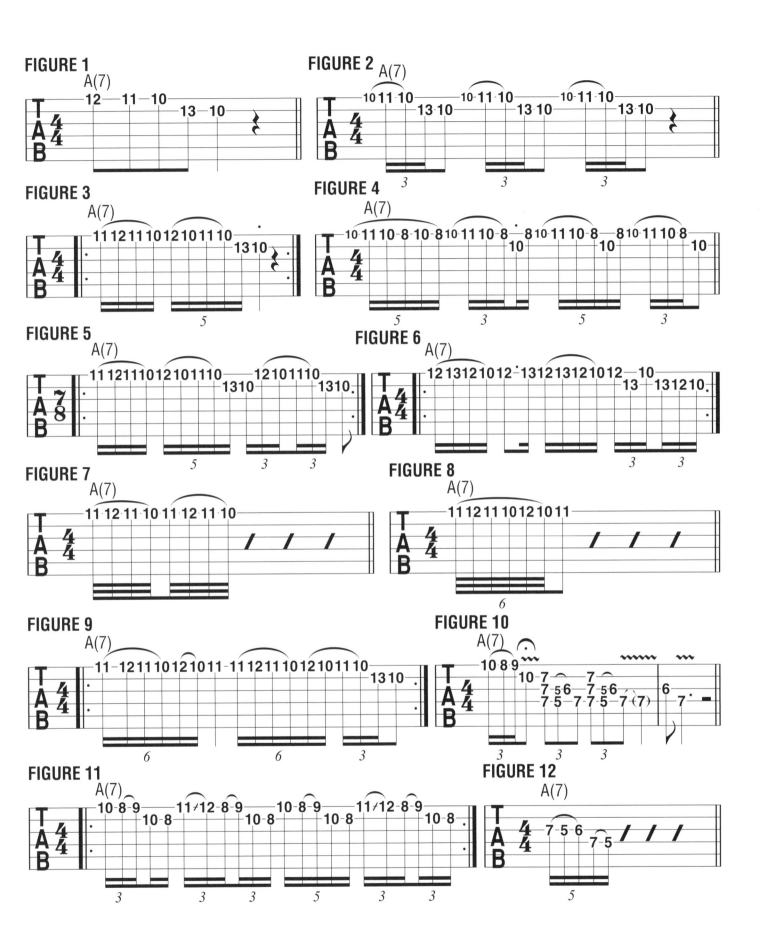

To Each Is Own

Finding your path to musical individuality

When it comes to evaluating a musician, individuality is the characteristic that I hold in highest regard. We all have our heroes and favorite players from whom we've learned a great deal through trying to emulate their playing styles. In rock, for example, most players list Jimi Hendrix, Jeff Beck and Jimmy Page as major influences, and in metal it's not uncommon to hear the names Eddie Van Halen, Randy Rhoads, Zakk Wylde or Dimebag Darrell mentioned as primary influences.

In that sense, many of us have learned from the same sources. The trick is to take those influences and push yourself in your own unique and distinct direction. Though it may be easier to learn other people's solos—which is fine if that's the goal you're pursuing—I believe it's much more rewarding to go out on a limb and take some musical chances, just to see what new and different sounds you can discover in the pursuit of forming a style that you can eventually call your own.

For example, playing fast is not the be-all and end-all of anything. In fact, it's utterly unimportant. But if you are like most guitar players, you'll want to be able to play fast, because everyone wants to play fast. So to my mind, you might as well try to do it in a way that's cool and different from everyone else. The first step to playing fast in a unique way is to find things that are easy for you to play. For this, I suggest using patterns rather than things that you hear on recordings or have found in a book or magazine.

FIGURE 1 is a pattern built from four notes—D C♯ B♭ A—that is played between the B and G strings quickly, using hammer-ons and pull-offs, and can be thought of as something one might play over an A chord. Notice that the order of the notes is altered slightly as the lick progresses, which gives it its "unpredictable" sound. Just the fact that this phrase is not constructed from an identifiable repeated pattern makes it appealing to me right away.

If we use this type of idea as a jumping-off point, we can move it up the fretboard and change one of the notes in the pattern. **FIGURE 2** is played in fifth position and can be thought of as working over a C chord, Am or even A7. The one twist I add here is to alternately change one of the notes on the B string from F to G. My penchant is to constantly change the order of the notes to create a random feeling and sound.

In **FIGURE 3**, I elaborate on the idea of using F to E and Df to C by playing lines based on the C Phrygian-dominant mode (C D♭ E F G A♭ B♭). In **FIGURE 4**, I take a simple idea based around a B7 arpeggio (B D♯ F♯ A) and add a few passing tones to make the phrase more interesting.

It's fine to copy other players just to learn about the guitar and to see how things tick. Ultimately, though, what's most important is to find your own musical identity. Hopefully, these examples will help get you on your way.

—reprinted from *Guitar World*, July 2014

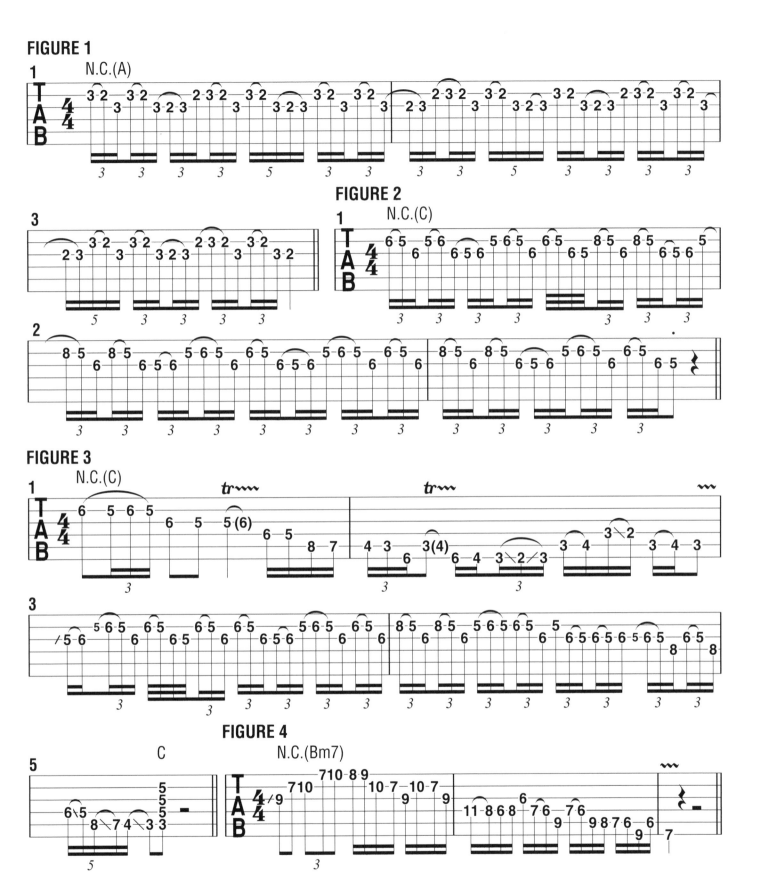

Swept Away
How to play fast and musical arpeggio-based licks without sweep picking

I've often been associated with players that use specific picking techniques, such as sweep picking, economy picking, hybrid picking and so on. In truth, I have no idea what any of these terms mean. Sweep picking does not appeal to me at all. To my ears, it sounds like, "bdLOOP, bdLoop, bdLOOP, bdLoop," as notes go up and down, over and over again. It's nothing more than a fancy technique that guitar players learn so that they can play fast arpeggios up and down.

To my ears, it's very unmusical. In my music, you will hear some insane, fast arpeggio-based lines, but it's never simply straight up and down through the arpeggios, the way sweep picking usually is performed. This month, I'd like to demonstrate some cool ways you can achieve the effect of fast arpeggio-based sounds while avoiding the predictability of standard sweep-picking licks.

My preference is to use a little bit of repetitive arpeggio-based lines and then grab some cool notes, bends or vibratos. I try to never lean on any one technique too much and always try to play with an ear toward melody. Playing straight triads up and down is, to me, neither creative nor melodic. Any monkey can learn how to execute a fast technique on the guitar, but technique in and of itself is not music.

FIGURE 1 is based on the notes of a Bm7 arpeggio: B D F♯ A. In bar 1, I outline the basic melodic "shape." I begin on the third string with a hammer-pull between F♯ (11th fret) and A (14th fret). Following the D (fourth string/12th fret), I hammer-on from F♯ up to A and end the phrase with three ascending notes, B D F♯. In bars 2–5, I elaborate on the idea by repeating the lick over several beats, adding a half-step bend and vibrato from the ♭5 (flatted fifth), F, in bar 4. I end the phrase with a half-step bend from A♯ to B, which I adorn with some vibrato.

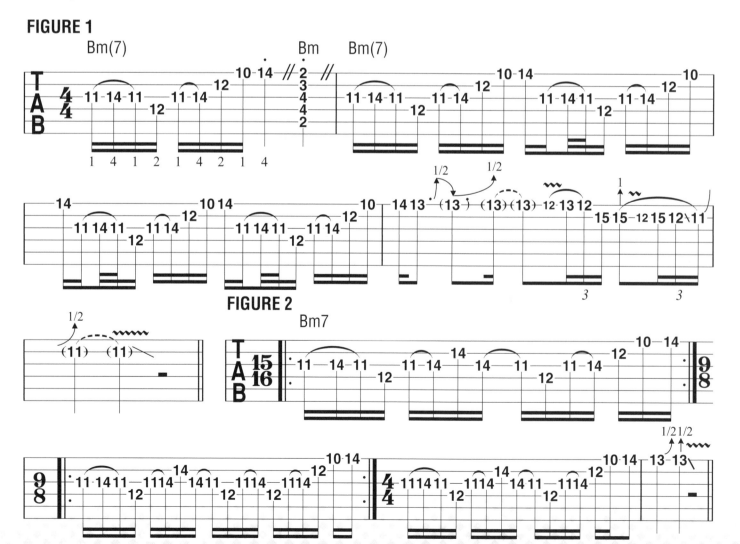

FIGURE 1

FIGURE 2

Now that you have the idea, try the same premise, but change the end of the lick. For me, elaboration on a basic idea is the most natural and musical way to play. Incorporating the arpeggio licks into melodic lines is far more interesting than an arpeggio that simply is repeated in an up-and-down fashion.

Let's wrap up with a few permutations of our initial idea. In **FIGURE 2**, I change the shape of the lick a little, and the result is odd-metered lines in 15/16 and 9/8 meters. In **FIGURES 3–8**, I take a basic G triad idea and morph it into Gmaj7 and Gm-maj7 ideas.

I certainly understand why guitar players are into speed. When I first started playing, I heard Alvin Lee—who was notoriously fast—and thought it was the coolest thing I'd ever heard. Since then, I've found that playing fast is only cool when you can't do it. Once you can, you'd rather play something musical.

—reprinted from *Guitar World*, August 2014

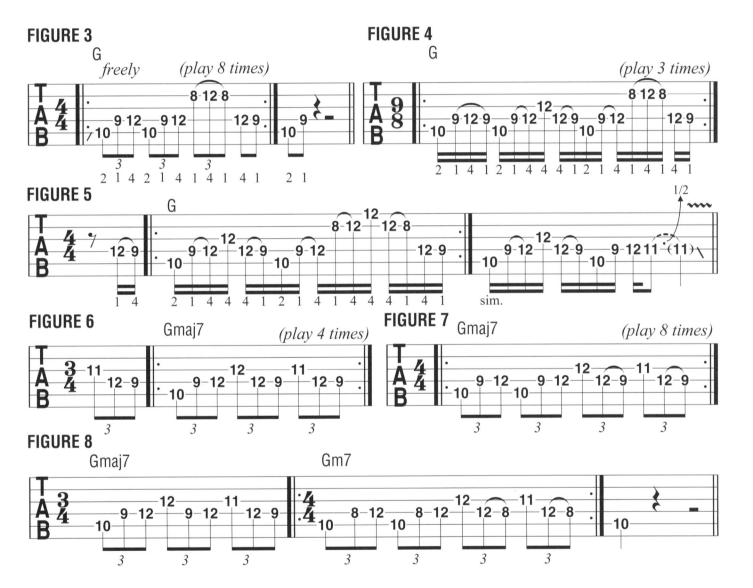

Melodic Moods

Using various articulation techniques to expressively interpret a melody

An essential element of guitar soloing, one that to me separates the grownups from the kids, is the player's ability to interpret single-note melodies in a musical way, with emotion and expression. There are countless ways in which one could play a note or series of notes on the guitar, and if you do not focus on being in control of how each note sounds, you're wasting an opportunity for *expression*, via *articulation*, which is one of the most important tools that is available to you as a soloist. The little details in the manner by which you choose to play each note in a melody is what will give you the opportunity to sound different than any other guitar player and develop a unique sound and musical "voice."

Using articulation as an expressive element is the one thing I concentrate on the most when playing live or recording, simply because there are so many options. The way in which you ultimately interpret a

FIGURE 1 "Devil Take Tomorrow" intro ♩ = 124

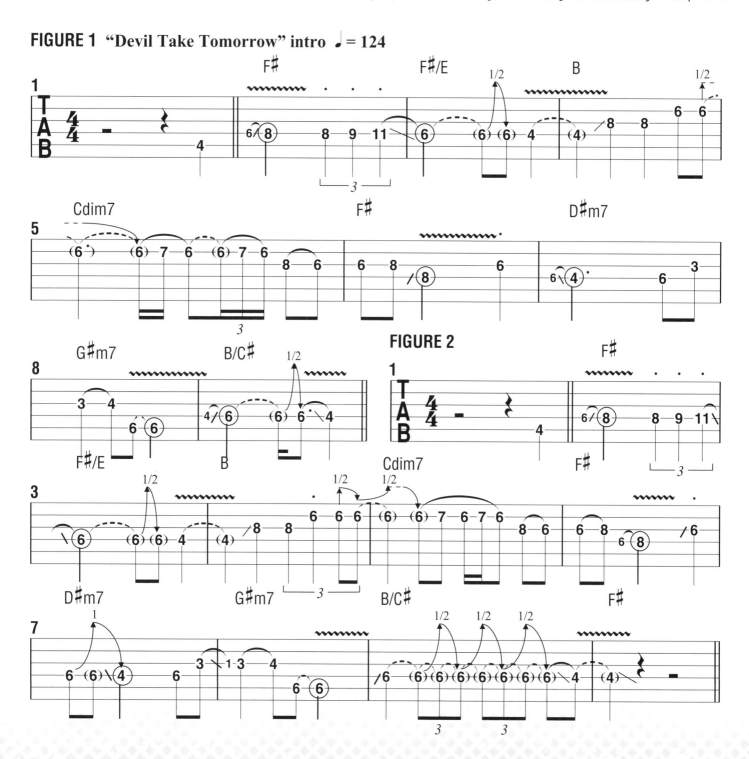

melody is the way you reveal your musical personality, which, to me, is the whole point in making music in the first place!

As an example, I'll use the melody to a song of mine called "Devil Take Tomorrow." I'll begin by playing the melody in a straightforward manner, and then I'll demonstrate a few different ways in which it could be varied by using different articulations.

FIGURE 1 illustrates an approach to playing the melody that is similar to how I play it on the studio recording of the song. This vocal-like melody is comprised mostly of half notes, quarter notes and eighth notes, so there are plenty of notes that sustain, leaving room for subtle variations in interpretation as the melody progresses. The song is played in the key of F# major and is based on the notes of the F# major scale: F# G# A# B C# D# E.

In this first performance of the melody, I use subtle slides, bends, hammer-ons, pull-offs and vibratos to exude an expressive feeling. In FIGURE 2, I offer very subtle variations in phrasing and articulation, specifically in the manner in which the melody is performed over the Cdim7, D#m7 and B/ C# chords. In FIGURE 3, I push things a little further by altering the phrasing and articulation in just about every bar, taking more liberties as I move along.

Now that you have the idea, try playing this melody in as many different ways as you can think of, using various combinations of the techniques mentioned above. Then try doing the same thing with other melodies that you know or, even better yet, with your own.

—reprinted from *Guitar World*, September 2014

FIGURE 3

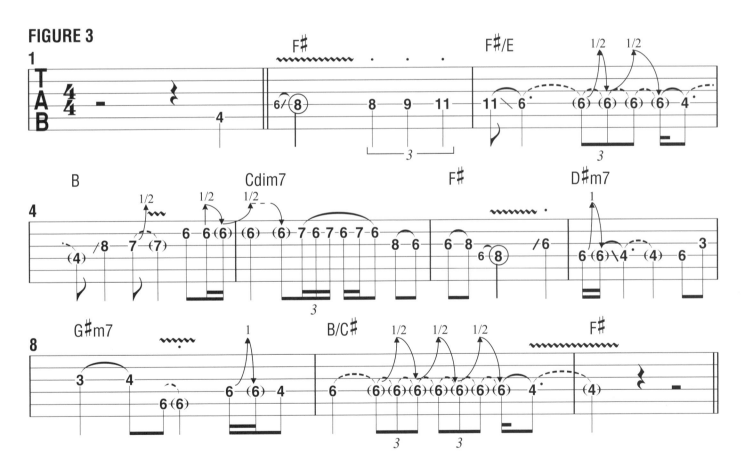

Bend to Your Will

Using string-bending and vibrato techniques to personalize a melody and make it more musical

Two of the most essential techniques for all aspiring guitarists to master are *string bending* and *vibrato*. The electric guitar affords us the opportunity to express musical statements that can evoke and rival the sound and qualities of the human voice, with string-bending and vibrato techniques as the primary elements necessary to achieve vocal-like sounds and phrasing. In this column, I'd like to detail a few of the string-bending and vibrato techniques I use and the applications that appeal to me the most.

You can bend a string in many ways, and I like to employ just about every method imaginable. Drawing from a variety of string-bending techniques provides me with more options for how to interpret whatever I'm playing.

Let's begin with a simple melody, and I'll then demonstrate a handful of ways I might interpret it using different string-bending and vibrato techniques. **FIGURE 1** illustrates a very simple three-note phrase, played in the key of A minor, comprising the notes E (the fifth) and G (the flatted seventh) and ending with a bend from G up one whole step, to A (the root note). A common approach that many guitarists take is to employ a *unison bend* for each note, as demonstrated in **FIGURE 2**. While one note is fretted with the index finger on the B string, another is fretted with the ring finger two frets higher, on the G string, and that note is then bent up a whole step to match the pitch of the B-string note. A unison bend is considered an *oblique bend* for which you have two notes on two strings, one of which is bent while the other remains stationary.

If you ever hear me play this unison bend lick, please shoot me. We just don't need another guitar player playing that way anymore. But if you like it, you should play that way; just don't let me play that way.

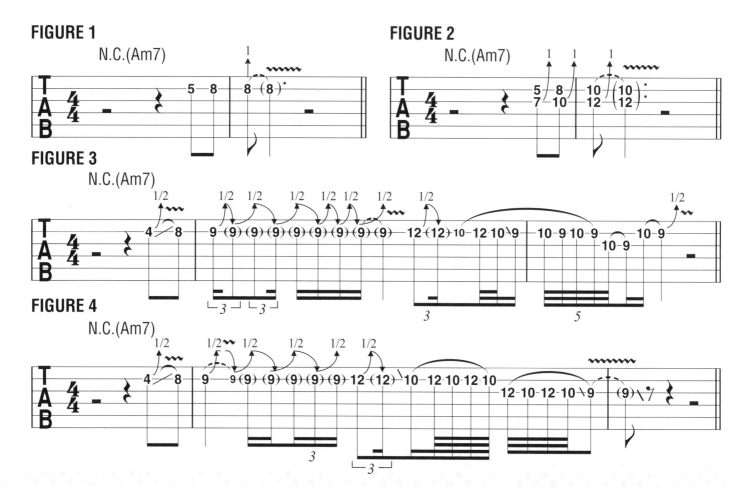

FIGURE 3 shows one of the many "Marty-style" options available when playing these three notes. Instead of simply fretting the first note, I place the index finger one fret lower and bend up to it from a half step below, from D♯ to E, then apply vibrato to the note. I then slide up to the G and execute half-step bends (and releases) between G♯ and A. Approaching a note from a half step below and bending up to it really appeals to my ear. It's a nice option to simply fretting the note. I then expand on the melodic idea by moving up to B and bending up a half step, to C, and then I release the bend and perform a series of quick hammer-pulls between A and G♯ on the B string. What had started as a simple and rather mundane three-note phrase is now something much more interesting and musical.

There are so many variations one could apply from here, and I've detailed a handful in **FIGURES 4–8**. I encourage you to use your musical ear and listen for variations and options that you find interesting and, most importantly, musically expressive and satisfying.

—reprinted from *Guitar World*, October 2014

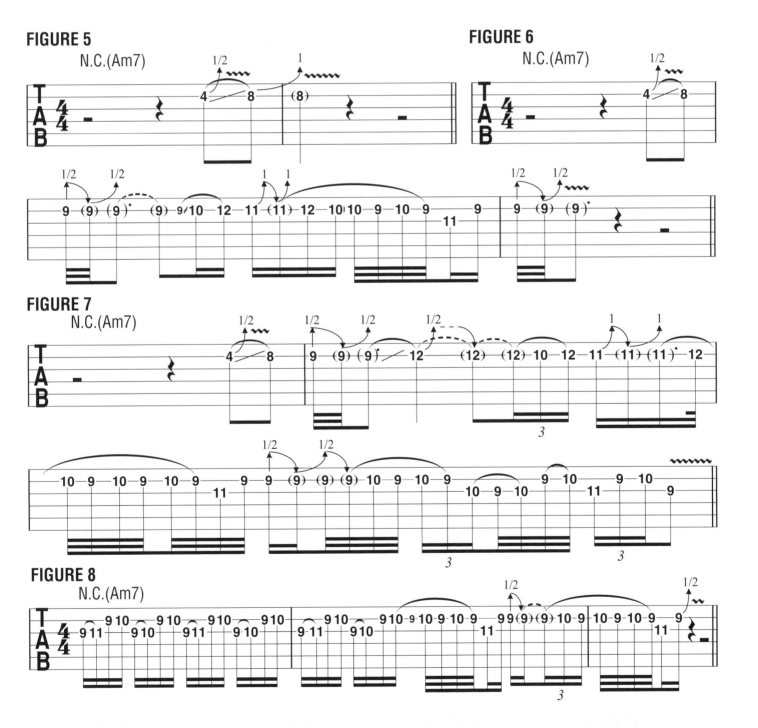

FIGURE 5

FIGURE 6

FIGURE 7

FIGURE 8

METAL SHOP

By Matt Bachand and Jon Donais of Shadows Fall

Ready to Rumble

The importance of warming up before hitting the stage.

MATT BACHAND It's very cool to have been asked to do this column, and we're definitely looking forward to it. It's also very intimidating, because it's something we've never done before, and when I see that the other columnists are players like Zakk Wylde and Kerry King, I can't help but think, Why am I here? Hopefully we'll be able to pass on some good advice, and a lot of you will be into what we have to offer.

JON DONAIS I've been reading *Guitar World* ever since I was a kid, so for us to have our own column is unbelievable. I'm very excited about it, but, as Matt just said, it's going to be a little weird being in the back pages with people like Zakk and Kerry because they're two of my heroes! My bandmates and I have learned a lot in the time we've been together, and we've been lucky enough to have had some pretty experienced people teach us what they've learned the hard way so that we can avoid making the same mistakes. Hopefully we can do the same for you in Metal Shop.

BACHAND One of the biggest mistakes I see guitarists make is going onstage without warming up. A♯ far as I'm concerned, warming up before a gig is crucial, regardless of how long or short your set is. When you play the sort of stuff we do, you need a good 20 to 30 minutes to get warmed up to the point where you're firing on all six cylinders as soon as you hit the stage. I hear players who don't warm up saying things like, "Well, the first half of the set was a little rough, but it got better as it went on, and the second half was great." Well, that's because they didn't warm up, and as a result they ended up playing half of their set to only half their potential because they were warming up onstage. I always play for at least half an hour before we go on so I can be ready to go from the first note. At Ozzfest, this meant that my warm-up was longer than our five-song, 20-minute set!

DONAIS Matt's 100 percent correct—warming up is very important. I used to be one of those guys who didn't bother to warm up before a gig, and as a result, the first two or three songs of those shows never went very well at all; they invariably ended up being a big slop-fest, and that's not fair to the other members of the band or the audience. I always warm up now. In fact, I approach warming up as a professional athlete would. Those guys wouldn't just go out there and do their thing without warming up and stretching, and it's the same thing for us. Plus, you can injure yourself by diving into a physically demanding activity cold. There are so many guitar players who used to be great but can't play anymore because they learned the wrong techniques or tried to play super fast without warming up right. I never want to be that guy.

I normally warm up with some chromatic stuff because it makes me use all my fretting fingers. I start off by using just the two high strings and playing a pattern like the one shown in **FIGURE 1**, taking the pattern all the way up the neck to, say, the 12th position, and then bringing it back down again. I start slowly and then, when I'm warmed up enough to burn it pretty fast, I'll do a chromatic thing across the strings, such as the run shown in **FIGURE 2**. I learned this exercise from a book written by Dream Theater's John Petrucci.

BACHAND My warm-up is all about my picking-hand technique; I just noodle around with my fretting hand. I jump on some riffs and repeat them over and over, starting off slowly and then building up speed so my hands get nice and loose. I'll begin with a straight down-picking riff, like the one shown in **FIGURE 3**, and then I'll do the same with a gallop riff (**FIGURE 4**). I'll also do some fast alternate picking (down, up, down, up, etc) death metal–style mania, like the triplet groove in **FIGURE 5**, and then mix them all up.

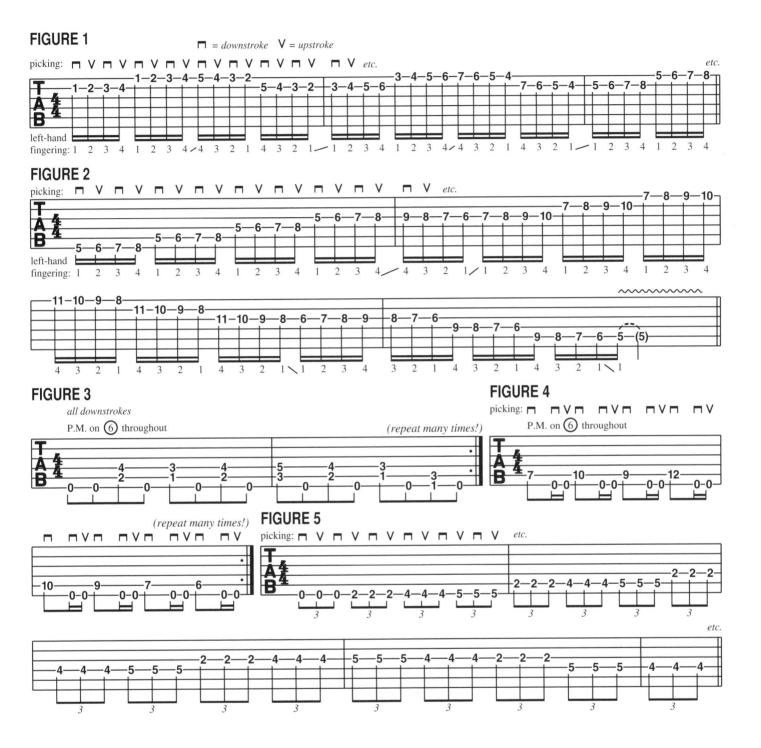

Harmony Central, Part 1

How to work out harmony lead lines in parallel fourths and fifths.

MATT BACHAND We've covered a lot of ground in this column recently by zoning in on some pretty basic but essential topics, like the importance of warming up, dialing in a good tone and how to use down-picking and palm muting to add chunk to a riff. Now that we've laid a pretty firm technical foundation, we're going to get into some more intricate and interesting subjects, such as this month's topic, creating *harmony guitar lines*.

JON DONAIS I know from talking to people at shows that there are a lot of guitarists out there that are really interested in using harmony lead lines but aren't really sure how to go about working them out. When I started taking lessons I learned some pretty simple but useful stuff about creating harmony lines that I wish I'd known about much earlier on. Hopefully, over the next few columns we'll be able to pass on some of this knowledge and save you a lot of the grief and frustration that I went through before I learned those few important guidelines!

BACHAND As far as I'm concerned, harmony guitar lines have always been a big part of the metal sound. When it comes to this subject, many players our age immediately think of bands like In Flames and, of course, Iron Maiden, but what a lot of them don't realize is that bands like Thin Lizzy and Boston were doing harmony lead lines way back in the Seventies, and not just as flashy parts of a guitar solo either but often as the very basis for a song—almost like a main rhythm part but a little different. Iron Maiden has always had that element too, where harmony lead lines actually become main riffs, and that's one of the things that got me into it.

DONAIS I got into harmonies from listening to the bands I grew up on, like Iron Maiden, Metallica and Megadeth. At the time I didn't know squat about music theory, but I managed to learn a bunch of harmony lines by ear anyway, even though what I was playing didn't really make any sense to me. Then, after I started taking lessons and had learned some of the theory behind harmonies I went back and studied exactly what bands like Iron Maiden and Thin Lizzy were doing, and it made sense. It's been part of my playing ever since.

BACHAND When I started out, I was pretty much just an ear player for a long time. I was never really big into theory. I'd always learn things by ear because it kept me interested. Let's face it, when you're 12 years old and you've just started playing you don't want to be learning how to play the C major scale all over the neck; you want to be hammering out "Master of Puppets"! That said, even though a lot of my learning was initially by ear, through playing with other people, like Jon, who actually knew some theory, I eventually picked up quite a few things about how to find different harmony notes, like thirds and fifths.

DONAIS The intervals I use the most when I'm coming up with a harmony line are thirds, fourths and fifths. [*The term interval refers to the musical "distance" between two notes.*] I don't always stick with one type of interval either; I always let my ear decide what sounds best, and then I'll mix and match them accordingly. Of the three I've just mentioned, fourths and fifths seem to be the easiest to work out.

To find a harmony note a fourth above any given note, move up five frets on the same string. A fifth is seven frets higher up the neck on the same string.

BACHAND To illustrate exactly what we're talking about here, let's take the simple A minor line shown in **FIGURE 1** and work out a harmony line to it a fourth above. If what Jon has just said makes sense to you, you'll have figured out how to do this already; all you've got to do is play the same exact pattern five frets higher up the neck, as shown in **FIGURE 2**. To hear what the two parts sound like together, record yourself playing **FIGURE 1**, then play **FIGURE 2** along with the playback, or have a friend play one of the parts.

DONAIS Either way, don't forget to count yourself in, otherwise you won't know when to start playing the harmony line or how fast to play it.

BACHAND To play a harmony line to **FIGURE 1** that's a fifth above it, all you've got to do is play the same exact note pattern seven frets higher up the neck, as depicted in **FIGURE 3**.

DONAIS As each of these options (**FIGURES 2** and **3**) has you harmonizing every single note in the line exactly a fourth or a fifth higher, they're called *parallel* harmony lines. **FIGURE 2** is the *parallel fourths* harmony to **FIGURE 1** and **FIGURE 3** is the *parallel fifths* harmony.

BACHAND FIGURE 4 shows another line that we'll harmonize, this one in G minor. **FIGURE 5** is the parallel fourths harmony above it, and **FIGURE 6** the parallel fifths harmony.

DONAIS Try to work out the harmony lines to **FIGURE 4** by yourself before peaking at **FIGURES 5** and **6**. Then try and do the same thing with some of your own single-note lines.

—reprinted from *Guitar World*, May 2004

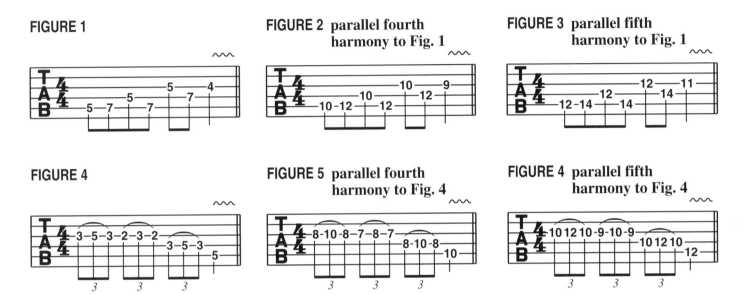

Harmony Central, Part 2
Diatonic Thirds

MATT BACHAND Greetings from Wolverhampton, England! We're writing this installment of Metal Shop while backstage at a show we're doing tonight with our good friends in Killswitch Engage, Chimaira and God Forbid—a tour we're calling the New Wave of American Heavy Metal. The tour's been going very well, with many of the shows, like this one, being sold out in advance.

JON DONAIS In addition to the tour, we're also doing some of the big European summer music festivals, like the Dynamo festival in Holland, which was a blast. After this European run we'll be back in America to continue touring and to give people a sneak preview of our upcoming new album, *The War Within*, which is due out on September 21.

BACHAND As you know, over the past few columns we've been going over parallel fourths and fifths harmony lines and have shown you some easy ways to work them out. This month we're going to get into thirds, which are probably the most common harmonies of all. They're definitely the ones you hear most when you listen to Metallica, Megadeth and Iron Maiden, as well as older bands like Boston and Thin Lizzy.

DONAIS As I mentioned a few issues back, when I first got into harmonies, it was from listening to bands like the ones Matt just mentioned. I didn't have a clue what I was doing in terms of theory, but I learned the lines anyway, and a lot of the harmonies I learned were *diatonic thirds*, especially the Iron Maiden ones. Then I learned the theory behind them by taking lessons, which opened up all sorts of doors for me because I was able to work out harmony lines to my own ideas without it being an exercise in "trial and error."

BACHAND I was never really a big theory head, so when I first started out I'd always learn by playing by ear. When I was 12 I had no interest in learning scales; I just wanted to be able to pound out some Metallica riffs! But by playing with other musicians who actually did know some theory, like Jon, I eventually learned how to create the third harmony of whatever was going on. Believe me, it's much easier once you know what you're doing!

DONAIS Just in case the term *diatonic thirds* has freaked you out, don't worry—it's not as complicated as it sounds; all "diatonic" means is staying within a certain seven-note scale and not using any chromatic passing tones (i.e., notes not in the scale you're using). This means that whenever you work out a diatonic third harmony to a run you *only* use notes from the same scale the original run is in. In fact, all you have to do to work out the diatonic third harmony line is know the scale being used and be able to count to three!

BACHAND Yeah, it really is that easy. Provided you know the notes of the scale used in the run you're harmonizing, it's just a case of counting up three notes in that scale, with the note you're harmonizing being "note number one."

DONAIS The best way to illustrate what we're talking about here is by showing you an example or two: let's work out the diatonic third harmony to a simple run that's based on the A natural minor scale [A B C D E F G A], as shown in **FIGURES 1** and **2**.

BACHAND FIGURE 3 depicts the A natural minor line we're going to harmonize. As you can see, the first note is A, so, counting that as note number one, the note in the scale three notes above it is C. So, that's the diatonic third harmony note to A. Likewise, the note three notes above the second note in the run, C, is E; and the note three notes above the third note, B, is D...and so on.

DONAIS FIGURE 4 shows you the diatonic third harmony to the run in **FIGURE 3**. As this example hopefully illustrates, working out the diatonic third harmony to a line really isn't that hard as long as you know the scale being used. In fact, you don't even need to know the note names—as long as you know the fretboard pattern of the scale (e.g.: **FIGURE 2** in the case of A natural minor) and can count to three, you're good to go!

BACHAND FIGURE 5 presents a slightly longer A natural minor run. Your homework is to figure out the diatonic third harmony line to it.

DONAIS And while you're at it, try experimenting with runs of your own that are based on different scales. Next month we'll discuss this subject more and look at some familiar examples from *The Art of Balance*. See you then.

—reprinted from *Guitar World*, September 2004

FIGURE 1 A natural minor scale (A B C D E F G)

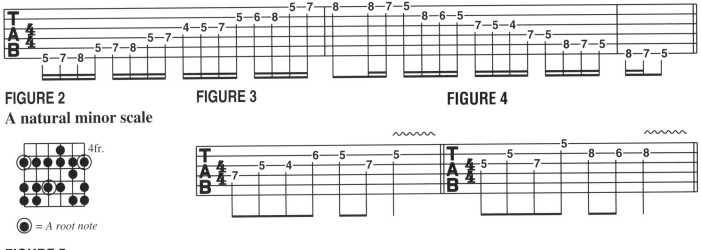

FIGURE 2
A natural minor scale

⦿ = A root note

FIGURE 3

FIGURE 4

FIGURE 5

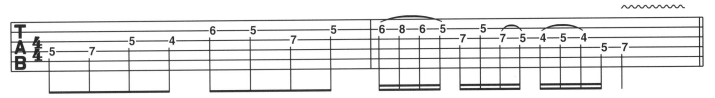

Training Secrets
Tips on keeping your chops in tip-top shape

JON DONAIS Generally speaking, I don't have a practice regimen. Instead of working on specific scales or riffs, I prefer to pick up the guitar and let my fingers do the walking, which allows my hands to loosen up according to what they feel like doing.

I'll usually start out by playing a bunch of *legato* licks with lots of hammer-ons and pull-offs. In **FIGURE 1** I'm playing 16th-note triplets with double hammer-ons, repeating each three-note pattern and moving across the strings, starting on the low E and moving across to the high E. The fret-hand index finger frets F at first fret, which is picked with a downstroke. I then hammer the middle finger onto G, third fret, followed by hammering the pinkie onto A, fifth fret. I repeat this three-note sequence and successively move the double hammer-on pattern over to each higher string, switching to the second, third and fifth frets on the D and G strings to stay within the F major scale (F G A B♭ C D E). As with any warm-up lick or exercise, start out slowly and allow every note to sound clearly before cranking up the tempo.

To warm up my picking hand, I like to start by playing two-string patterns of 16th-note triplets, like the two shown in **FIGURE 2**. I'm playing three notes per string in each case, so the picking pattern on the B string is down-up-down, followed by up-down-up on the high E string. The first shape (bars 1 and 2) has you fretting with the index finger, middle finger and pinkie; in bars 3 and 4 the fret hand alternates index-middle-pinkie on the B string, with index-ring-pinkie on the high E string.

From here, I like to move on to sextuplets (six-note groups) that are alternate-picked, as shown in **FIGURE 3**: this run, a descending pattern based on the E Dorian mode (E F♯ G A B C♯ D), uses shapes that feature three notes per string. I play the notes straight down in bar 1, and in bar 2 I repeat the first sextuplet group twice before continuing down the scale.

When picking fast like this, I prefer not to rest any part of my picking hand on the guitar. Instead, I keep it floating freely above the guitar, which helps me to glide across the strings more effortlessly and generate more speed.

When warming up, I also like to practice playing trills, and I'll play something like **FIGURE 4** across the top two strings. Using my first three fingers, I begin by pulling off from the ring finger to the middle to the index, and then trill quickly between index and middle. I then do the same thing on the high E string and alternate between the two strings.

FIGURE 5 is another alternate-picking exercise I like to perform: this one is played in a straight 16th-note rhythm and also has you alternating between the top two strings, starting with an index-ring-pinkie shape in fifth position and then shifting up to seventh position and switching to an index-middle-pinkie shape on beats three and four.

MATT BACHAND Between answering zillions of emails every day and attending to band business, I have barely any time to practice these days. So when I do, I like to perform exercises that get the blood flowing in the right hand, because I'm primarily the rhythm guitarist in Shadows Fall. Because of this, I'll work on riffs that specifically address either downpicking or alternate picking. For instance, I'll alternate-pick some 16th-note-triplet riffs across the bottom two strings, as in **FIGURE 6**, using the same "floating" pick-hand technique that Jon uses. I'm not even thinking of a specific riff or pattern here; I'm just concentrating on loosening up my right hand.

When I have time, I'll work on down-picking chugging patterns, like the one in **FIGURE 7**, which is based on sliding power chords. When I can play a pattern like this clean at extremely fast tempos, I know I'm warmed up.

To me, preparing to play is like running a marathon: you've got to stretch the muscles before going full speed. Though to be honest, I got my pick-hand speed together by throwing on Metallica's Master of Puppets and obsessively trying to keep up with James Hetfield's right hand. Instead of playing slowly, I'd spend four hours playing it fast until I'd scream, "Alright! I've got it!"

—reprinted from *Guitar World*, June 2007

FIGURE 1 legato exercise

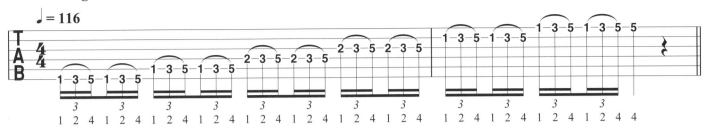

FIGURE 2 alternate picking triplets

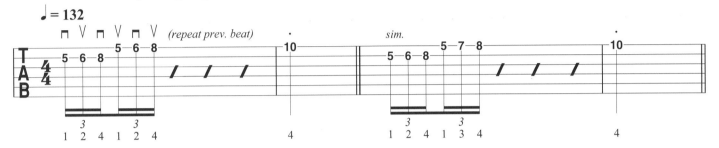

FIGURE 3

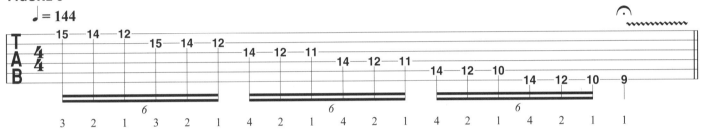

FIGURE 4

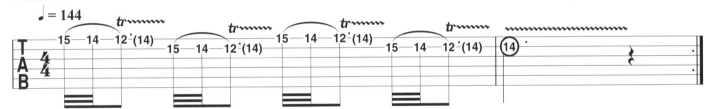

FIGURE 5 alternate picking 16th notes

FIGURE 6 alternate picking

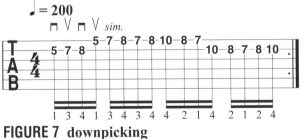
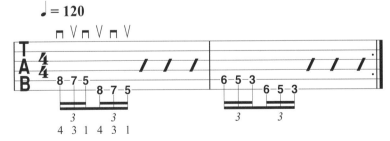

FIGURE 7 downpicking

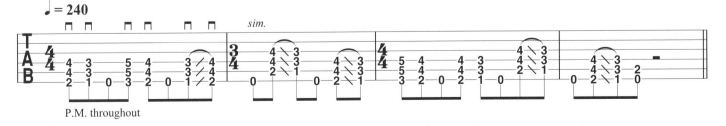

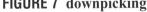
P.M. throughout

Get Your Motor Running
Inspiration, Guitar Harmonies, Vibrato and Pinch Harmonics

FINDING INSPIRATION

JON DONAIS Riffs come to me a lot of different ways. I might throw on some music, jam along and try to figure out the guitar parts, but usually I'll figure them out incorrectly, which inevitably sends me down my own path to writing something of my own. Often I'll have the TV set to a music channel, like one of the arena rock or metal stations, and I'll leave it on as background music. I'll start to jam along, and sometimes some new song ideas come together.

CREATING GUITAR HARMONIES

DONAIS Usually after one of us comes up with a guitar line we'll decide if we think it needs to be harmonized. If so, we'll try the standard approach, which is to use diatonic thirds, fourths or fifths (diatonic means that all of the notes are derived from a specific scale structure). We'll try each approach and see what sticks.

MATT BACHAND There's really no secret to it. We can tell pretty quickly within the context of a song which harmony will work best.

DONAIS And we won't necessarily go with what's theoretically "correct." We may try doubling the line using thirds, which may suit the key, but it won't always sound right to us. In that case, we'll move on to fourths or fifths, or even some other weird interval. Sometimes we *have* to hit the "wrong" note, because there are times when "wrong" sounds right! It might not make sense to someone else, but if we like it, that's what we'll use.

VIBRATO

DONAIS When you're a kid, all you want to do is play fast; when I was 14, that's all I cared about. As you get older, you realize that properly intonated string bends and finger vibrato are just as important as speed (**FIGURE 1**). There are fast, wide vibratos (**FIGURE 1**, bar 4, beat 1), where you shake the string back and forth as much as possible, or slow, narrow vibratos (**FIGURE 1**, bar 4, beat three) where you just move the string a little bit. The point is that you need to develop the control so that you can effectively use either approach. A good vibrato can say a lot, sometimes more than just burning up the neck.

There are so many different kinds of vibrato, such as the half-step-bend type (**FIGURE 2a**), in which you slowly bend and release the string one half step. Or, you could do the big one-and-one-half-step bend (**FIGURE 2b**) when you really want to scream. You could also use multiple string bends in conjunction with wide vibratos, like this (**FIGURE 2c**). When bending the top three strings at once, I try to snag all three strings under the tip of my ring finger. This is something you hear George Lynch and Stevie Ray Vaughan do all the time (**FIGURE 2c**, bars 1 and 2). I've always loved the ugliness of the notes clashing with each other.

PINCH HARMONICS

DONAIS Getting some of the edge of the pick-hand thumb into the pick attack is what makes a pinch harmonic happen; I especially like doing it on the G string (**FIGURE 3a**). The specific harmonic pitch is determined by where you pick along the length of the string, so you need to experiment a little by picking at different spots in the area over the pickups. Here's one on the B string (**FIGURE 3b**, bar 1), but the "classic" ones are on the low wound strings (**FIGURE 3b**, bar 2).

Pinch harmonics really sound cool when you add some "shake," or vibrato. That's when they really come to life and just scream (**FIGURE 3c**).

—reprinted from *Guitar World*, August 2007

Tune down one whole step (low to high: D G C F A D)

All music sounds one whole step lower than written.

FIGURE 1

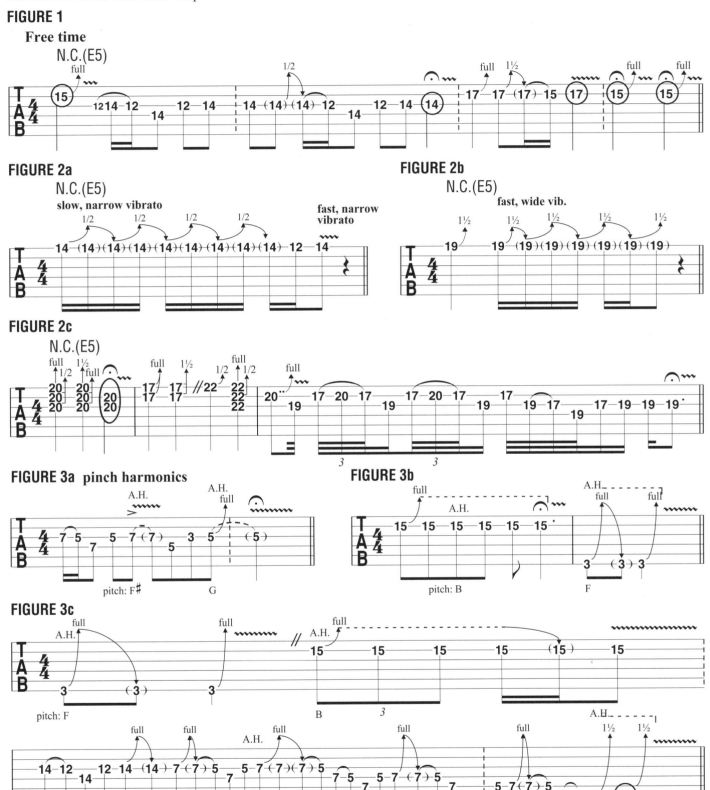

AXENDANCY
by Matt Heafy of Trivium

Lessons Learned

The importance of learning from others and warming up every time you play

I grew up with a monthly subscription to *Guitar World*, and as I was curious about other guitarists' techniques, I studied the columns religiously. Some of the most influential columns for me were the ones written by the mighty Dimebag Darrell, Kirk Hammett and John Petrucci. I can still specifically remember some of the best lessons I learned from these columns, and it's stuff that I still apply to this day. For example, Kirk once said something along the lines of "When you start learning guitar, use your pinkie." Coming from my hero, I heard the message loud and clear: from that day on I focused on using and strengthening my pinkie. Dimebag taught me to use the pinkie, too. He always played tremendous wide-stretch leads, which I love, and they're all about pinkie dexterity. Dime's column also taught me how to play pinch harmonics and his trademark whammy "squeal" dive. And I learned all about accuracy and the discipline of working with a metronome from John Petrucci.

Being asked to do a column for *Guitar World* is quite an honor, considering the many important lessons I learned from some of the greats. My band's other guitarist, Corey Beaulieu, will be joining with me in this column, and I just hope that we can teach you all something decent! Because playing fast music requires much warming up, I'm going to start things off by showing you a couple of warm-up exercises that also force you to use your pinkie.

To me, warming up makes all the difference in my playing. When I don't warm up, I'm a mess, and while some people may not notice, I can tell. My preshow warm-up regimen usually clocks in between 15 and 45 minutes, depending on how I'm feeling or sounding in the dressing room that day. We're currently in the studio recording our next album, and I spend about two hours a day with a metronome doing exercises from John Petrucci's *Rock Discipline* book (the one that came with the tape). I pretty much go through the entire book on a daily basis, using a slow-medium-fast tempo graduation. After that, to nail some sweeps, I'll go over the arpeggio section of Jason Becker's "Altitudes," and then it's off to improvising solos to our new songs until my fingers and wrists hurt.

FIGURE 1 is a G major/E minor exercise that's good for a number of things, such as developing left/right-hand coordination, learning the modes and playing with triplet and sextuplet rhythms. As shown above the tab, the exercise covers four different modes: Ionian, Dorian, Phrygian and Lydian. As with any warm-up exercise, start slowly and use a metronome or tap your foot on each beat. Think three notes per beat and use alternate picking (down, up, down, up, etc). Make sure you master ascending and descending each mode perfectly before moving up to the next one. Then bring the tempo up a few metronome clicks and do the same thing again.

The next exercise is a repeating pattern with wide stretches that uses the two symmetrical fingering patterns shown in **FIGURE 2**. As you'll hear, it has that Dimebag "Cowboys from Hell"/"Domination" solo vibe to it. Don't be afraid to start out really slow with this one if you can't quite nail the riff. It's all about mastering it slowly and then building up speed a little at a time. Do this, and you'll eventually accomplish your goals.

—reprinted from *Guitar World*, August 2006

FIGURE 1

G Ionian mode: G A B C D E F♯

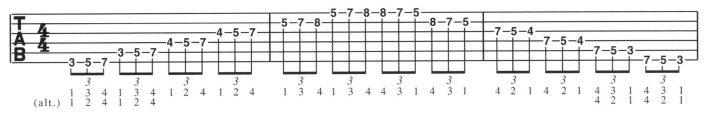

A Dorian mode: A B C D E F♯ G

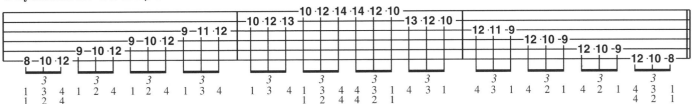

B Phrygian mode: B C D E F♯ G A

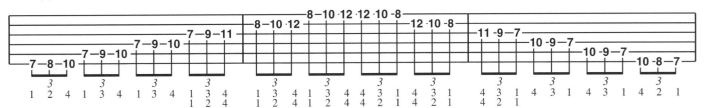

C Lydian mode: C D E F♯ G A B

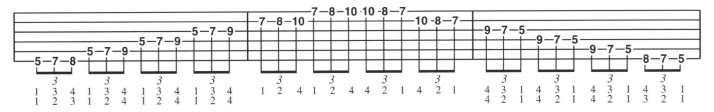

FIGURE 2

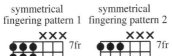

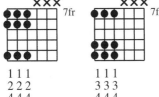

FIGURE 3

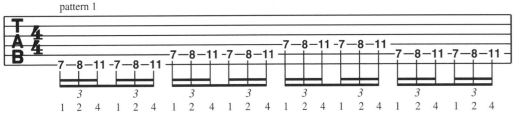

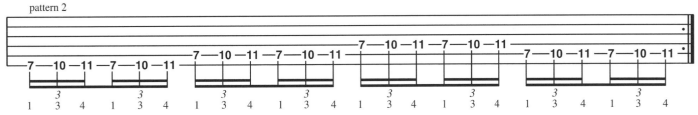

The One-Three Punch

Playing twin-guitar harmony lines in thirds

I'm writing this month's column in Osnabruck, Germany, on a welcome day off. We just launched our mini headlining tour across Germany, and things have been fantastic. We're enjoying some amazingly successful European festival shows, including the legendary Download Festival, in Donnington, England, and playing in front of ridiculous amounts of people.

This month I'm going to talk about harmony guitar lines, which are becoming widely used again in metal after an absence of quite a few years. I find that Iron Maiden provide a great source of inspiration and guidance when I'm arranging harmonies. So many of their songs feature two lead guitars wailing away on melodic lines that blend so sweetly and soar over great bass and drum riffs. That sound is created by having one guitar play a distinct melody while a second guitar plays a line that has the same rhythm and phrasing but with different notes. This can be accomplished by the second guitarist harmonizing with notes from the scale utilized by the first guitarist, playing them higher or lower than the main melody. The middle riff in our song "Rain" is a good example of what I'm talking about. In the song I'm playing a main melody line while Corey is playing a harmony part around it, with some of his notes being higher than the ones I'm playing and some of them lower. Corey is essentially playing the same line as me but using different notes from within the scale upon which the melody is based, D natural minor (D E F G A B♭ C).

I've never had any formal musical schooling, but I'll do my best to explain what I'm talking about here in conceptual terms that, hopefully, will be clear and easy to grasp. The term *interval* refers to the distance, or number of half steps and whole steps, between two notes. You can get a sweet sound by having a harmony note be the interval of a *third* above a melody note. A *major third* is two whole steps (equal to four frets), and a *minor third* is one and one half steps (equal to three frets). So how do you know whether to play the major or minor third? First, you need to determine what key you're in and the scale upon which your melody line is based on. Having established that, have the harmony guitar play a note that's two scale tones above the first melody note, carefully staying within the scale. This will give you an interval that's either a major or a minor third, depending on what scale degree the melody note is on. Most scales are built from an asymmetrical combination of whole steps and half steps, and this dictates a particular pattern of major and minor thirds for that scale when you go to harmonize it. This is known as *diatonic* (scale-based) harmony.

Metallica and Maiden have used major and minor thirds a lot to make pleasingly sweet, but dark, harmony lines. **FIGURE 1** is a fairly simple example of such a two-part lead guitar harmony in the key of E minor. As you can see, I'm playing a melody while Corey is playing a diatonic harmony line above it, with each of his notes either a major or minor third higher than the note I'm playing, depending on where we are in the scale. He is simply playing the same kind of melodic contour as me but three notes higher in the E natural minor scale. Notice how the major thirds sound brighter and happier, and the minor thirds sound darker and scarier.

This type of harmony line is easily worked out by staying within the melody's scale (in this case, E natural minor: E F♯ G A B C D) and playing the third note above each melody note; this third note will be a major or minor third interval, and it will sound harmonically correct. For example, if you're in the key of E minor and want to play a diatonic third harmony to the E note at the 12th fret on the high E string, play the note that's two notes higher in the E natural minor scale; this would be G at the 15th fret, which is a minor third (see **FIGURE 2**). If the melody note is C at the eighth fret on the high E string, the third above that would be E at the 12th fret, which is a major third interval (see **FIGURE 3**).

We'll continue this exploration of harmony leads next month. In the meantime, try coming up with some E minor harmony lines like this on your own.

—reprinted from *Guitar World*, October 2006

All gtrs. tuned to drop-D (low to high: D A D G B E)

FIGURE 1 harmony run using thirds
in E minor

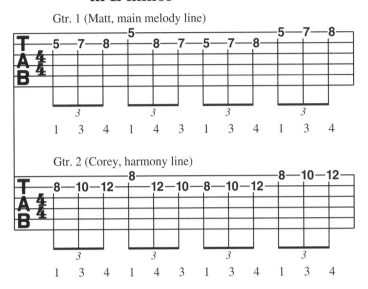

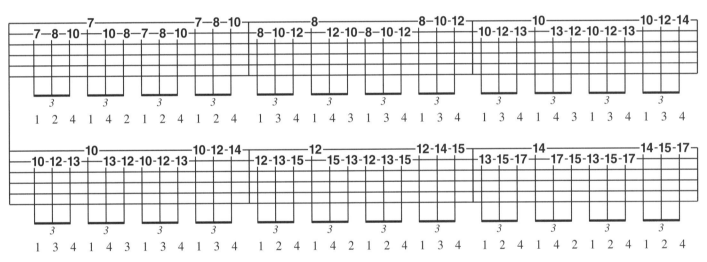

FIGURE 2   **FIGURE 3**

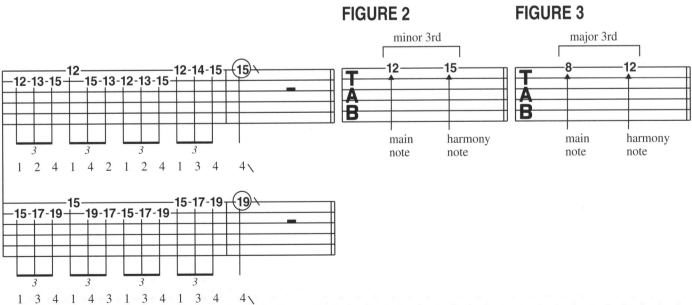

Maiden Heaven

More on dual-guitar harmonies with thirds

by Corey Beaulieu of Trivium

Last month, Matt introduced you to dual-harmony guitar leads, a topic that I will continue to explore this month. While I could mention numerous examples of great harmony guitar leads, my favorites are those by Iron Maiden; I think Dave Murray and Adrian Smith are responsible for some of the coolest harmony lines ever written. If you want to learn how to play harmony guitar, my advice to you is simple: buy some Iron Maiden albums! *Somewhere in Time* is a great place to start.

When creating harmonies, you can use several *intervals*, such as thirds, fourths, fifths and octaves. They can also be employed in various combinations, depending on the part you're harmonizing and the sound you want to achieve. Maiden frequently use thirds, which, as Matt explained last month, are rather easy to work out, especially if you are familiar with the scale you're using. To create a third harmony to a root note, simply play the note two degrees higher in the same scale. For example, if you're in the key of E minor and your melody line is based on the E natural minor scale (E F♯ G A B C D), the third harmony to E is G, and the third to A is C. **FIGURE 1** shows a simple E minor line (Gtr.1 part) to which another guitar (Gtr.2) plays a harmony line a third higher. Try to work out the Gtr.2 part without looking at the tab, then check your work to see if you got it right.

Another good example of the Iron Maiden influence is in our song "A Gunshot to the Head of Trepidation," particularly the first half of the big dual-harmony part we play after our solos. The part is played over a Maiden-style bass line, and the main guitar line (Gtr.1) is very melodic, flowing and straightforward, with no unusual notes. It's in D natural minor (D E F G A B♭ C), and the harmony line I play (Gtr.2) is a third above Matt's all the way through.

In the second half of that long harmony section, we swap roles: I play the main line and Matt plays the higher harmony. We do this because I came up with the main line in **FIGURE 1** and Matt came up with the main line that follows it. We showed each other our original melodies and then worked out our harmony lines. We both find it much easier to teach the other guy our main line and then work out the harmony ourselves because we already know the original part inside out.

It's always fun to work out harmonies with another guitarist, but you can do it by yourself if you have a tape recorder. I used to do this all the time with an eight-track tape recorder. I would practice and compose by recording a rhythm track and layering harmony lines over it. I'd do that for hours because I love the sound of two guitars harmonizing each other.

—reprinted from *Guitar World*, November 2006

FIGURE 1

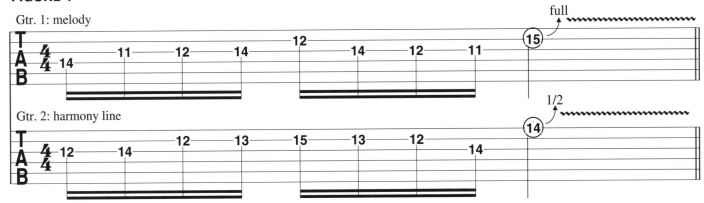

METAL FOR LIFE

By Metal Mike Chlasciak

Single-Note Carnage
How to use an open-string pedal tone to build heavy single-note riffs.

Hello everyone, and welcome to my new instructional column. Over the course of the next few months I'd like to demonstrate a variety of cool, useful metal ideas and techniques that can be applied to every aspect of guitar playing within the context of hard rock, classic metal and beyond.

For this lesson, I've put together a series of melodic riffs that could potentially be used for a song's intro, verse, chorus, bridge or solo section, and that utilize an open low E-string *pedal tone*. A pedal tone is defined as a long held or rearticulated note around which other parts move. As applied to the guitar, a pedal tone usually represents the tonic, or root note, and is played on the lower, often open, strings.

For each example in this column, the open low E string is used as a pedal tone throughout the riff. In **FIGURE 1**, I play a melodic line on the A string against the open low E pedal. The line is derived primarily from the E Phrygian scale (E F G A B C D) and is played in steady 16th notes, four notes per beat. I begin by striking the open low E along with a D note, fifth string/fifth fret, fretted with the index finger, followed by a hammer-on with the ring finger up to E, seventh fret. This hammer-on idea is carried through the riff as I move either higher or lower on the fifth string. The lower note is always fretted with the index finger: if the higher note is two frets above, I hammer-on with the ring finger; if it's one fret above, I hammer with the middle finger. When the open low E string is played by itself, I use pick-hand *palm muting* for a more percussive attack.

On beat four of bar 2, I move the fretted notes over to the low E string, fretting A, sixth string/fifth fret, followed by a hammer-on up to B♭ at the sixth fret. The use of this "flatted fifth," or *tritone*, interval lends the riff a bluesy quality, as it is part of the E blues scale (E G A B♭ B D). Found three whole steps above (or below) the root note, the tritone was once called, in Latin, *diabolus in musica* (the devil in music). It is an interval often employed in metal for its dark, somewhat dissonant quality. To me, this riff recalls the sound of Megadeth's *Rust in Peace* album, specifically the track "Holy Wars."

FIGURE 1 ♩ = 156

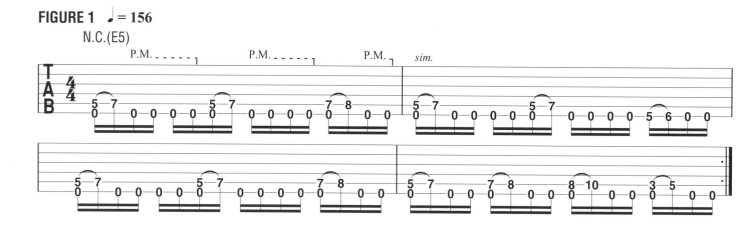

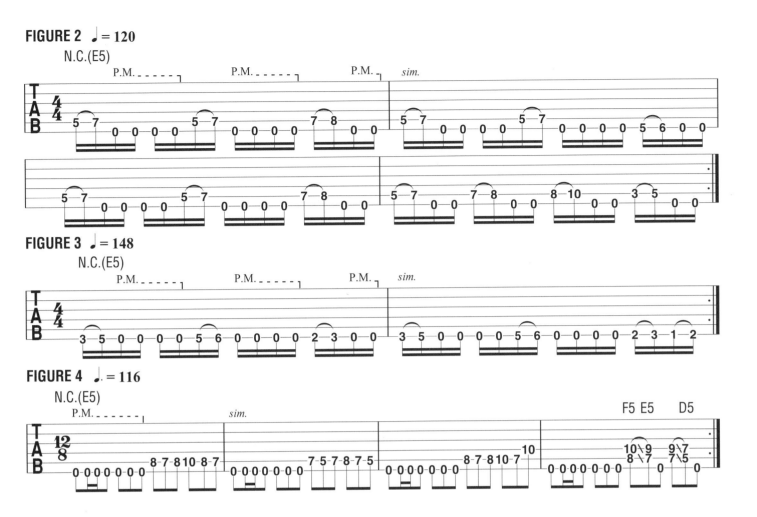

The phrasing of this line is also interesting in that the hammered notes are always followed by four consecutive open low E pedal notes, with the exception of bar 4, where I switch to two consecutive open E notes between hammered notes. Another way to play this riff is with a clear separation between the fretted notes and the open E pedal, à la **FIGURE 2**. Try both approaches and notice the difference in sound.

Now let's look at a different riff using the same concept and phrasing, as shown in **FIGURE 3**. Here, the fretted notes are all played on the low E string and are based essentially on the E blues scale, but I add the second, F♯, as well as the "flatted" second, F natural, to the line, which serves to lend it an overall atonal quality. This harmonically "free" approach—creating a riff that is not based entirely on one specific scale—is very common in metal, exemplified on such albums as Metallica's *Master of Puppets*.

Let's try one more permutation of this idea, shifting to 12/8 meter, as shown in **FIGURE 4**. Like **FIGURE 1**, this riff is based on E Phrygian, and the melody is played primarily on the A string and against the open low E pedal. To make the riff more dramatic, I switch back and forth between palm-muting the open low E notes and allowing the notes on the A string to ring clearly. This riff ends with sliding two-note power chords, fretted on the fifth and fourth strings.

I'll be back next month with more tips on strengthening your metal chops. See you then.

—reprinted from *Guitar World*, April 2011

Power Surge

How to build power chord variations for maximum sonic effect.

This month, I'd like to cover a topic that my guitar students continually ask me about: how to break away from the typical root-fifth power-chord rhythm figures that are used so prominently in rock and metal. My solution is to devise a variety of different two-note chord shapes—built from pairs of notes, like root-fifth power chords—that sound great when applied to metal, even though these chord shapes can be, and are, used in virtually every style of guitar-based music.

So how does one devise these two-note chord shapes? To me, the simplest and most effective way is to first take a look at metal's most commonly used scale, natural minor, and then create note pairings that are built from various degrees of that scale.

FIGURE 1 shows the A natural minor scale (also known as the A Aeolian mode) in fifth position. The idea is to build two-note chords from different combinations of these scale degrees: FIGURE 2a illustrates a standard root-fifth A5 power chord, which combines the root note, A, and the fifth, E. FIGURE 2b combines B and D to create a two-note B minor chord voicing, FIGURE 2c combines A and F to create F/A, and FIGURE 2d combines C and E to create a C voicing. FIGURE 3 shows these chords used within the context of a progression.

Now that we've identified these four two-note chord voicings, let's create some metal-style rhythm parts that utilize them. In FIGURE 4, I play the same chord progression but add palm-muted eighth-note triplet accents on the bass note of each chord throughout. Also, I've added one more two-note voicing, E5, sounded by barring the index finger across the bottom two strings at the seventh fret.

Let's pick up the tempo and apply this concept to a hard-driving rhythm part. In FIGURE 5, I add palm-muted eighth-note accents on the bass note of each chord, creating a syncopated feel by accenting many of the power chords on the eighth-note upbeats.

Many metal bands feature a two-guitar lineup, and often the guitarists will play the same rhythm part but use different chord voicings to fill out the sound. FIGURE 6 represents the same rhythm pattern shown in FIGURE 5 but utilizes open strings and second-position chords instead.

Another twist is to *displace* one of the notes of a two-note pair an octave higher, which will change the sound and texture of the chord dramatically while retaining its underlying harmonic quality. In FIGURE 7, I again play the same rhythm pattern and chord progression but change the C chord voicing by moving the C note up one octave so that the chord becomes C/E.

Now let's apply this concept to another key. FIGURE 8 shows the E natural minor scale (E F♯ G A B C D), and FIGURE 9 depicts a chord sequence devised of two-note shapes built from the notes of this scale. There are only three different chord voicings used in this example—Em, C/E and D/E, all played against the open low-E-string *pedal tone*. The only deviation is found in bar 4, wherein I incorporate the open G string to fill out the sound, resulting in the Dadd4 and C chord voicings.

For all the shapes used in these examples, you'll notice that the notes are either one or two frets apart and that the shapes occasionally "flip," meaning that while one voicing places the index finger on a lower string than, say, the ring finger, in the next voicing the ring finger will be placed on the lower string.

I encourage you to apply this approach to other scales and see how many different two-note voicings you can come up with. There are a great many interesting sounds to be discovered once you begin to break away from the tried and true.

—reprinted from *Guitar World*, May 2011

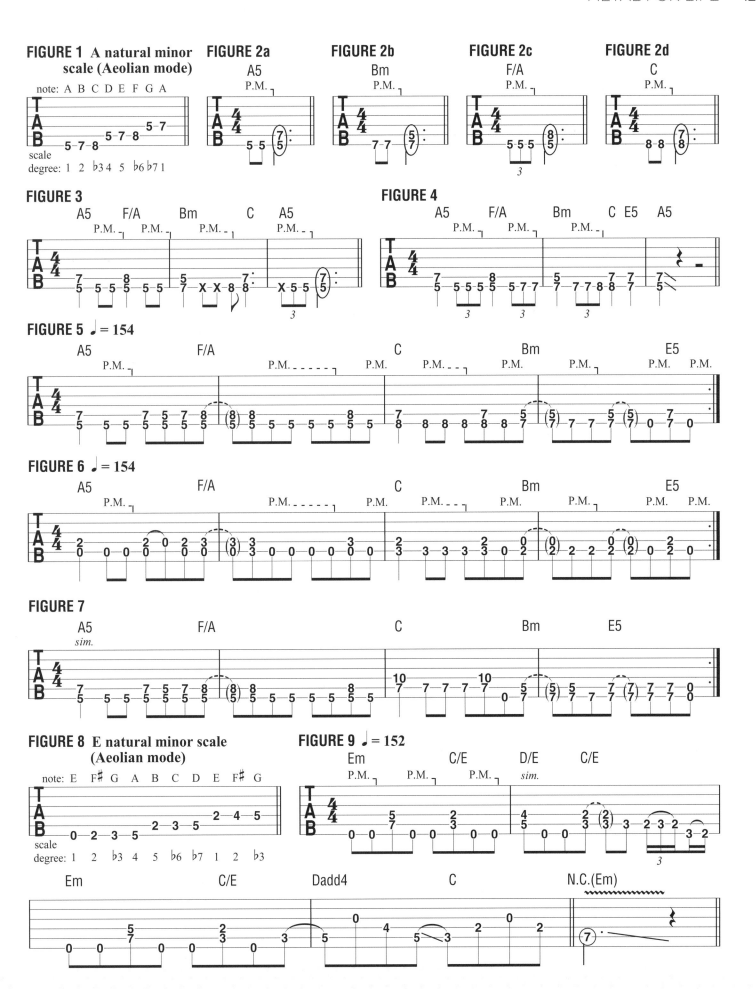

Rhythm Nation

Tips for getting the most out of your metal rhythm guitar parts.

In this month's column, I'd like to show you some simple and effective ways to make your metal rhythm guitar parts sound bigger, heavier and more powerful. These ideas are useful in many different ways, and I think you will find them applicable in live performance as well as when overdubbing and layering tracks.

Let's start with a basic metal-type chord progression, using standard two-note root-fifth power chords, fretted on the fifth and fourth strings and played against an open low E pedal tone (**FIGURE 1**). I start with an E5 power chord, made up of the root note, E, and the fifth, B, followed by two palm-muted open low E notes. I then move down to C5, alternated against the open low E pedal in the same way, and wrap up the progression on B5 before returning to the I (one) chord, E5.

Now, how can we take a fairly standard rhythm part like this and make it sound bigger and more exciting? One effective way to do this is to take the two-note power chord and move either the root or the fifth to a different string, trying different combinations while listening closely to how these subtle differences can alter and fill out the sound.

An easy way to fatten up this rhythm part is to drop the fifth, B, down to the sixth string while keeping the E root note on the fifth string. As shown in **FIGURE 2**, I barre my index finger across the bottom two strings to sound each power chord in the progression, shifting my hand up and down the neck and lifting my finger off the strings to sound the open low E notes between the chord accents.

Already, this riff sounds a little heavier and more sinister, so we are on the right track. Now, let's double the fifth by adding B, fourth string/ninth fret, to the root-fifth shape played in **FIGURE 2**. This new, three-note power chord driven progression is shown in **FIGURE 3**.

Let's continue this idea by stacking another root note onto the previous fifth-root-fifth power-chord stack, adding a high E, third string/ninth fret, which results in a four-note power-chord voicing. A♯ shown in **FIGURE 4**, this simple progression now sounds much wider and bigger than it initially did, in **FIGURE 1**.

For our last example, I'd like to expand each power chord to a different type of four-note voicing. This next technique is used often by Dream Theater guitarist John Petrucci, and it involves stacking the ninth on top of each three-note power-chord voicing introduced in **FIGURE 3**. Applied to the first chord, E5, the result is the four-note Esus2 voicing that kicks off the rhythm part shown in **FIGURE 5**. When moved down to third and second position, the resulting chords are Csus2 and Bsus2, respectively. I think of these sus2 voicings as "progressive metal" chords, because, though they still sound very tight like a typical power chord, the inclusion of the ninth lends the chord a wider and more unusual flavor. They do require a bit of a stretch, however, so make sure your fret hand is warmed up before reaching for these types of chords, especially in the lower positions. I'll be back next month with more useful ideas on how to expand your metal guitar techniques and approaches.

See you then.

—reprinted from *Guitar World*, June 2011

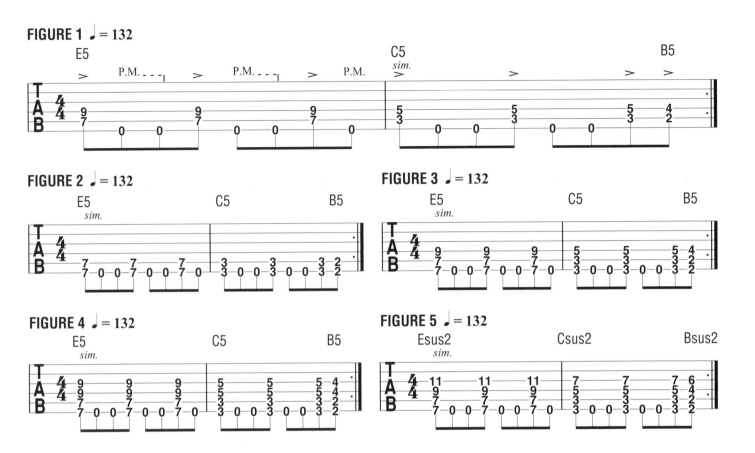

Across the Board

How to expand pentatonic lick patterns up and down the neck.

Most rock and metal guitar players are well familiar with the minor pentatonic scale, by far the most prominently used scale for heavy riffs and soloing. But it's not uncommon for many players to reach a point where they feel "stuck in a rut" and find themselves playing the same, or very similar, riffs. In this month's column, I'd like to show you a few useful ideas for breaking out of that rut by exploring new and different ways to approach the minor pentatonic scale.

For reference, let's begin by looking at the standard 12th-position E minor pentatonic "box" pattern shown in **FIGURE 1**. When I play this scale in this position, I like to use my index finger and pinkie to fret the notes on the sixth, second and first strings, and the index and ring fingers to fret the fifth, fourth and third strings.

A great way to break out of the "box" is to stay on the top two strings only and move up or down the neck (as opposed to across it), using fragments of adjacent "box" patterns on these strings, as demonstrated in **FIGURE 2**. I begin two frets lower, in 10th position, play a four-note pattern, then quickly shift up to 12th position, play four ascending notes and then shift up once more, to 15th position to play four more notes.

A good way to break away from the "bluesy" sound of minor pentatonic and into more of a "metal" sound is to play repetitive figures that incorporate wide stretches, including some of the notes that fall outside the standard minor pentatonic box. In **FIGURE 3**, a repeating four-note descending pattern is played in straight 16th notes on the top two strings, first with a wide stretch between the 17th and 12th frets on the high E string—fretted with the pinkie and index finger—followed by the standard box pattern, moving between the 15th and 12th frets, using the ring and index fingers. I end the phrase with a whole-step bend and vibrato on D, second string, 15th fret.

Now let's take this idea and expand on it by incorporating descending patterns that consist of six-note groups. In **FIGURE 4**, I begin in the same manner as **FIGURE 3**, but, starting in bar 2, I descend the notes of E minor pentatonic in six-note phrases, moving between the 15th and 12th frets on the top two strings (as well as the sixth string), and between the 14th and 12th frets on the third, fourth and fifth strings.

Zakk Wylde is a master at incorporating these kinds of quick, seamless position shifts into his solos very effectively. His solo on Ozzy Osbourne's "Miracle Man" is a great example. **FIGURE 5** offers a solo played in this style: across the first three bars of this example, I steadily move repeated four-note patterns up the fretboard, from 10th to 12th to 15th position, culminating with fast 16th-note triplet phrases based on the E natural minor scale (E F♯ G A B C D).

Our last example, **FIGURE 6**, consists of repetitive six-note phrases that entail a wide fret-hand stretch and move through three octaves. Using the pinkie and ring and index fingers to fret all the notes, I begin on the top two strings and descend—A G E E D B—and play this pattern twice. I then move those notes down an octave and play them on the G and D strings, then down another octave to the A and low E strings.

Try incorporating these lick ideas into your own solos, moving through various keys and fretboard positions. You'll find that the possibilities are endless, and that new sounds and licks are just waiting to be discovered.

—reprinted from *Guitar World*, July 2011

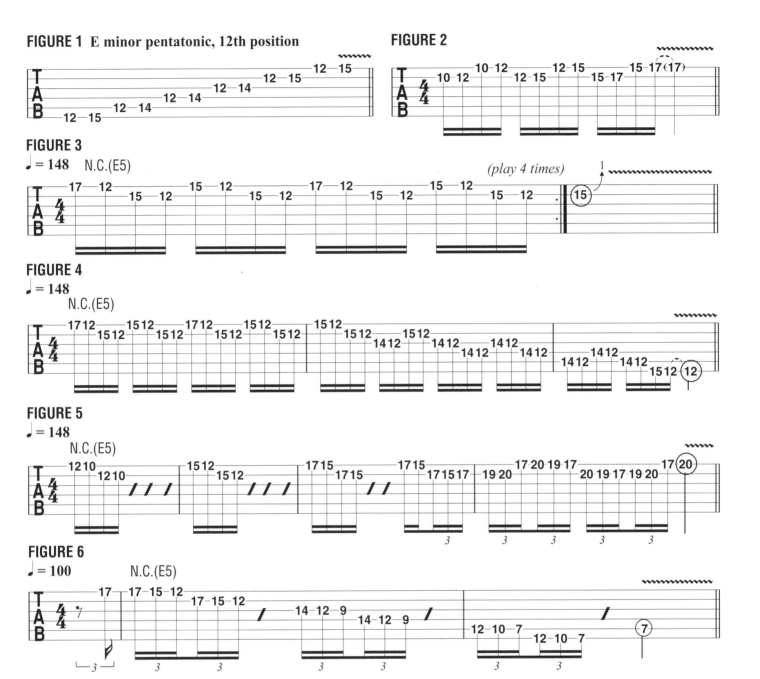

FIGURE 1 **E minor pentatonic, 12th position**

FIGURE 2

FIGURE 3

♩ = 148   N.C.(E5)

(play 4 times)

FIGURE 4

♩ = 148

N.C.(E5)

FIGURE 5

♩ = 148

N.C.(E5)

FIGURE 6

♩ = 100   N.C.(E5)

Pent-Up Demand

Traversing the fretboard using the minor pentatonic scale.

The minor pentatonic is the "go-to" scale for hard rock and metal soloing. Last month, I illustrated several different ways to combine and connect various scale positions of minor pentatonic in the quest to "break out of the box," and I demonstrated ways to generate fresh pentatonic-based licks. This month, I'd like to show you a few more techniques that make it possible to view larger areas of the fretboard all at once, while also giving you some new, cool licks to play.

A great way to expand on a minor pentatonic idea is to move either up or down the fretboard on only two strings, using a four-note melodic "shape," or "module," that changes according to the specific scale structure of minor pentatonic in each position. For example, **FIGURE 1** illustrates this idea as applied to the top two strings, staying *diatonic* to (within the scale structure of) A minor pentatonic (A C D E G). There is, however, one note that falls outside the A minor pentatonic scale—the B note sounded by the open second string—but to me, this pitch—which is the second, or ninth, in the key of A minor—actually makes the lick sound more interesting.

A neat twist on this approach is to stay on the high E string exclusively and combine *double-picking* with *palm muting* (P.M.), as demonstrated in **FIGURE 2**. Here I play four-note groups of straight 16th notes, picking the first three notes down-up-down, followed by a pull-off to the open string, which serves as a pedal tone. Each four-note group is played twice, after which I move down one fretboard position, staying diatonic to the A minor pentatonic scale. I then take this concept and move through five scale positions of A minor pentatonic, ending the run with a wide, one-and-a-half step bend and vibrato, from E up to G on the B string's 17th fret.

Now let's take this idea and apply it to the E natural minor scale (E F♯ G A B C D), staying on the high E string only and alternate picking every note (see **FIGURE 3**). This lick, by the way, is similar in style to Kirk Hammett's lead work on the first few Metallica albums.

Another great way to use E natural minor is to play ascending four-note patterns while climbing up a single string, as shown in **FIGURE 4**, ending with a high whole-step bend and vibrato from high E to F♯, the ninth. You can hear licks like these in many of Yngwie Malmsteen's neoclassical-style solos.

Now that you've gotten the idea, try moving these licks over to other strings and applying these ideas to different scales and various keys.

—reprinted from *Guitar World*, August 2011

FIGURE 1

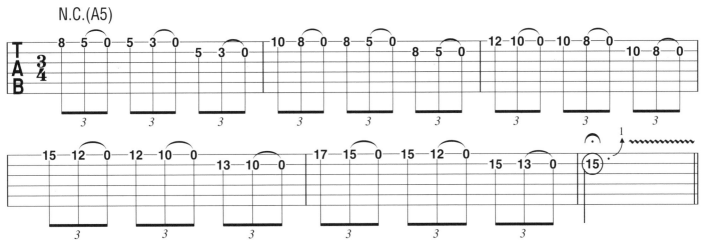

FIGURE 2

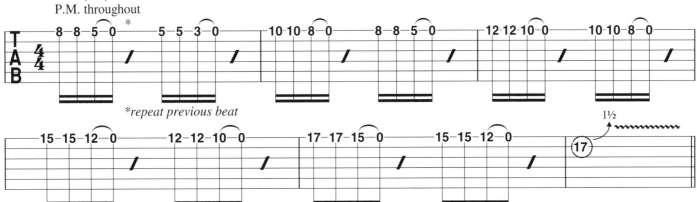

*repeat previous beat

FIGURE 3

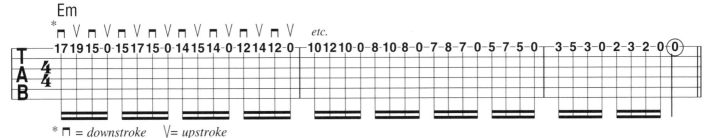

* ⊓ = *downstroke*   ⋁ = *upstroke*

FIGURE 4

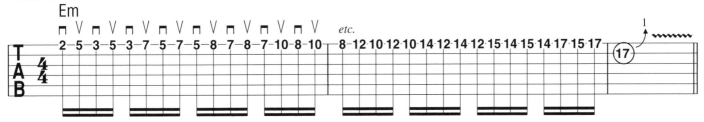

Reinventing the Steel

Discovering new ways to use the minor pentatonic scale.

I'd like to pick up where we left off last month by investigating some new and different ways to use minor pentatonic scales in order to break away from the "bluesy" sound with which the scale is so often associated.

A great way to discover new minor pentatonic sounds on the fretboard is to expand common "box" patterns. A♯ shown in **FIGURE 1**, E minor pentatonic (E G A B D) is played in two connecting positions: when ascending, I play the scale in seventh position; when descending, I play it in 10th position.

Let's now combine both of these forms into a single fretboard pattern, as shown in **FIGURE 2**. Here, I use a wide fret-hand stretch to cover all the notes of E minor pentatonic in seventh and 10th positions, using three notes per string.

A cool approach is to take this "expanded" fingering of E minor pentatonic and leave out the middle note on each string, as demonstrated in **FIGURE 3**. On each string, I use hammer-ons to move from a note fretted with the index finger at the seventh fret to a note sounded on the 12th fret with the pinkie. The one exception is the B string, where I hammer-on from the eighth fret to the 12th in the same manner.

Now let's see what happens when we move this wide-stretch approach to minor pentatonic up and down the fretboard. A♯ shown in **FIGURE 4**, I begin by "cycling" the seventh-to-12th-fret hammer-ons on the bottom three strings, and then, in bars 2 and 3, I move the idea up to the ninth and 10th positions. Be sure to keep your fret hand relaxed throughout this passage, as the wide stretch can build up tension in the hand muscles.

One thing I like about this pattern is that, when you really get it moving quickly, it sounds almost like a keyboard or synthesizer. A good way to build up speed is to work on moving between pairs of strings repeatedly, as I do in **FIGURES 5** and **6**.

Another great way to make use of this approach is to stick to just one string. In **FIGURE 7**, I play repeated pairs of eighth-note triplets on the high E string, combining two different scale positions in each bar, culminating with the open high E string.

Due to the great number of wide stretches and hammer-ons/pull-offs, this lick sounds almost as if it's performed with fretboard tapping. This is a great way to achieve the wide intervallic jumps associated with tapping but without actually employing the technique.

—reprinted from *Guitar World*, September 2011

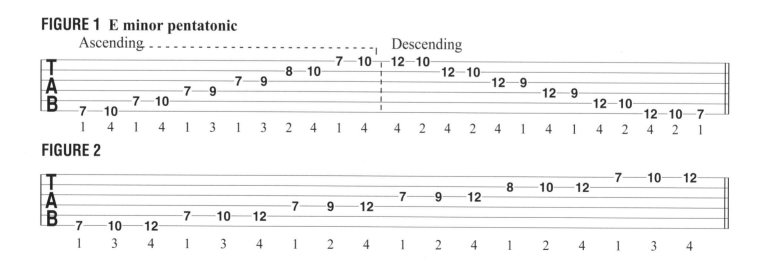

FIGURE 1 **E minor pentatonic**

FIGURE 2

FIGURE 3

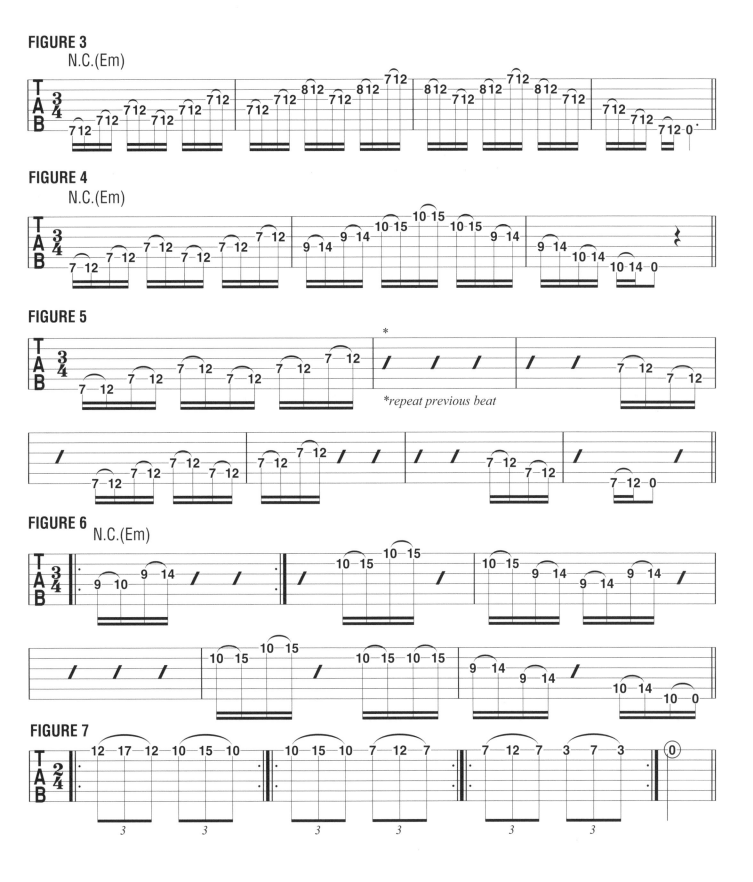

FIGURE 4

FIGURE 5

*repeat previous beat

FIGURE 6

FIGURE 7

Northern Darkness

A look at Scandinavian black metal and death metal styles.

In this month's column, we'll be traveling to the cold and dark lands of Norway and Sweden to investigate the brutally heavy riffage of black metal and death metal. So get ready—it's going to get extreme!

A while back, I spent some time with Nergal, from the Polish extreme metal band Behemoth. Among other things, we talked about how he creates a majestic, epic, symphonic sound without using keyboards. Nergal showed me a few of his techniques, and I'd like to share them with you.

In this first example, shown in **FIGURE 1**, I combine an open low E pedal tone with full-voiced chords, wherein I sweep, or *rake*, the pick across all the strings on Fm and E5 chord voicings. Across beats one and two, I quickly alternate-pick the open low E pedal. On beat three, I fret a fifth-string-root Fm chord but include both the open low and high E strings in the voicing, and rake the pick in a sweeping motion across all six strings, moving from the low E to the high E. I then shift the fretted shape back one fret while opening up the B string, sounding an E5, and articulate this chord with a reverse rake, sweeping the pick across all the strings in the reverse order, from the first to the sixth. These slashing strum patterns make the rhythm part sound very big and dramatic. I then wrap up the riff with a dark-sounding single-note line, utilizing the notes C, D, B and B♭.

Now let's look at a death metal–style riff. The great thing about death metal is that the guitar is an open canvas. Most often in death metal, the guitar lines do not follow any particular scale or tonality; the best and most powerful riffs have a jagged, atonal quality that is both unsettling and truly heavy. When devising these types of riffs, you are free to use your ear to choose which notes will best evoke the feeling and sound you are looking for, without any adherence (if you choose) to any scale or modal structure.

In **FIGURE 2**, I alternate-pick straight 16th notes throughout, forgoing any palm-muting techniques so that the riff sounds as wide open as possible. With reference to the key of E minor, I begin with chromatic movement from the open low E to F, the flatted ninth, followed by chromatic movement from C♯, the sixth, to C, the flatted sixth. On beat four, I alternate between C and B♭, the flatted fifth, in trill-like fashion. Bar 2 is the same for beats one and two, but on beats three and four I move from G, the minor third, to D♯, the major seventh! A♯ you can see, this riff is all over the place, harmonically speaking. Bar 3 is a recap of bar 1, and bar 4 ends on the major third, G♯, which lends a really weird twist to the riff overall. Pay close attention to the palm muting: I release the palm mute to open up the sound and give a "spike" to each note at the end of a phrase.

Let's wrap up with a heavy rhythm part in E minor, built from two-note chord voicings on the fifth and fourth strings and played in conjunction with the open low E string (see **FIGURE 3**). Using mostly downstrokes in a steady eighth-note rhythm (with occasional 16th notes added), I maintain an E octave sound in each chord with the presence of the open low E and the E note one octave higher, on the A string's seventh fret. Melodic interest is created on the D string, where I shift different notes up and down in a free manner, making reference to Em, Esus2, C/E and E5. The statement then ends with reference to F major.

—reprinted from *Guitar World*, October 2011

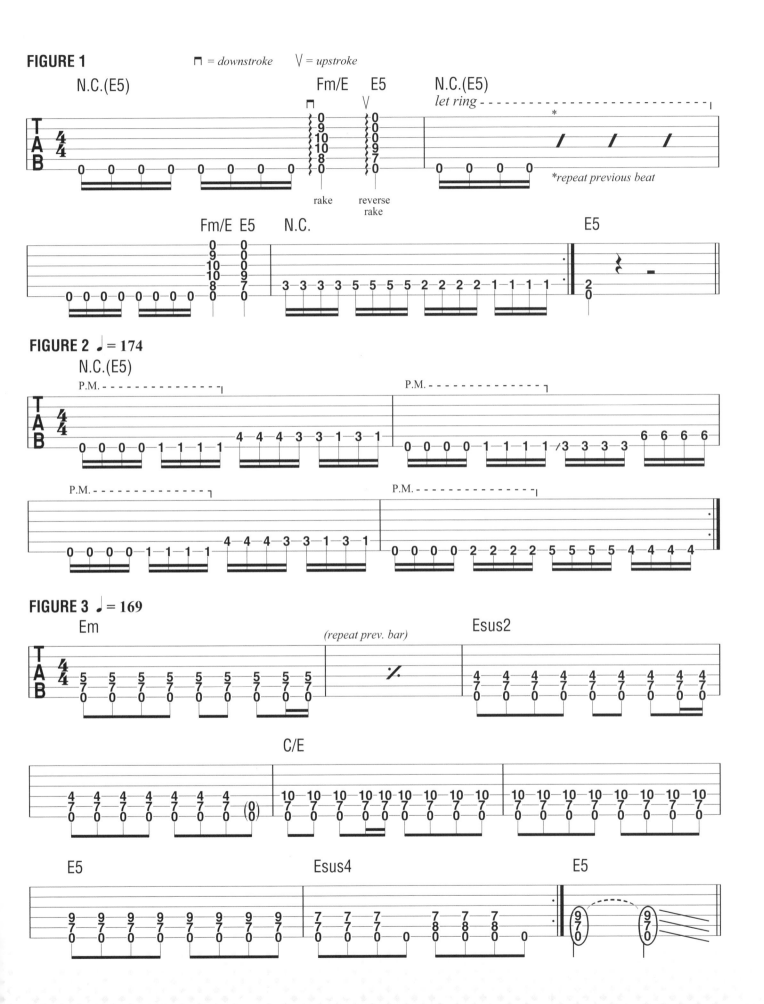

Minor Technicalities

Incorporating different minor scales into riffs and rhythm parts.

Without a doubt, the most commonly used scale in metal is the minor scale. Each minor scale has its own distinct characteristics, and it's essential for all guitarists to know the basic minor scales all over the fretboard and to be aware of the sometimes subtle differences between them. This month, I'd like to detail the most prevalent minor scales in metal: natural minor (also known as the Aeolian mode), the Dorian mode, the Phrygian mode and the harmonic minor scale.

To begin, let's play each of these scales in the key of E, starting with E natural minor. **FIGURE 1a** illustrates this scale played in one octave, starting from the open low E string and staying on the bottom two strings. You can see the *symmetry* in the fingering pattern, as the second, third and fifth frets are played on both the low E and A strings. The same type of symmetry occurs in the second octave, as shown in **FIGURE 1b**, as well as in the third octave (see **FIGURE 1c**). Now let's put it all together and play E natural minor across three octaves, as shown in **FIGURE 2**.

Another essential minor scale is the Dorian mode. **FIGURE 3** illustrates this scale in three octaves. Be aware that, as compared to natural minor, there is only one note that is different in Dorian: the sixth scale degree. In natural minor, the sixth is minor, or "flatted," whereas in Dorian, the sixth is major, or "natural."

The Phrygian mode, illustrated in **FIGURE 4**, sounds slightly darker than natural minor and Dorian minor. The intervallic structure of Phrygian is almost identical to natural minor, with the exception of the second scale degree, which in Phrygian is minor, or "flatted"—F in the key of E, as opposed to the major second, F♯, present in natural minor.

One of my favorite things about the Phrygian mode is that it can be used to conveniently play long runs of symmetrical licks across all six strings. A♯ shown in **FIGURE 5**, I can play fast triplet figures articulated with pull-offs on every string and create a seamless sound while moving down through three octaves.

Also essential to metal guitar is the harmonic minor scale, shown in the key of E in **FIGURES 6a** and **6b**. Harmonic minor is also very similar to natural minor, with the exception of the seventh scale degree. In harmonic minor, there is a major, or "natural," seventh, which in the key of E would be D♯.

Harmonic minor is a great scale to use for heavy single-note licks, as demonstrated in **FIGURE 7**. A great twist is to play double-stops, or two-note figures, against the open low E pedal, as I do in **FIGURE 8**. You will hear harmonic minor used in this way in the music of In Flames and At the Gates.

—reprinted from *Guitar World*, November 2011

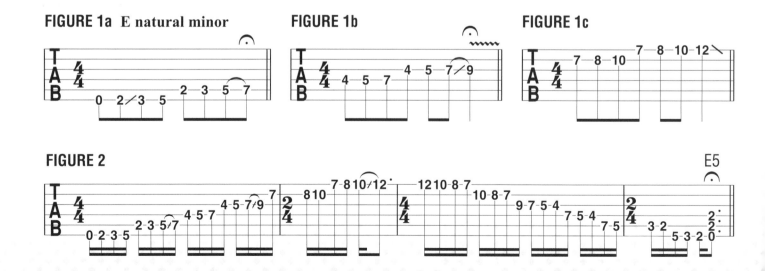

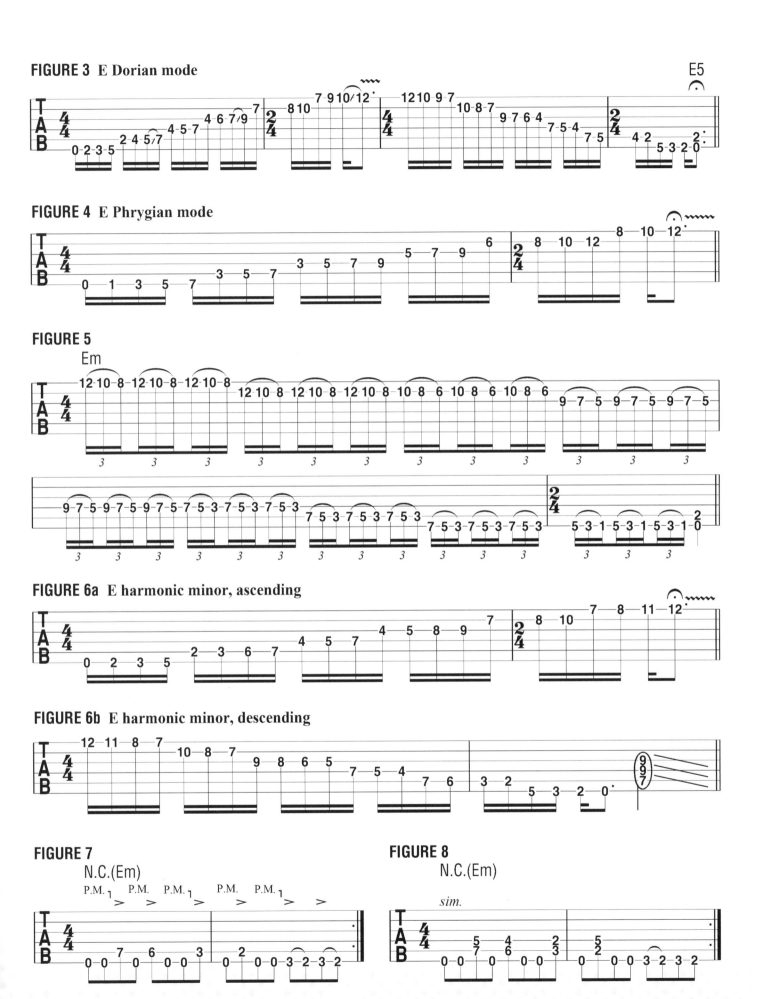

FIGURE 3 E Dorian mode

FIGURE 4 E Phrygian mode

FIGURE 5

FIGURE 6a E harmonic minor, ascending

FIGURE 6b E harmonic minor, descending

FIGURE 7

FIGURE 8

Scream For Me, Long Beach!

Getting the most out of high-pitched natural harmonics.

In this month's column I'd like to demonstrate several licks that utilize natural harmonics. A natural harmonic (N.H.) is sounded by picking an open string while lightly touching it with a fret-hand finger directly above a given fret. The natural harmonics that are easiest to produce and are most commonly used are those found directly above the 12th, seventh and fifth frets.

When executed properly, a natural harmonic should have a bell-like chime that rings clearly and sustains. Let's begin by lightly resting the ring finger across all six strings directly above the 12th fret and picking each string individually, as shown in **FIGURE 1**. I then proceed to do the same thing at the seventh and fifth frets. (Remember, the finger must touch the string directly above the fret.)

Some of my favorite natural harmonics—the ones I use most often to create cool-sounding licks—are found on the G string between the second and third frets. As shown in **FIGURE 2**, I rest my ring finger directly above the third fret to sound a high D natural harmonic and move back slightly to a point just ahead of the midpoint between the second and third frets (indicated as 2.6 in the tab) to sound a high F natural harmonic. I then move back a hair more to just behind the midpoint (indicated as 2.4) to sound a G, four octaves higher than the pitch of the open string. I then play the natural harmonic directly above the second fret, which is a very high A. These higher, "stratospheric" natural harmonics are not as loud as those at the 12th, seventh and fifth frets and are more challenging to sound clearly. You can help bring them out by using your guitar's bridge pickup and lots of gain.

For each of these harmonics, I use the whammy bar to add vibrato, which also helps the note to sustain a little longer. I can then depress the bar to get the harmonic to quickly drop, or "dive," in pitch.

A very cool natural-harmonic technique—one that players like Dimebag Darrell, Joe Satriani and Steve Vai have gotten a lot of mileage out of—is to pull off to the open G string while simultaneously dropping the whammy bar, and then lightly touch the string at different points while raising the bar to get a great ascending-harmonic sound.

In **FIGURE 3**, I quickly pull off with the index finger at the second fret of the G string to get the string vibrating, dropping the whammy bar simultaneously, after which I lightly touch the string directly above the third fret to sound the natural harmonic located there. This is often referred to as a "touch harmonic" and is indicated by the abbreviation "T.H." In **FIGURES 4** and **5**, I move slightly behind the third fret (2.6) and to the second fret to sound even higher, screaming natural harmonics.

Another great technique is to play the high G harmonic located above the fifth fret of the G string along with the high F♯ harmonic located above the seventh fret of the B string, as I do in **FIGURE 6**. Notice that I again use the whammy bar to shake or lower and raise the pitch of the harmonics.

In **FIGURE 7**, I repeatedly pull off to the open G string from different points along the fretboard so I can add natural harmonics at the 12th, ninth, seventh, fifth and fourth frets, as well as just behind the third fret, adding two quick whammy-bar scoops as each harmonic sounds. Lastly, in **FIGURE 8** I use the same technique to get the G string ringing but quickly "flick" the whammy bar to get a fast warble on each harmonic, followed by a whammy-bar dive.

—reprinted from *Guitar World*, December 2011

FIGURE 1

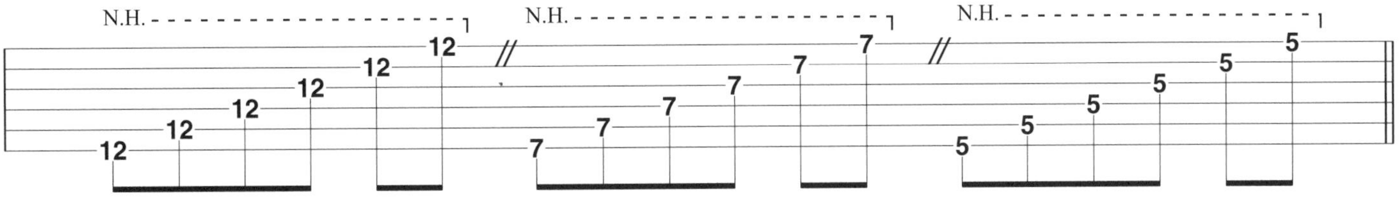

FIGURE 2

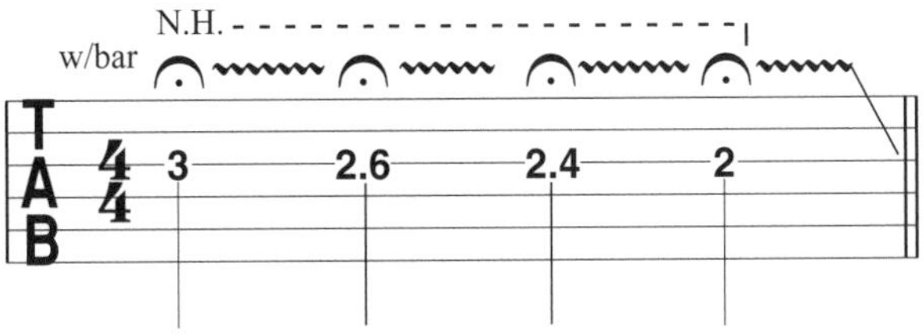

FIGURE 3

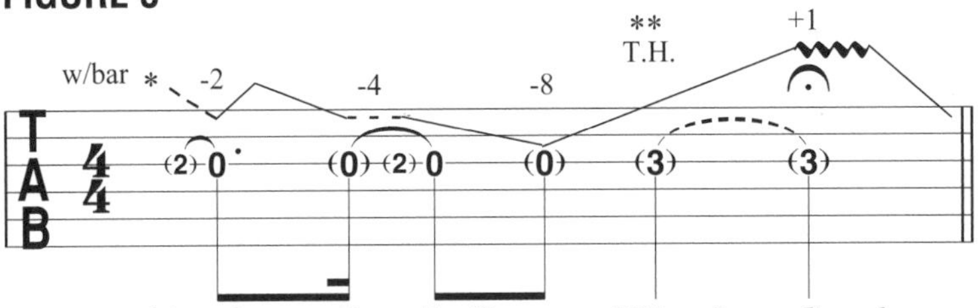

*Simultaneously pull-off to
open str. while depressing bar*

**Touch str. directly
over 3rd fret while
releasing bar*

FIGURE 4

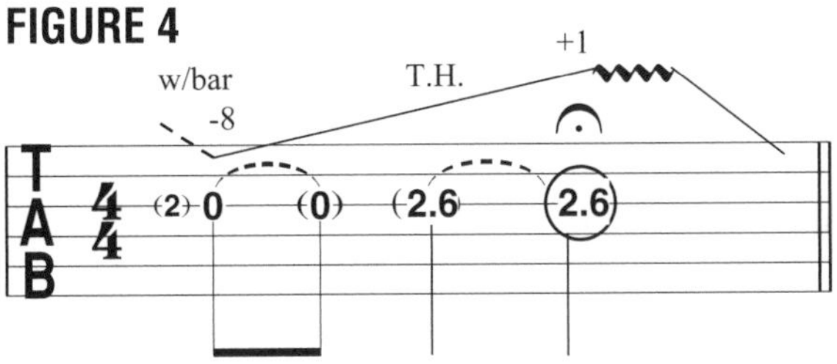

FIGURE 5

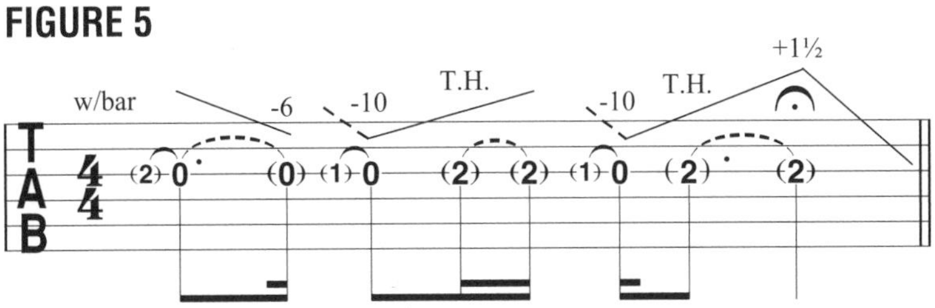

FIGURE 6

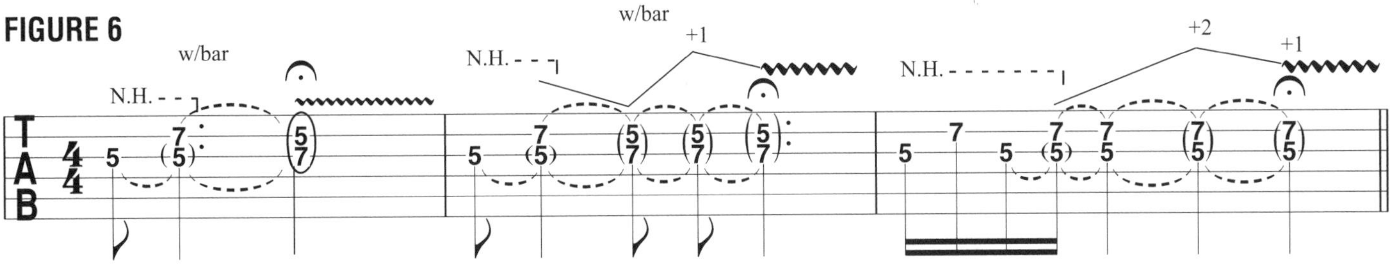

FIGURE 7

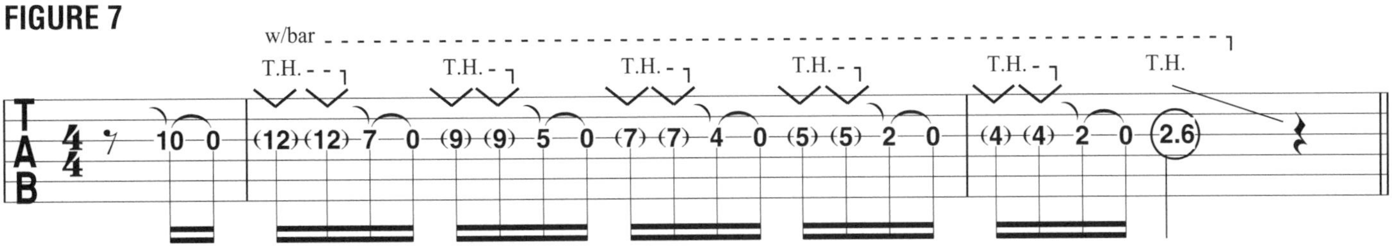

FIGURE 8

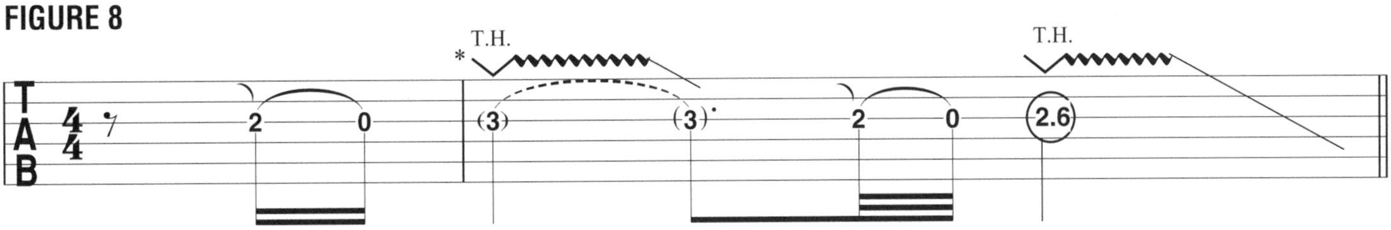

depress and flick bar

The Mad Butcher

Utilizing consecutive downstrokes to create the heaviest metal riffs.

I've decided to call this month's column "The Mad Butcher" because the focus here is on pick-hand technique, specifically the constant downstroke "chopping" necessary to execute the heaviest metal riffs of all time, like those made famous by Metallica, Megadeth and Slayer. I'd like to show you a few riffs that will help you to develop the ability to play metal rhythm parts like these with precision, stamina, control and power.

I've seen many players who, when performing rhythm parts that require consecutive downstrokes for more than a couple of bars, strain after just a short while in an effort to keep the riff even and precise. The muscles and ligaments in the pick-hand forearm tighten up, and they start to lose the rhythm. The trick to performing steady downstrokes with precision and power is to "open up" the picking motion when you are picking the strings, because this is the only way you will be able to get all of the notes to sound even and uniform as the riff progresses.

A great way to get a handle on this technique is to start with the example shown in **FIGURE 1**, which is executed with a consistent downpicking motion and moves between open A and open low E root-note pedal tones. In bars 1 and 2, I alternate between the D and A strings in even eighth notes, with the accents on the fretted D-string notes falling on the downbeats (one-two-three-four) and the accents on the open A string falling on the eighth-note upbeats (one-*and*-two-*and*-three-*and*-four-*and*). In bars 3 and 4, the same pattern simply moves over to the bottom two strings.

Throughout the pattern, the lower of the two strings is always palm-muted while the higher string is allowed to ring. Be sure to really punch out the higher notes, which function as a melodic line, and do not let the two strings ring together. At the end of the pattern, I play a B♭5 chord as a quarter note, just to give the pick hand a temporary break.

In **FIGURE 2**, I use a similar idea but instead double-pick the low E-string pedal tone consistently as the riff progresses. I begin by barring my index finger across the bottom two strings at the second fret and play a melodic line on the A string against the steady pedal tone on the low E string. In bars 3 and 4, I sound *pairs of notes* on the accents, instead of just single notes on the A string, and end the phrase in bar 4 with alternate (down-up) picking.

In the last example, **FIGURE 3**, I switch to pairs of notes, fourths apart and barred across the A and D strings, played against an open low E pedal tone. I again use all downpicking through this riff, with reference made to F5 and G5 as the line moves up the neck, even though I maintain the open low E pedal tone throughout. In bar 4, I switch to a fast pull-off riff, moving quickly between the A and low E strings, but still use only downpicking whenever I strike the strings.

The best way to develop your downpicking technique is to start slowly and try to stay as relaxed as possible—which is good advice for everything you practice! Take your time in building up the tempo, and soon enough you will be mastering "mad butcher" licks of your own.

—reprinted from *Guitar World*, Holiday 2011

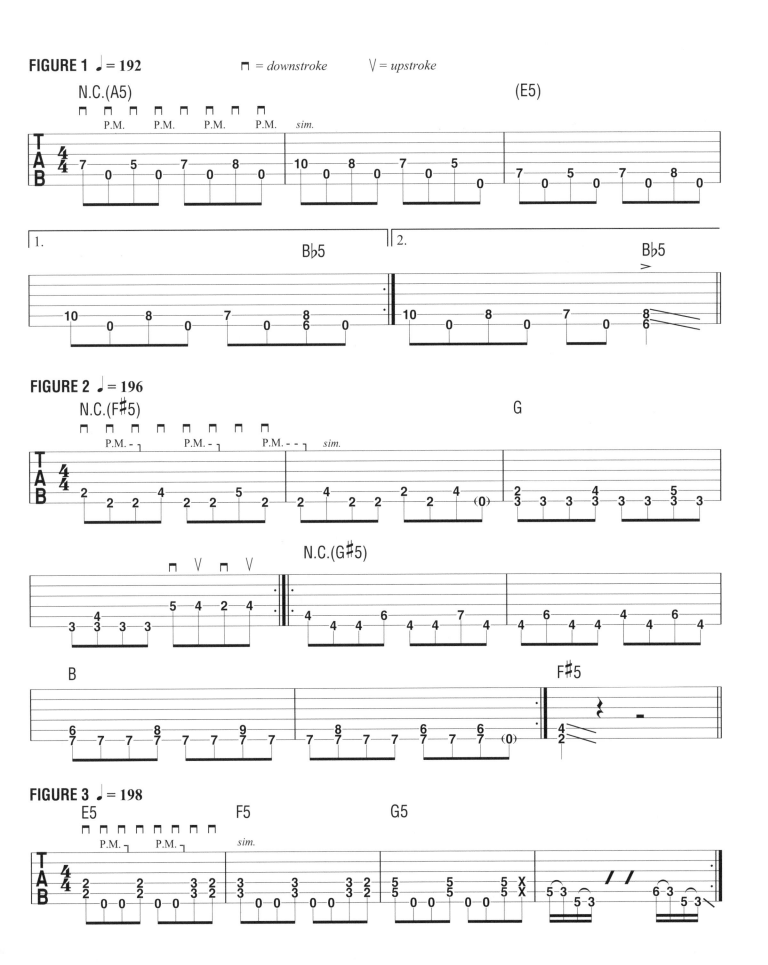

THE CAT IN THE HAT

by Slash

Armed and Ready

My pre-gig warm-up strategy

In this month's column I'd like to talk about my pre-show warm-up routine. Making sure I'm properly prepared to play before I go onstage helps me turn in a solid and convincing performance. This is especially true if I have to play something really fast in one of the first few songs, because it helps me play the notes cleanly and at the proper speed. Prepping before a show loosens me up, increases my coordination and my control over my instrument, and raises my confidence so that the guitar doesn't feel like a foreign object in my hands.

I usually warm up for 30 to 60 minutes before a gig. While my comfort level onstage is determined by a lot of things, such as the sound in the room and the vibe of the venue and crowd, everything seems to fall together under any circumstances when I'm relaxed and ready to play.

Having said that, I can't just sit in the dressing room and mindlessly practice scales or technique as a way of warming up. Those things have nothing to do with helping me get ready for a show. Besides, playing scales just doesn't work for me, because I get distracted quickly. I'm much better off warming up with a riff or something that actually engages me.

So most of the time, I'll noodle around with a new riff I'm working on or take an idea and expand on it. Other times I'll try to play a lick that I hear in my head. Whatever I do, it has to be musically worthwhile. There isn't one particular pattern or technique that I focus on every time, since my mindset on any given day is pretty different. I like playing more than practicing, so if I can find something to play that is a good warm-up and also entertaining to me, that's what I'll go with.

For example, lately I've been warming up with a run I play at the end of "Do It for the Kids," from Velvet Revolver's *Contraband*. **FIGURE 1** is along the lines of the run I'm talking about. I'm not exactly sure what scale it's based on [*D harmonic minor (D E F G A B♭ C♯)*], but it's got an East Indian kind of vibe and fits the song really well. When I play it fast I'll use a lot of pull-offs and only pick every third or fourth note, but when I feel up to the task or am practicing it slowly, I'll try to pick every note. Generally, I don't like a run like this to have a staccato pick attack on every single note. It sounds good if it's done precisely, but I'm not the best picker in the world, and I know my limitations, so if I don't think I can smoothly pick every note, I'll use hammer-ons and pull-offs. Having said that, if I practice picking every note of the run for a couple of minutes, my picking tends to become smoother and more precise, and that gives me an incentive and goal to shoot for.

Although I generally find running scales boring because there's no emotional content, I'll do it occasionally, for lack of anything better to do. **FIGURE 2** is a technically challenging two-octave chromatic scale exercise I came up with to keep both hands busy. If I can think of something more creative to do, I will, but in a pinch, I'll fall back on a scale exercise like this one.

Another thing I've realized is that it's important to spend a few minutes before a show playing while standing up, because your posture sitting down is completely different. The guitar is at a different height relative to your hands and body when you're sitting, and so you have to adjust once you get onstage, especially if you perform with your guitar hanging low, like I do.

—reprinted from *Guitar World*, January 2008

FIGURE 1

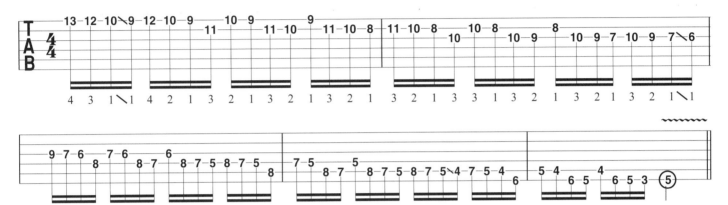

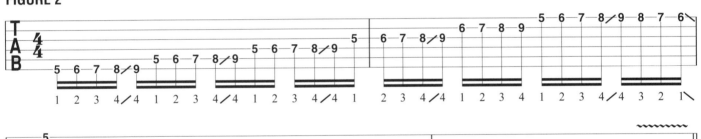

FIGURE 2

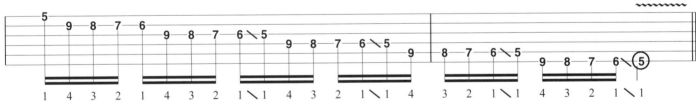

Bending & Stretching
Using the pinkie, and different fingerings for string bending.

I'm writing this month's column on my way to Rock 'n' Roll Fantasy Camp in Las Vegas. I'm only spending a day there, and I've got no idea what to expect, apart from the fact my friends Roger Daltrey, Joe Walsh and [producer] Mark Hudson are going to be there. Mark talked me into it, and Roger told me, "It's a hoot!" I'll let you know.

In this month's column I'm going to discuss how, when bending strings, the choice of which finger you use will influence the sound you get. I play pretty hard and am not what you'd call a "finesse guy." I like using fairly thick strings so that there's a bit of "fight" with the guitar. I tune down a half step (low to high: Eb Ab Db Gb Bb Eb) and use .011, .013 and 0.18 gauge strings for my high E, B and G strings, which are definitely on the heavy side. This is a key factor in this month's topic.

Even though I naturally tend to use my pinkie for certain fingering patterns and wide-stretch licks, it never really comes into play when I'm bending strings. I do use my index, middle and ring fingers for bends, and find that each one gives me a different form of expression. They each feel very different, too. For example, if I use my ring finger as opposed to my middle when bending the high E string up a whole step at the 19th fret, it feels very different (see **FIGURE 1a** and **PHOTOS A** and **B**). As you can see in **PHOTO A**, when I bend with my ring finger, like a lot of other players do, I support it with my middle finger. But when I bend with my middle finger (PHOTO B), I do so without any help from my index finger; the middle just seems to work pretty well on its own. And when bending with your index finger you obviously don't have the option of reinforcing it!

This same approach applies to bends anywhere on the neck and on any string—check out **FIGURES 1b** and **1c** and you'll hear and feel what I mean. The difference isn't just a matter of string tension and finger strength either; it's also about intonation and the way you approach the same bend, depending on the finger you're using. For example, I have a natural tendency to over-bend (beyond a whole step) with my ring finger, and even though my middle finger is pretty strong I rarely overbend with it.

The difference in feel when bending with my ring or middle finger is so noticeable to me that I'll often deliberately switch fingers. Once again, to hear and feel what I'm talking about here, try playing **FIGURE 2** using the two different fingerings indicated, first with your middle finger then with only your ring finger. Try doing the same with **FIGURE 3**, and then with some licks of your own.

The three fingers I use to bend strings each offer a different kind of parameter for control when it comes to vibrato. My index finger has a certain type of vibrato that I've found I can get really wild with, much more so than I can with my ring finger, which is definitely more controlled, as is my middle finger. Once again, experiment and let your ears decide which finger works best within the context of a particular bend or lick. It all depends on the feel and vibe you're going for.

Another thing to bear in mind is this: sometimes the position of your hand at a certain point during a solo will effectively determine which finger you use to bend a particular note. So, in addition to the different feel each finger will give to a bend, being adept at bending with every finger is definitely a useful skill.

—reprinted from *Guitar World*, February 2008

PHOTO A

PHOTO B

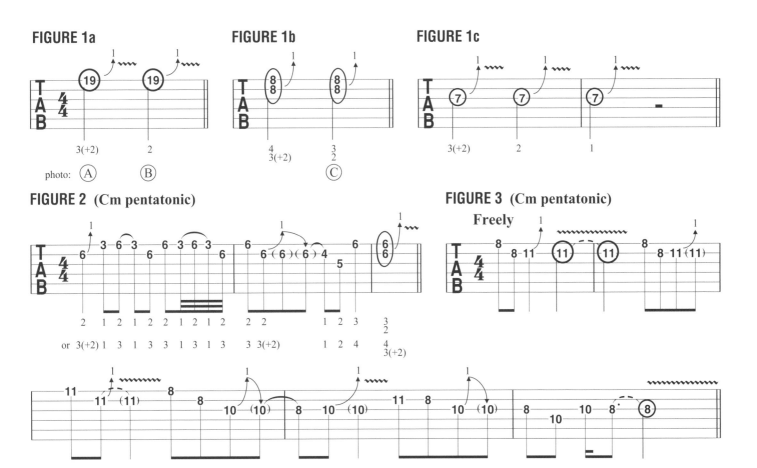

FIGURE 1a

FIGURE 1b

FIGURE 1c

FIGURE 2 (Cm pentatonic)

FIGURE 3 (Cm pentatonic)

The Rock Box

Playing the pentatonic scale in different positions on the neck.

I'm writing this column the day before the final date of Velvet Revolver's tour with Alice in Chains. The show was originally supposed to take place at the end of October but it got postponed due to the wildfires in Southern California. We're going to include "American Man" in the set, which we've never played live before. We rehearsed it last night, and it sounded good, so we're going to throw that in between "Big Machine" and "Vaseline."

For this month's column I'd like to talk about some of the scales I use—or, as the case may be, don't use. You can sit around and practice scales all day long, but if you don't—or can't—in some way apply them to music, then they're of no real use. I always find that whenever I start to play something that sounds like a real song, I tend to take off and forget all about scales.

I have a lot of guitarist friends who are what you might call "technically evolved," and are amazing at incorporating scales into their playing. But that's just not me. One of these friends, Steve Lukather, is effectively my technical guitar mentor. Steve's always giving me lessons and tips on how to use different scales in weird positions and over various chords. He knows all these tricks about starting on different notes and using certain scales in certain keys. As fascinating as that stuff is, I have a hard time applying it because melodically it doesn't appeal to me. I just can't seem to play that technical stuff with any real feeling or emotion. Ultimately, the most important thing for me is to make sure what I play has some sort of melodic significance. For that reason, in any given song there are only a couple of different types of scales that work for me.

Obviously, my main thing is the rock sound, which revolves around what I think is the simplest scale, the minor pentatonic. I'll play this scale in different positions up and down the neck. Let's say, for example, I'm playing over a I-IV-V progression in C (C-F-G). **FIGURES 1–4** show four different positions, or "boxes," of the very basic C minor rock scale [C E♭ F G B♭] I would use as a framework to build a lead around. The other fairly standard scale you can use is the major pentatonic (**FIGURE 5**).

You can use any one of these positions or boxes at any given time, and you can also throw in passing tones or mix up the minor and major notes. The lick in **FIGURE 6** is a good example of a major run that ends on the minor seventh note [B♭], while **FIGURE 7** is major with a minor third [E♭] thrown in as a passing tone, which gives the lick a chromatic flavor. I would like to add, however, that it's also important to think outside the scale box. There are countless combinations of notes on the neck of your guitar, so the possibilities are virtually endless. Basically, whatever sounds good "works" for me, so use the boxes or shapes as a rough framework and let your ears dictate what other notes also work within the context of a particular song.

As you can see in **FIGURES 5–7**, I invariably transition between these different positions by going up or down a single string—kind of like "Chutes and Ladders." If you're just getting into playing rock lead guitar and are interested in learning some of the really basic but useful minor and major rock scale positions, check out Eric Clapton's playing. He uses them very well and usually at a speed you can follow! Clapton has used these scale patterns throughout his career, but the period I'm into mostly is his work with Cream and Derek and the Dominos. Cream's *Disraeli Gears* is a great album for that.

—reprinted from *Guitar World*, March 2008

FIGURE 1

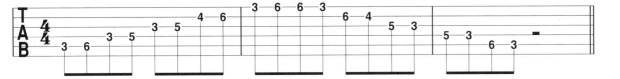

FIGURE 2

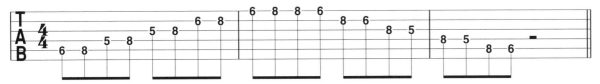

FIGURE 3

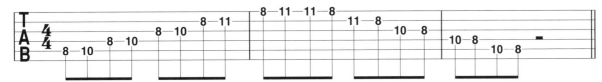

FIGURE 4

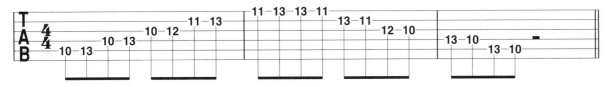

FIGURE 5

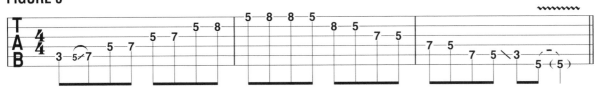
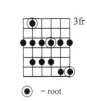

FIGURE 6

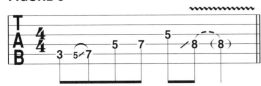

FIGURE 7

Thank you, and Good Night!

Readers' Poll results, answering a few questions and signing off.

I'm going to open up this column with a sincere "thank you" to all the readers of *Guitar World* for their praise and regard. I just heard that I've been voted "MVP of 2007" and "Best Rock Guitarist," and that *Libertad* was awarded "Best Rock Album" in the *Guitar World* 2008 Readers' Poll. That is such a huge, unexpected surprise, and I am honestly speechless. Thanks!

I'd also like to thank the guys at *Guitar World* for asking me to write this column, and encouraging me in the process. It's something that I honestly never expected to do. I'd read other players' columns in the magazine and think, How does that work? Well, now I know. It's been a great experience, and really fun and painless. It's also offered me more insight into my own playing. Until I started doing this, if someone had asked me in passing, "How do you do that?" I would've responded, "I don't know!" Now I'm able to analyze some of the stuff I do.

This is my final column for now, and I'm going to sign off by answering a few of the many questions that have been sent in and forwarded to me over the past 10 months.

A lot of your solos sound like they've been meticulously worked out and composed. Is that the case? Also, how do you go about coming up with a lead break? Do you practice along with a tape loop of the section you're going to solo over?

—Adam Leader

When it comes to the solo section of a new song, I usually hear the basic melody I want to play in my head. Then, every time Velvet Revolver practices the song as a band, I'll work on perfecting that idea and expanding upon it. Sometimes the rest of the solo will come naturally, and other times I'll hear something more in my head and work on grabbing it while we're rehearsing. Basically, it's during the actual writing of the song I begin to form the structure of my solos. But, as I've just mentioned, I invariably hear the basic melody first.

Sometimes a solo that sounds like it's been constructed is an idea that came totally spontaneously the very first time we played the song. Good examples of this are the solos in "Fall to Pieces" and "You Got No Right." Both are pretty much exactly what I played the very first time we performed each of those songs. I just stuck with my initial ideas, and by the time it came to record them I basically had all the notes in there, give or take a few.

In regards to working on a solo at home with a tape loop, I know there are some guys that do that, but I'm not one of them! I just don't have the patience.

I saw Velvet Revolver three times on your most recent tour. It seemed like you played your solos slightly differently at each gig. How do you approach soloing live?

—Chris Long

Every day is different because I go through so many different frames of mind when I'm onstage. Sometimes what I play is completely freeform, and sometimes it's a little bit more focused on certain tonal aspects and whatnot. There's a whole range of approaches. But, for the most part, everything has gotten to the point where it's really, really fluid.

There are certain "set" Velvet Revolver solos that I've actually been tearing away from these days. For example, the solo in "American Man" that I talked about a few columns back is one that's been evolving; its basic structure is still there, so you still get the vibe of the recording, but I don't play it exactly as it is on the record.

What can we expect from Velvet Revolver, and your own playing, in the near future?
                                                                          —John Rhodes

Right now we're gearing up to tour America, Australia and Europe, and we should be done with those dates by April. That's all we've got on the horizon for the moment in terms of touring, because everybody wants to really focus on making another record sooner than later. But you never know!

As for my own playing, Libertad probably features the improvisation I've done to date when it comes to leads. On the next album I want to record more solos that are more melodically structured than what I've done with Velvet Revolver so far. We're still growing as a band, and that's probably half the fun of doing it—trying to find that place where suddenly everything is completely in-sync and I can let it rip. That's what makes all the work worth it, and I think I'm always striving to find that blissful state where all the gears are turning together and everything just happens naturally.

In previous columns you've mentioned quite a few of your early musical influences. Are there any current players you admire?
                                                                          —Evan Drennan

I like Tom Morello a lot. I think he's a revolutionary guitar player. I like Jack White, too. And, of course, there's Jerry Cantrell of Alice in Chains, who we toured with recently. He's great. I like Dave Mustaine a lot, too. He's one of my favorite guitar players and a very articulate character and a brilliant riff writer. Dave's a very methodical and accomplished heavy metal player but way more interesting than "just a heavy metal guy." I see he's writing a column for *Guitar World* now, and that's really cool. Dave's vastly underrated in the general scheme of things, but he's a phenomenal player and songwriter.

To be honest with you, most of the recent guitar players I'm into are holdovers from the Nineties. There's been a real lack of rock lead guitar from the late Nineties into the new millennium. I just haven't heard any breakout lead players. I'm sure they're around, but they don't have record deals. Lead guitar is not really that in vogue right now, which is a shame.

Why do you often hold your guitar so that the neck is vertical and right by your face when you're playing lead?
                                                                          —Chris Fisher

That's actually a habit I never even noticed I had until I saw pictures of myself doing it. I think it's just because it helps me get in touch with the upper half of the neck a lot better than when the guitar is all the way down by my knees.

Well, that's it for me. Thanks for reading, everyone. Like I said, writing this column has really been a lot of fun!

                                                    —reprinted from *Guitar World*, April 2008

HEAVEN AND HELL

by Tony Iommi of Black Sabbath

Never Say Die

Overcoming overwhelming odds, and how to play "Paranoid" the right way.

Hello there! Welcome to my first *Guitar World* column. I'm looking forward to sharing with you in these pages my thoughts on playing, equipment and the music business. Actually, this isn't the first time I've written a column—I used to do one many years ago for an English music magazine called *Beat Instrumental*. I did it for about eight months and it was great fun, and I'm sure this one will be too.

NEVER SAY DIE

Although my handicap has received quite a bit of press over the years, a lot of people are very surprised when they find out that I'm missing two fingertips from my fretboard (right) hand. After all, that is a fairly serious affliction for a guitarist. Specifically, I lost the tips of my middle and ring fingers in an accident I had at work—they got caught in a piece of machinery and when I instinctively pulled my hand back I literally ripped the ends of my fingers off. Ironically, the day the accident happened was my last day at that job before turning professional musician as I was all set to go to Germany on tour with a band. The timing couldn't have been worse—not that there's ever a good time to cut off the ends of two of your fingers! As you can imagine, it was an awful experience and I went through a terrible period of depression because I was convinced that my guitar playing days were over for good. I went to dozens of different doctors and hospitals and they all said, "Forget it. You're not going to be able to play guitar again."

While I was down in the dumps though, a friend of mine, who happened to be my foreman at work, brought me a record of [*world-renowned Gypsy jazz guitarist*] Django Reinhardt who, at the time, I'd never heard of before. My friend said, "Listen to this guy play," and I went, "No way! Listening to someone play the guitar is the very last thing I want to do right now!" But he kept insisting and he ended up playing the record for me. I told him I thought it was really good and then he said, "You know, the guy's only playing with two fingers on his fretboard hand because of an injury he sustained in a terrible fire." I was totally knocked back by this revelation and was so impressed by what I had just heard that I suddenly became inspired to start trying to play again. I wanted to continue playing and the fact that Django was able to play so brilliantly with only two fingers gave me the hope I so desperately needed.

I tried playing right-handed for a while but that didn't work out for me so I bandaged my two damaged fingers together and started playing lefty again using just my first (index) and little fingers. I then decided to go a step further by trying to bring my two injured fingers back into the game. What I did was this: I melted down a Fairy Liquid [*a well known English dishwashing detergent*] bottle, made a couple of blobs of the plastic and then sat there with a hot soldering iron and melted holes in them so they'd fit on the tips of my injured fingers, kind of like thimbles. When I got the caps to fit comfortably, I ended up with these big balls on the ends of my fingers, so I then proceeded to file them down with sandpaper until they were approximately the size of normal fingertips.

It took me quite a while to get them exactly right because they couldn't be too heavy or thick but had to be strong enough so they didn't hurt the ends of my fingers when I used them. When I had sculpted my "thimbles" to the right size and tested them I realized that the ends weren't gripping the strings so I cut up a piece of leather and fixed pieces to the ends of them. I then spent ages rubbing the leather pads so they would get shinny and absorb some oils and would help me grip the strings better. I filed down the edges so they wouldn't catch on anything and it worked!

Once I had done this it took me quite a while to get used to bending and shaking strings with those two fingers because I obviously couldn't feel anything. It was difficult to even know where my fingers were and where they were going. It was just a matter of practicing and persevering with it, using my ears to compensate for my lost tactile sense.

In the years since my story was publicized more than a few musicians who have had similar afflictions have told me that my "never say die" attitude has inspired them to keep going. However bad something may seem at first, you've got to try to overcome it because sometimes the "impossible" is possible. A♯ I've already told you, after my accident literally everybody wrote me off. It was really depressing to hear that but, after hearing what Django was able to do with two fingers I just wouldn't accept defeat. I was sure there had to be a way around my problem.

"PARANOID" THE RIGHT WAY

Anyway, that's enough about my missing fingertips! Let's finish up this first column with some music talk. Over the years a lot of guitar magazines and books have transcribed my "Paranoid" [*Paranoid*] main riff but nearly all of them did so incorrectly. They invariably get the notes right but the position on the neck is always wrong. I saw one recently that made the same old mistake. Nearly everyone (most professional transcribers included) assumes that I play the E5 power chord that the riff is based around on the 5th and 4th strings at the 7th fret. Well, I don't! I play the chord on the 6th and 5th strings at the 12th fret. I play it here because, to my ears, the E5 power chord at the 12th fret definitely sounds darker and more ominous than the 7th fret grip.

Regarding the three grace-note hammer-ons that occur on the 5th string at the very beginning of the riff—they're definitely played by "feel" and will sound wrong if you perform them too quickly or too slowly. To get them right, listen to the recording carefully a few times until you've memorized the way that part of the riff sounds.

—reprinted from *Guitar World*, August 1997

Less Is More

Sabbath update, tone talk and the intro to "A♭ter Forever."

Alright, mate—how's it going? A♯ it's been a while since we last spoke, the chaps at *Guitar World* have asked me to fill you in with what's been going on with me lately. First, I'm delighted to announce that we've finished mixing the live Black Sabbath album, which was recorded at our two reunion gigs in our hometown of Birmingham, England, last December. We're still not sure what the album is going to be called yet, but it's definitely going to come out later this year.

In addition to all the live stuff there are also going to be two brand new Sabbath tracks on it featuring Ozzy, myself, Geezer [*Butler, bass*] and Bill [*Ward, drums*]. We wrote them in the studio while the live album was being mixed and they're called "Psycho Man" and "Selling My Soul."

Talking about the Black Sabbath reunion, we just played 15 or so gigs in Europe over the last month that went very well. Unfortunately though, Bill wasn't able to do 'em with us. What happened was, after we did the second rehearsal for the tour Bill said, "Oh, I feel really weird." Then, bloody hell, not long after that an ambulance came and we realized he'd had a heart attack. Thankfully he was up and about in no time, but he obviously couldn't do the tour. We brought him onstage at the Ozzfest show in Milton Keynes [*England, June 20*] to let the fans know he was okay and then pulled his trousers down in front of 60,000 people! Playing practical jokes, especially on Bill, is a Sabbath tradition.

Because Bill couldn't play we got Vinnie Appice [*who played drums in Sabbath from August 1980 to October 1982*] to fill in and he did a great job of getting the knack of all of Bill's parts. The way Bill plays is very different from how a typical rock drummer would play stuff—he's very unorthodox and rhythmically quirky. Listen carefully to any of our old albums and you'll hear exactly what I mean—Bill's drumming is definitely not normal! So I sat with Vinnie for quite a while to make sure he was getting the original feel of the songs. On more than one occasion we had a drummer come in and say, "Oh yeah, I know that one," and then start playing the song and it sounds nothing like the original version! And, as this was going to be a Black Sabbath reunion tour, we needed to make sure that the songs were going to sound right, which they did.

TONE TALK

I recently received a letter from a young reader named Ted Burger whose guitar teacher told him that if he wanted to sound anything like me he'd have to use as much distortion as possible. I had to laugh when I read that because what his teacher told him is really a load of rubbish! From my experiences I've found that whenever I turn up the gain too much, my sound gets smaller rather than bigger. The low end goes all mushy and the high end gets way too fizzy—basically, not a good sound at all!

Some people think that all you do to sound like me is plug into a decent valve [*tube*] amp and turn everything up full! To me, though, there's definitely an art to playing with distortion. Basically, you've got to let your ears decide what the best level of gain is because if you use too much distortion then the pure note isn't going to come through and that's what I want to hear. The last thing I want to do is sound like I'm playing through a bloody fuzz box! If anything, I tend to use less gain than most people think because I want my sound to be as full and natural-sounding as possible with a lot of note definition.

Like most serious guitarists I'm very fussy about my sound because it definitely affects the way I play. If I don't like my tone then my performance suffers. I also like to *feel* my sound onstage which means I tend to play a bit on the loud side! Sabbath has always been a pretty loud band and I think that goes back to when we were playing in bars during our early days. The people would be talking so loudly in those places you could hear them over the band, so after a while we went, "Sod this, the audience is louder than we are; let's turn it up so the bastards have to listen to us!"

The down side of playing loud for all this time is that it's buggered up my hearing to a point. There are certain things I can't hear too well on the top end. Standing with my head right next to the drummer's cymbals for many years probably hasn't helped either! I've tried those special ear protectors but I just didn't feel comfortable with them because they always make me feel like I'm listening to myself playing underwater! Regardless of what some people might say about ear plugs or filters, the ones I tried definitely messed with the way I hear. I like to hear the sound I'm getting and that's it. If you're not hearing that then you might just as well go back to the drawing board again—it's a no-win situation, it seems!

Getting back to the subject of distortion, when Sabbath first started out, distortion in an amp was unheard of. There wasn't an amp that existed back then with built-in distortion. You either had to turn a valve amp all the way up or try and use a fuzz box—and, as I've already said, I hate the sound of those things. I played through Laney amps on the first albums but I also used this treble booster pedal called a Rangemaster that I had modified. This guy came up to me at a gig and said, "I can adjust that to give you a bit more of a powerful sound." He did it and I said, "Bloody hell, I like that!" It sounded great because it was driving the input of the amp. From that point on, I kept trying to get guitar amp companies to build something into an amp that would create that sort of a sound. But they all went, "No, that's way too much. Nobody is going to want to buy an amp that does that!" Of course, since then all those companies have come out with boosters and God-knows-what-else built into their amplifiers. If only people would've listened back then, we'd have had all that years ago!

—reprinted from *Guitar World*, October 1998

Contracts: Heaven…or Hell?

Career advice, and my solo in "Paranoid."

Hello again. A♯ promised, this month we're going to start chatting about playing lead. First though, I'm going to answer one more of your questions because it is a fairly common one that more than a few of you have been writing in about. Here goes…

> *Like probably everyone who reads your column and owns a guitar, I'd love to be able to make a living playing music. You've managed to do so pretty successfully for a good 30 years, so I figured you'd be a good person to ask about it! Do you have any advice you'd like to pass on?* —Ryan Rhoads

I've been asked this sort of question quite a few times over the years and the first thing I almost say is this: learn three chords and then find yourself a bloody good lawyer! In fact, I recently read an interview with Deep Purple's Ritchie Blackmore and he even quoted me on that one, which was fairly flattering. Anyway, what I've just said might sound quite funny at first, but having a good lawyer in this business is really important because bands get ripped off all the time. Unfortunately, there are an awful lot of people out there who'll sign a band and then rob them blind because the guys in the group don't know a bloody thing about the industry. I mean, when Sabbath first went into this business, we did so because we really loved what we did and all we wanted to do was make an album and go on tour. We weren't thinking about the financial side of things at all, probably because we'd never made any dough playing anyway! The fact is, in this business you will meet people who are very interested in what happens to your money, and they can "take you for a ride," so to speak.

Because of this reality, I strongly recommend that you never sign any sort of contract you're offered unless it's been looked over by a really good music business lawyer. Unfortunately, having this done will cost you a few bucks because music lawyers don't exactly come cheap. It'll be well worth it in the long run, though. I'm not just saying this because I've seen it happen to other people; it's a lesson I had to learn the hard way! Believe me, Black Sabbath got taken to the cleaners in the early days because we didn't know any better. Sadly, it's all too easy to write your name on a piece of paper, only to realize before you know it that you're bound to the terms of that contract for bloody ever!

When you tell someone who's offering you a contract that you want a lawyer to look at it, they'll invariably try to pull the old trick of saying, "Well, if you don't trust me, forget it." That's an easy line to fall for, so watch out for it. When you think about it, if someone tries to pull that one on you then there's a good chance that the contract they're offering you is dodgy. Remember, these people are there to make money and some of them will go to any lengths to get as much as they can, so always bear that in mind. It's all too easy to get taken in by someone being nice to you and promising you the world by saying, "You're gonna get this and you're gonna get that…you'll all have Rolls Royces in a year!" Do yourself a favor—get it in writing because anyone can make empty promises like that. We had that happen to us loads of times in the first few years and we always fell into the trap. Hopefully you'll learn from our mistakes and be careful!

The only other thing I can say about trying to make it into this game is this: first and foremost, you've got to go out there and really enjoy what you do. It gets to be a bit of a sorry state when you end up asking yourself, "What's the 'in' thing right now? Right, I'll play that and make a bloody fortune." I think you've got to go where your heart is and believe in what you're playing. That way, if you don't make it, then at least you can look back on what you did with pride! At the end of the day though, it's in the lap of the gods as to whether you'll get the right breaks or not. So enjoy yourself and good luck!

"PARANOID" POINTERS

A lot of you have written in asking about the solo I play in "Paranoid" [*Paranoid*], beginning at 1:23. I usually like to leave a bit of room for improvising when I play certain solos live, but with this one, I always play something that is pretty much the same as the lead break on the record. I feel I have to do this because so many fans know the solo note-for-note and if I deviate from it even slightly they immediately think I've made a bloody mistake! It's a rather easy solo to play and it features a few moves—like using finger slides to move smoothly up and down the neck and fast trills—that have definitely become a part of my soloing style over the years.

—reprinted from *Guitar World*, December 1998

Chromatic Man

The latest on Black Sabbath's Reunion tour, plus more ways to move around the neck.

Bleedin' hell. Where does the time go? It seems like only yesterday that I was finishing off my last column and I'm already handing this one in. No rest for the wicked, aye! A♯ I'm sure you've probably guessed, we've been hard at work rehearsing for the upcoming U.S. Black Sabbath *Reunion* tour. In fact, we've just finished a nice little stint at a rehearsal studio in Wales, England. Everything's going really well—we're having a load of fun and I'm happy to report that Bill [*Ward, drums*] is doing great. He's made a wonderful recovery from the heart attack he had last summer. In fact, the only problem we're having right now is what bloody songs to play on tour! We've been rehearsing so many different tracks that we've ended up with way too many to choose from. I know an awful lot of you are dead keen to find out what songs we're going to be playing, but I'm going to keep my mouth shut for now.

PLANET PANTERA

As I'm sure you know, Pantera is going to be doing the whole tour with us. I'm looking forward to seeing them again; they're a great band and a really nice bunch of lads. They do a pretty good version of "Planet Caravan" too! In fact, when an English guitar magazine recently asked me to show them how to play that song I told 'em to give Dimebag Darrell a call because he probably knows it better than I do at this point! Actually, I just found out that Pantera has also done covers of "Hole in the Sky" and "Electric Funeral" for rock radio stations to tie in with the tour. I can't wait to hear what they've done—I'm sure both of their versions are very good.

TRILLING AROUND

Last month we chatted about using finger slides to help you move smoothly around the neck. Today we're going to look at a couple of other ways you can do this. One way is to simply move a trill (like the short E minor run shown in **FIGURE 1**) up or down a string. I do this sort of thing quite a bit—it's really an easy way of moving to a different place on the neck. **FIGURE 2** shows another E minor trill run—one that's played on the G string and moves in the other direction.

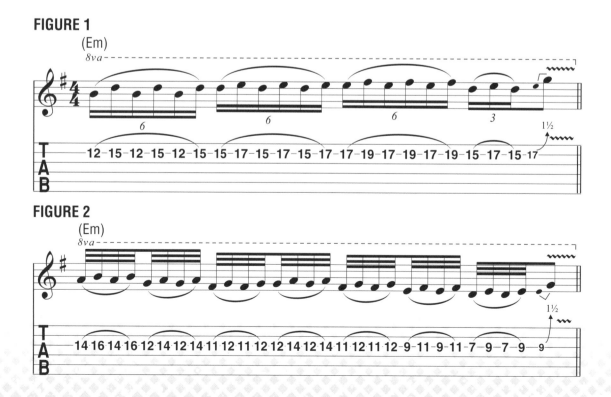

FIGURE 1

FIGURE 2

ONE STEP AT A TIME

Another thing you can do to get from one place on the neck to another is to move a trill pattern up or down the neck one fret at a time. The word used to define this type of movement is chromatic. **FIGURE 3** is a good example of this technique and approach. A# you can see, all I'm doing is playing a trill in the key of A minor on the G and D strings and then moving it quickly up the neck, one fret at a time. **FIGURE 4** shows an E minor lick (one I'm sure you've heard a hundred times before) being moved down toward the nut. Chromatic movement can add a nice bit of tension to a solo and once again, you can move in either direction on the fretboard—up or down.

FINISH WHEN YOU WANT

Hopefully you'll have noticed that both of the chromatic examples I've just shown you finish up on notes that are in the exact same key they started off in. It would be a bit pointless if they didn't—unless you want your solo to end up sounding like a right old mess, of course! To my way of thinking, it really doesn't matter how far up or down the neck you take this approach, providing you end up somewhere that makes some kind of sense. The best thing to do is let your ears and your better artistic judgement decide where and when you should stop.

We'll talk some more about making the most of your fretboard next month. Cheers mates...see you on the road.

—reprinted from *Guitar World*, March 1999

Chromatic Man Part II

News from the road and more chat about chromatic runs.

Happy New Year, mates! I'm happy to report that the New Year's Eve show I told you about last issue that we did in Phoenix with Soulfly, Slayer, Megadeth and Pantera went great. It was a real good event and the whole thing seemed to go really well for us, despite the horrendous sound situation onstage. Apparently, they've never had a band play at Bank One Ballpark in Phoenix before and the sound we were hearing while performing onstage made it a bit difficult for us. We all played well, though, and everyone I spoke to afterward said it sounded great out in the audience, which was a relief to hear. Hell, even the reviews were phenomenal, which is a bloody rare thing for us because the press normally give us a right old slagging, so it must've sounded fine!

The stadium had one of those roofs that can be opened or closed and although it was closed when we played, at the end of the night we opened it up and let a load of fireworks off to celebrate the New Year. Mind you, it wasn't exactly midnight when we did that, it was something like 12:30! We didn't want to stop halfway through our set and say "Happy New Year everybody, let's hold hands and sing 'Auld Lang Syne,'" you see. That would've been a little bit too much like a bleedin' cabaret show for our liking, so we decided to call our own New Year at the end of the show instead.

ON THE MOVE

As you recall, in the last few columns we covered fast trills and using finger slides to help you move smoothly around the fingerboard. **FIGURE 1** is an example of an E minor run that employs both of these techniques. Last month we looked at moving trills and licks up and down the neck, including moving them chromatically (one fret at a time). **FIGURE 2** is a good example of this and is a rather ominous-sounding chromatic trill run on the low E string that sounds really good when it's done really fast.

FINGER FITNESS

As well as sounding pretty good in solos (providing you use 'em with thought, of course), this type of run is also a good little exercise that can help you develop speed and finger strength. The patterns shown in **FIGURES 3** and **4** are great little warm-up exercises for your fretboard hand. Try taking them both all the way up the neck and then back down again and you'll definitely see (and feel) what I mean.

DOUBLE YOUR TRILL

Thinking up examples to show you for this column has actually reminded me of a little trick I used to do that I haven't done for bloody ages. I call it a "double trill" and I haven't seen that many people do it. **FIGURE 5** illustrates what I'm talking about here; as you can see I'm hitting the B and high E strings at the same exact time as I'm doing the trill.

USE YOUR HEAD

Like I told you last month, using chromatic runs like these is a great way to add tension and excitement to a solo. They also provide you with a convenient and musical way to move from one place on the fretboard to another. You can take these ideas as far up or down the neck as you think sounds good...it's entirely up to you. Just make sure you don't end up on a duff note for the obvious reasons. Also, like any effect or trick, don't overdo this sort of thing or it'll lose all of its impact. See you out there on the road. Cheers.

—reprinted from *Guitar World*, April 1999

FIGURE 1

l.h. fingering:

FIGURE 2

continue up
the neck

FIGURE 3

continue up
the neck

FIGURE 4

continue down
the neck

FIGURE 5

BREWTALITY

By Zakk Wylde

Playing the Numbers, Part 3

Switching melodic patterns in the middle of a run.

Over the last couple of months I've been showing you a simple and cool way of making scales sound more interesting by numbering the notes and then creating note patterns based on number patterns. So far we've checked out "threes" and "fours" and, hopefully, you've been able to come up with some cool patterns of your own with five- and six-note sequences. I'm gonna quickly show you two more pattern ideas and then I'll get into mixing and matching some of these ideas. Once again, we're gonna stick with the A minor diatonic scale (A B C D E F G) and use the three-note-per string pattern illustrated in **FIGURE 1**, with each note numbered from low to high.

First, I want to turn you on to you a pattern we haven't looked at yet: "twos." Here's how it goes: 2-1, 3-2, 4-3, 5-4, 6-5, etc. **FIGURE 2** shows it going up, and **FIGURE 3** shows it coming down (17-18, 16-17, 15-16, 14-15, 13-14, 12-13, etc). In case you're wondering, we can do the same kind of "backward" deal with "threes" too; instead of going 1-2-3, 2-3-4, 3-4-5, 4-5-6, etc., like we did last month (**FIGURE 4**), we can go 3-2-1, 4-3-2, 5-4-3, 6-5-4, 7-6-5, etc., as demonstrated in **FIGURE 5**.

FIGURE 6 shows the same "backward threes" idea going back down (16-17-18, 15-16-17, 14-15-16, 13-14-15, 12-13-14, etc). All four of these new runs will probably sound pretty familiar to you because sections of them have been used by pretty much everybody, from Jimmy Page to Michael Schenker to Randy Rhoads to Dimebag Darrell. This said, let's get into mixing and matching some of these patterns.

FIGURE 7 shows an A minor run that uses the wide-stretch A minor scale box illustrated and numbered out in **FIGURE 8**. This one mixes up three different number pattern ideas: "threes" going up (1-2-3, 2-3-4, 3-4-5), "threes" going down (6-5-4, 7-6-5, 8-7-6) and a 9-8-9, 10-9-10 pattern before finishing with a string bend at the eighth fret on the B string. **FIGURE 9** is another run that's based on the same exact A minor box shape (**FIGURE 8**). This one mixes patterns of "twos," "threes" and "fours" together to create a cool, flowing run that definitely doesn't sound like you're merely running a scale up and down across the strings like a moron.

As these last two examples demonstrate, the new run ideas you can come up with by mixing up number patterns are endless. So, get to it and come up with your own runs.

—reprinted from *Guitar World*, July 2003

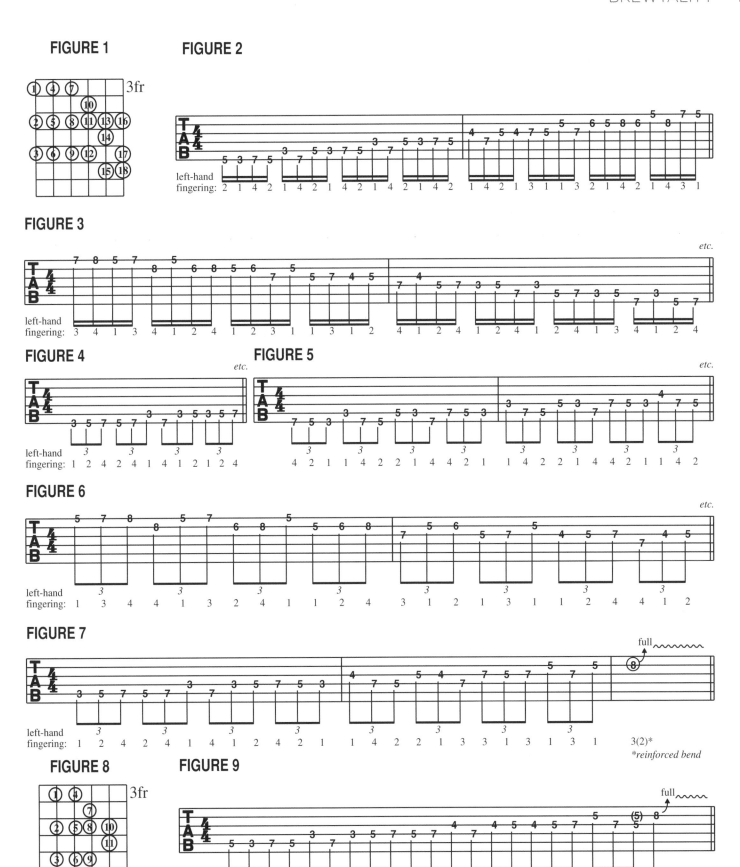

Diminished Capacity
Symmetrical insanity and the "clown show" run.

Hey Zakk, I was at the Ozzfest in Nashville, and thanks to the "mosh pit" area in front of the main stage, I was able to watch you play from only a few feet away. In between two of the songs you did an amazing, off-the-cuff lead solo on your Randy Rhoads Jackson ax that was mainly in E minor, and during it you did a couple of things I'd love to know how to play. One was a really wide stretch run with a diminished vibe where you took the same fingering pattern right across the neck from the low E string to the high E. The other was a chicken-pickin' thing that one of my friends said he'd once read that you call your "clown show" lick.

—Keith Victor

I've gotta be honest with you, Keith—I have no idea what I played there! That was just me going off in between songs. From your description, though, my money is on the wide-stretch run you're talking about being something like the one shown in **FIGURE 1**. As you can see in the photos on the top of the next page, all I'm doing is taking a six-note, wide-stretch fingering pattern on two strings and moving it across the neck. My index finger is at the ninth fret, my middle finger's at the 12th and my pinkie covers the 15th fret. You'll notice that as I move the pattern across the neck, my fret hand stays in the same exact position and I keep playing the same three frets with the same three fingers. If you're not used to doing wide stretches like this then this run will give your fretting hand a good workout.

FIGURE 1

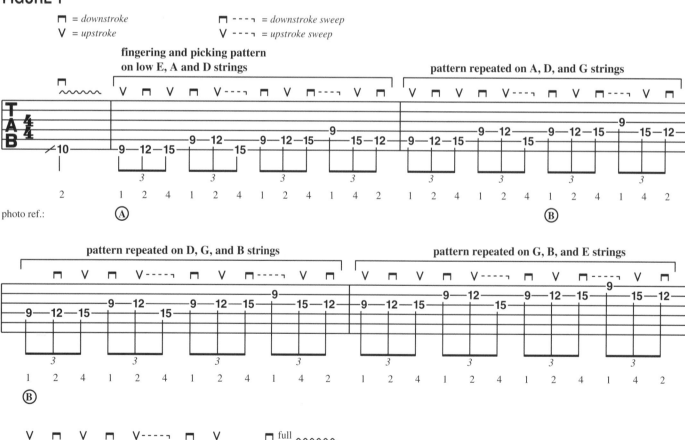

FIGURE 2 shows a fretboard diagram of the fingering pattern I'm using in this run, and because I'm playing the same three frets on each string, a lot of people call this kinda fingering pattern "symmetrical." Eddie Van Halen does this kinda symmetrical shit a lot, as does my buddy, Dimebag. Check out "I'm the One" from *Van Halen* or the beginning of Dime's solo in "Cowboys from Hell" and you'll hear exactly what I'm talking about.

FIGURE 2

Even though I'm big on alternate picking, I don't alternate pick this particular run because everything I do is geared for efficiency—check out the picking marked above **FIGURE 1** and you'll see what I do here. We'll talk more about this kinda picking approach next time out.

Although this run sounds diminished, it isn't really a diminished scale or any sort of scale for that matter; it's just a fucked-up pattern that sounds slamming, provided you play it with some balls.

Try coming up with some musical-sounding symmetrical ideas of your own. If you play something like you mean it and at least start and finish it in the right zip code, there's a good chance that it will work out well for you.

FIGURE 3 The "clown show" chicken pickin' lick

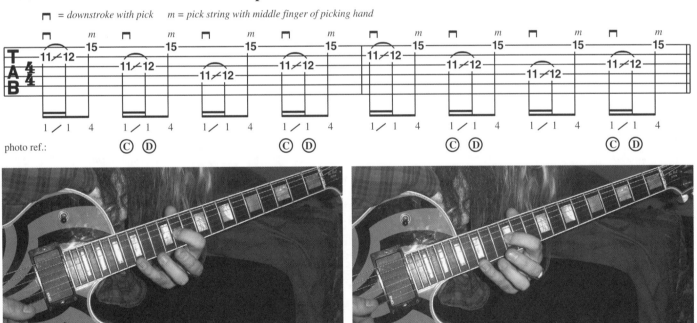

As for the "clown show" chicken-pickin' lick, I bet it went something like the run shown here in **FIGURE 3**, which does kinda sound like something you'd expect to hear at a clown show. This lick is something I've been doing for years; in fact, I'm pretty sure you can hear me doing it during my solo spot on the live Ozzy Osbourne record *Live and Loud*, which was recorded more than 10 years ago! A♯ you can see in **FIGURE 3**, all I'm doing is keeping my pinkie on the G note at the 15th fret on the high E string and then sliding from the 11th fret to the 12th with my index finger on the B, G and D strings. I use my pick to hit the sliding notes on the B, G and D strings and I pick the high E string with my middle finger. As I've said before in this column, one of the really cool things about chicken-pickin' is that it allows you to haul some serious ass on string skipping licks like this, licks that would be pretty hard to play as fast using regular picking.

—reprinted from *Guitar World*, December 2004

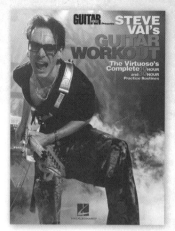
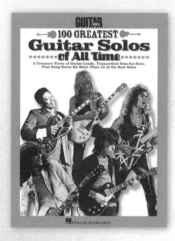
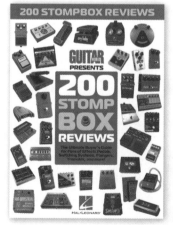

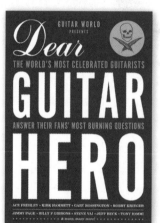
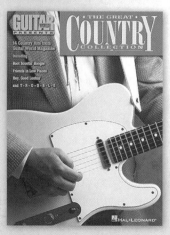